The structure of phonological representations

Linguistic Models

The publications in this series tackle crucial problems, both empirical and conceptual, within the context of progressive research programs. In particular *Linguistic Models* will address the development of formal methods in the study of language with special reference to the interaction of grammatical components.

Series Editors:
Teun Hoekstra
Harry van der Hulst
Michael Moortgat

The structure of phonological representations
(Part I)

Edited by
Harry van der Hulst
INL, *Dutch Lexicological Institute, Leyden*
Norval Smith
Institute for General Linguistics, *University of Amsterdam*

1982
FORIS PUBLICATIONS
Dordrecht - Holland/Cinnaminson - U.S.A.

Published by:
Foris Publications Holland
P.O. Box 509
3300 AM Dordrecht, The Netherlands

Sole distributor for the U.S.A. and Canada:
Foris Publications U.S.A.
P.O. Box C-50
Cinnaminson N.J. 08077
U.S.A.

ISBN 90 70176 53 X (Bound)
ISBN 90 70176 54 8 (Paper)

© 1982 by the authors.
No part of this book may be translated or reproduced in any form, by print, photoprint, or any other means, without written permission from the publisher.

Printed in the Netherlands by Intercontinental Graphics, H.I. Ambacht.

Table of Contents

Harry van der Hulst and Norval Smith
An Overview of Autosegmental and Metrical Phonology 1

John Goldsmith
Accent Systems 47

Morris Halle and Jean-Roger Vergnaud
On the Framework of Autosegmental Phonology 65

Shosuke Haraguchi
On Schane's Linear Theory of English Stress and Rhythm 83

Bruce Hayes
Metrical Structure as the Organizing Principle of Yidin^y Phonology   97

Larry M. Hyman
The Representation of Nasality in Gokana 111

Paul Kiparsky
From Cyclic Phonology to Lexical Phonology 131

William Leben
Metrical or Autosegmental 177

John J. McCarthy
Prosodic Templates, Morphemic Templates, and Morphemic Tiers . 191

Marina Nespor and Irene Vogel
Prosodic Domains of External Sandhi Rules 225

References 257

Index of Names 267

Subject Index.. 271

Preface and acknowledgements

The idea of putting together a volume of articles on non-segmental phonology originated during the fourth phonology meeting in Vienna (1980) where a section was devoted to this topic. It became apparent in Vienna that there was a strong need for an accessible collection of original work in this fruitful new research area.

In the course of 1981 a number of phonologists were invited to write contributions for the volume. This initiative met with unexpected enthusiasm, which made it necessary to put the contributions together in two volumes. They appear under the same title as Part I and Part II (Part II will appear as *Linguistic Models 3*).
We thank all authors for their cooperation.

An Overview of Autosegmental and Metrical Phonology *

Harry van der Hulst and Norval Smith
INL, Leyden and University of Amsterdam

CONTENTS

1.	Introduction	2
2.	Autosegmental phonology	5
2.1.	General remarks	5
2.2.	The representation of tone	6
2.2.1.	Contour tones	6
2.2.2.	The autosegmental solution	8
2.2.3.	The 'problem-solving efficiency' of autosegmental phonology	9
2.2.4.	The independence of autosegmental tiers	10
2.2.5.	Association principles	11
2.2.6.	Tone-bearing segments and 'projections'	16
2.3.	Extensions of the autosegmental theory	16
2.3.1.	Complex segments	17
2.3.2.	Harmony	18
2.3.3.	Three dimensional phonology	22
2.3.4.	Non-concatenative morphology	23
2.3.5.	Length	27
2.4.	Recapitulation	28
3.	Metrical phonology	29
3.1.	General remarks	29
3.2.	The metrical theory of stress	29
3.3.	Extensions	36
3.3.1.	Syllable structure	36
3.3.2.	Downdrift	39
3.3.3.	Phonological domains	40
4.	Autosegmental and metrical theory	41
4.1.	Syllable structure again	41
4.2.	Foot structure	42
5.	Concluding remarks	43

* We would like to thank Morris Halle, Teun Hoekstra, Jan Kooij, Michael Moortgat and Deirdre Wheeler for their helpful comments on an earlier version of this article. We alone are responsible for any shortcomings.

> "In this study, suprasegmental features (pitch, stress, juncture) have not been seriously considered. Ultimately of course, these phenomena must be incorporated into any full syntactic theory, and it may be that this extension still requires a more elaborate system of representation." (Chomsky 1955: 29)

1. INTRODUCTION

The history of generative phonology up until now can be divided into two phases. In the first phase the focus was on the rule system that related underlying phonological structures to phonetic structures. This we may call the *derivational* aspect of the theory. Central topics were questions of rule formulation, rule application, rule ordering and the degree of abstractness of underlying representations. In the second phase attention has shifted to the structure of the phonological representations themselves. The reason for this shift appears to be twofold. On the one hand discussions within the derivational paradigm had reached an unfruitful stage, in that the participants in these discussions no longer adhered to the same set of theoretical assumptions, but in fact disagreed about fundamental aspects of the theory. In particular the abstractness debate gave rise to this kind of schism. Several 'natural' or 'concrete' phonological theories were advanced in which the idea was given up that one rule type could be used to account for all distributional regularities. Although natural and concrete phonologists were apparently unable to convert the proponents of more abstract analyses it is certainly true that the spirit of some of their ideas has been incorporated in recent elaborations of the standard theory, subsumed under the name 'lexical phonology' (cf. Kiparsky, Part I), where part of the phonological rules has been transferred to the lexicon to form an integrated aspect of the morphological component.

It is interesting to note that the emergence of lexical phonology has a close parallel in syntax, where we have witnessed a similar transference of syntactic rules to the lexicon, giving rise to 'lexical syntax'. For an extensive discussion of the emergence of lexical syntax as well as an illustration of some of the striking similarities between lexical phonological rules and lexical syntactic rules we refer to the Introduction in Hoekstra, Van der Hulst and Moortgat (1980).

On the other hand, a second reason for shifting attention to representations was that generative phonologists had become seriously interested in 'suprasegmental features'. An immediate result of extending the empirical domain of the theory in this direction was the recognition of the fact that the standard view of phonological representations was oversimplified. These two factors have resulted in a large amount of energy being invested in the development of new ideas concerning the structure of phonological representations. Two lines of research have proved to be of particular interest and the goal of this volume (and its sequel: *The Structure of Phonological Representations. Part II*) is to inform the reader about these and other closely related developments.

In this introductory article we will present an outline of the two lines of research mentioned above, which have led to the development of the theories known as *Autosegmental Phonology* and *Metrical Phonology*. We will pay special attention to the kind of arguments that have been used to introduce new theoretical notions. This, we hope, will provide the uninitiated reader with the necessary background. Anticipating the more detailed discussion in the following sections we will sketch here briefly the questions that are at issue.

In the standard theory phonological representations consist, at every level, of a linear arrangement of *segments* and *boundaries*. Segments are conceived of as unordered sets of features (with a feature-specification). The boundaries interspersed between the segments are, with respect to their 'nature' and location, dependent on morphological and syntactic structure. They partition the string of segments into substrings that constitute possible domains for phonological generalizations. The *hierarchical* aspect of the morpho-syntactic structuring is only of limited importance for the application of phonological rules, with the one exception of stress rules. It is important to note that the segments are not grouped in terms of any other hierarchical structure, such as e.g. syllables. This standard view is oversimplified in several ways, two of which directly relate to the geometry of phonological representations.

First, it has been shown that the 'scope' of one feature need not be exactly one segment, or, to put it more precisely, that not all features that characterize some property of a segment are synchronized by the same temporal function (cf. Anderson, Part II). Both *sub*segmental and *supra*segmental phenomena have led to the recognition of the untenability or undesirability of the 'strict segmental theory'. In the theory of Autosegmental Phonology it is proposed that the standard *one-tiered* representation be split up into several *tiers*, each constituting a linear arrangement of segments. Segments in different tiers are linked to each other by *association lines* that indicate how they are to be coarticulated. The autosegmental theory was originally designed to handle tonal phenomena, which were problematic for the standard theory, and a number of fruitful analyses have been proposed. The ability of this theory to deal with subsegmental phenomena caused fresh attention to be paid to the treatment of complex segments in general, since these segments had been problematic for the standard theory from the beginning. The extension of the autosegmental theory to non-tonal phenomena has been most significant, however, in the area of vowel and consonant harmony. Finally, the autosegmental principles have even led to a new morphological theory that seems well equipped to deal with non-concatenative morphological operations, especially those involving various kinds of 'copying'. In section 2 the autosegmental theory will be discussed more fully.

A second major modification of the standard paradigm concerns the organization of segments into larger units. It has become clear that the partitioning of the segmental string dictated by the morpho-syntactic structure of an utterance is insufficient to allow for the expression of all phonological generalizations. In the theory of Metrical Phonology the nature of a different kind of hierarchical organization is explored, one that is based on phonological principles, though not without its relations to the morpho-syntactic (grammatical) hierarchy. In the phonological hierarchy segments are grouped together into syllables, syllables into 'feet', feet into phonological words etc. The metrical theory was originally introduced as a new theory of stress, but it soon appeared that it had a much wider scope. In this case also the new theory was capable of solving a number of 'old problems' such as the proper treatment of syllable structure and phonological boundaries in general. A slightly unexpected extension of the metrical theory involved the application of some of its principles in the analysis of vowel and consonant harmony. In section 3 we will discuss the metrical theory.

Ideally, autosegmental and metrical phonology should complement each other. In practice there are areas of disagreement, or doubt, about the treatment of a number of phenomena. One such area is vowel and consonant harmony, as we have seen above. Clearly, both theories have extended their empirical domain to a point where they now intersect. There are several ways in which this conflict can be resolved and we will discuss some of these in section 4.

It is well known that nonsegmental theories are not a novelty in phonology. Outside the framework of generative phonology, and even before this theory was proposed, we can find both theoretical and descriptive work based on ideas that are very similar to those being discussed in these volumes, although it is equally true that autosegmental and metrical phonology differ from all these other theories in a number of essential ways. To keep this introductory article within reasonable limits we have not tried to relate what is being discussed here to other approaches. This does not mean that we think that nothing could be gained from a careful study of these other theories, however.

2. AUTOSEGMENTAL PHONOLOGY

2.1. General remarks

The standard theory is characterized by what Goldsmith (1976) has called the 'absolute slicing hypothesis'. A representation of the sound flow starts with exhaustively splitting it up in 'slices'. The slices or *segments* are linearly ordered and defined as having no ordered subparts (cf. Clements 1976). Each segment then is an unordered set of specified features, which can be interpreted as characterizing functions from points in time to states of the articulatory organs (or, alternatively, to acoustic properties of sounds). In most cases the features are interpreted in terms of a constant state, but in some cases a changing state is involved. A well know example is the feature [delayed release], used for affricates as in German *Pfeife* [p͡f] or *Zeit* [t͡s]. But there have also been suggestions that features like [prenasal] for sounds like [m͡b], or [diphthong] are necessary. We refer to Ewen (Part II) for more examples and discussion. In the German dialect of Zürich affricates function like units at the underlying level, but at later levels it is necessary to refer separately to the constituent parts (i.e. the *internal structure*) of these sounds, which would be impossible if atomic features, like [delayed release], were used (Van Riemsdijk and Smith 1973). The suggestion that another characterization of complex segments is called for can be found in a number of publications, most recently in Anderson (1976, 1978). In general, what is suggested is some sort of linear arrangement of features within the segment, thus characterizing the beginning and end points of the segment (and sometimes even a point in between). This is in conflict with the conception of segments mentioned above.

The segmental theory has also been attacked from 'the other side'. Complex segments involve *sub*segmental structure. The study of tonal phenomena in particular has revealed that we also have to recognize *supra*-segmental structure. Tones can 'spread' over several tone-bearing segments (i.e. several vowels in a sequence may have the same tonal specifications), and it has been suggested that such phenomena can best be dealt with by removing the tonal features from the tone-bearing units and placing them on a 'higher level' from which they can be superimposed onto several tone-bearers at a 'lower level'. But a theory incorporating this idea also comes into conflict with the standard segmental theory.

We will now discuss both attacks on the integrity of the segment in more detail, turning our attention first to tonal phenomena since problems surrounding the treatment of these were the main reason for rejecting the absolute slicing hypothesis.

2.2. The representation of tone

2.2.1. Contour tones

Tones that involve a 'changing state' are termed contour tones. Contour tones are opposed to level tones, which involve a constant pitch. Contour tones may be rising tones or falling tones or rising-falling etc. Level tones are high, mid or low.

Segments that bear a contour tone are comparable to affricates and features like [rising] or [falling] are comparable to features like [delayed release] or [prenasal]. The characterization of changing states in terms of an atomic feature, formally indistinguishable from other features like [high] or [round], has certain disadvantages, that disappear if it is decided to characterize contour tones in terms of a sequence of level tone features, e.g. [+high], [-high] for a falling tone. This position has been defended by Woo (1969).

One of the crucial arguments involves the formulation of phonological rules. It appears to be the case that a falling tone will behave like a low tone when acting as a left context in a rule, and like a high tone when acting as a right context. The following example will illustrate this.

Many African tone languages exhibit a phenomenon termed *downdrift*. Downdrift involves a gradual decrease in pitch of tones that belong to a single utterance and that are, phonologically speaking, the same. The example is from Igbo:

(1)   ó nà áŋwà ínyà ígwè

$$\begin{bmatrix} \text{H} & \text{L} & \text{H} & \text{L} & \text{H} & \text{L} & \text{H} & \text{L} \\ \rule{0.3cm}{0.4pt} & & & & & & & \\ & & \rule{0.3cm}{0.4pt} & \rule{0.3cm}{0.4pt} & & & & \\ & & & & \rule{0.3cm}{0.4pt} & \rule{0.3cm}{0.4pt} & & \\ & & & & & & & \rule{0.3cm}{0.4pt} \end{bmatrix}$$

(H and L stand for high tone and low tone)

From a phonological point of view both *áŋwà* and *ígwè* have the same tonal pattern (HL), but the phonetic realization of their tonal pattern differs. The distance between the H and L is the same in both cases, but the H (and L) of the first word has a higher absolute pitch than the H (and L) of the second word. The usual means of describing this is to write a rule that drops the pitch of every H tone after a L tone:

(2)   H → !H / L —
(!H stands for 'lowered H')

In languages that have both downdrift and falling tones it is usually the case that H tones are dropped not only after L tones but also after falling tones. If the latter is characterized in therms of an atomic feature (e.g. Falling or F) the downdrift rule would have to be complicated:

(3)   H → !H / $\left\{ \begin{array}{c} F \\ L \end{array} \right\}$ —

This is only one example of a conjunction of F and L, and it might very well be an accident that the two are associated here. However it turns out that such conjunctions show up again and again, and in fact constitute the norm under such circumstances. When the context bar is on the right L appears together with F, when it is on the left L appears together with R (rising tone). Conjunctions that turn up in several rules suggest that a generalization is being missed (cf. Chomsky and Halle's "weak clusters"). There must be something that the conjoined environments have in common. In this example the property that is shared by the conjoined environments is revealed if falling tones are characterized in terms of the two level tones H and L. Now one can see why a falling tone behaves like L when it is a left context and like H when it is a right context.

This proposal does not necessarily entail that the segmental theory is abandoned but if it is not, the theory predicts that contour tones cannot occur on short vowels. Recall that the segmental theory does not allow sequences of features within one segment. Long vowels pose no problems if they are represented as two short vowels: each short vowel can contain one part of the feature sequence that characterizes a contour tone. And there are languages that forbid contour tones on short vowels. Note that this state of affairs is difficult to account for if atomic features are used for contour tones, since in that case there is no formal difference between level tone features and contour tone features. Within the two-feature approach it is possible to say that languages that forbid contour tones on short vowels have a constraint to the effect that each vowel may be associated with only one tone feature. In fact, working within the segmental theory this constraint would follow automatically. However, there also are languages that allow contour tones on short vowels. How must this type of situation be accounted for if the two-feature approach is accepted but if, at the same time, the segmental theory is maintained? Several 'possibilities' come to mind:

(4)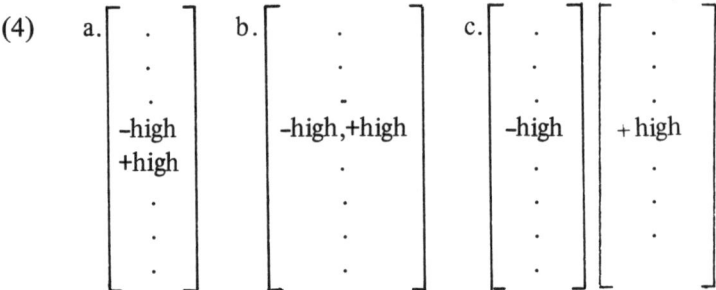

(a) is unsuited to characterize a rising tone since it could just as well represent a falling tone; after all the features are unordered. (b) tries to capture the ordering of the two features, but it violates the definition of a segment. (c) cannot be taken as characterizing a short segment, without giving up the normal assumption (cf. above) that two adjacent feature bundles represent a long segment. The conclusion seems to be that short vowels with contour tones cannot be accounted for in the segmental theory, unless the two-feature approach is rejected, but this, as has been shown, is well-founded.

2.2.2. The autosegmental solution

The autosegmental solution is a simple and a radical one. Within this theory the idea is given up that there is only one string of segments that characterizes the sound flow. Rather it is proposed that a phonological representation consist of several layers or *tiers*. Each tier constitutes an independent string of segments. This view implies that a horizontal segmentation 'precedes' the vertical segmentation. In the first segmentation the tonal part of the utterance is separated from the rest. Then both tiers are separately subject to a vertical segmentation:

(5) tonal tier   [+high]   [-high]   [+high]   .....

segmental tier $\begin{bmatrix} +cons \\ -voc \\ \vdots \end{bmatrix}$ $\begin{bmatrix} -cons \\ -voc \\ \vdots \end{bmatrix}$ $\begin{bmatrix} +cons \\ -voc \\ \vdots \end{bmatrix}$ $\begin{bmatrix} -cons \\ +voc \\ \vdots \end{bmatrix}$ .....

The phonological representation now resembles the score of a song. The tune is on one line and the text on the other.

The autosegmental theory does not require that there should be an equal number of segments on each tier. Furthermore sequences of identical segments (e.g. two low tones) are usually avoided, in the sense that such sequences are assumed to be marked. If in the course of a derivation two identical tones come to stand next to each other they will be collapsed automatically into one 'segment', according to what is referred to as the *Obligatory Contour Principle*. The theory is called autosegmental since it regards tones as autonomous segments (autosegments).

A short vowel that bears a contour tone can be characterized as follows:

(6)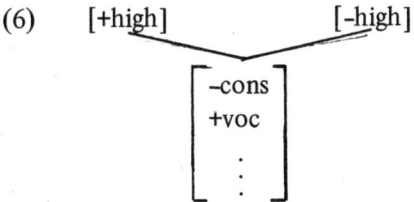

(From now on we will use H and L as abbreviatory symbols for tonal feature bundles, just as we use 'C' and 'V' for feature bundles containing non-tonal features. We will call the CV-level the 'segmental' level, though it should be kept in mind that the tonal level is really segmental too. Later in this article the symbols 'C' and 'V' will receive a different interpretation). The lines that connect the tonal segments to the non-tonal segment indicate how segments on different tiers are co-articulated. The essence of the autosegmental theory is encapsulated in this idea of association or co-articulation and it is easy to see that the theory has solved the problem of contour tones. In the next section we will discuss how the autosegmental approach, originally designed to solve the problem of contour tones, has lead to the solution of seemingly unrelated problems.

2.2.3. The 'problem-solving efficiency' of autosegmental phonology

Within a 'multi-tiered' framework the phonological representation of lexical entries may consist of two tiers:

(7) $\begin{bmatrix} \text{LHL} \\ \text{CVCVCV} \end{bmatrix}$

The tonal pattern and the segmental make-up are both independent properties of a lexical entry. Imagine now a tone language that allows words of type (8a) but not of type (8b); cf. the example given in Leben (1971):

(8)   a.   i.   CṼC   ii.   CV̀CV̂C   iii.   CV̀CV́CV̀C
     *b.   i.   CṼC   ii.   CV́CV̌C   iii.   CV́CV̀CV́C

(The diacritic ' ´ ' indicates H, ' ` ' indicates L; ' ᷈ ' thus means LHL). If there is a separate level for the tonal melodies it becomes apparent that all words of type (a) have the melody LHL, whereas all words of type (b) have HLH. In an autosegmental model only one statement is needed to rule out type (b). Within a segmental model it is necessary to repeat the constraint three times since the number of segments is different in the three possible word types. This problem of missing an obvious generalization does not exist in an autosegmental model.

In addition there is another problem that disappears, viz. the question why, in this example, contour tones on three-syllabled words are absent. The autosegmental model explains this fact:

$$(9) \quad \text{i.} \begin{bmatrix} \text{L H L} \\ \diagdown\!\!\!\diagup \\ \text{CVC} \end{bmatrix} \quad \text{ii.} \begin{bmatrix} \text{L H L} \\ \diagdown\!\diagdown \\ \text{CVCVC} \end{bmatrix} \quad \text{iii.} \begin{bmatrix} \text{L H L} \\ \mid \diagdown\diagdown \\ \text{CVCVCVC} \end{bmatrix}$$

The contour tones result from a situation in which the number of tones is greater than the number of syllables. Of course, it is assumed here that tones are mapped onto the vowels in one particular way: from left to right in a one-to-one fashion as far as possible. The mapping-relation will be discussed in more detail in sect. 2.2.5.

Another point in favor of the autosegmental model is that the existence of morphemes lacking either the tonal or the segmental tier is predicted given a model in which tonal and segmental properties are encoded independently. Segmentless morphemes can be found indicating for example tenses of verbs. A particular melody (say L) is associated with verbs without any change at the segmental level. For examples we refer to Goldsmith (1976). Morphemes that lack the tonal tier in their lexical representation are equally common. Usually such toneless morphemes are affixes. They receive tone at the surface from the base they are attached to.

Within a segmental model the representations of 'defective' morphemes requires the use of archisegments, i.e. in this case segments that have blanks for the tonal features or for all features except the tonal ones. Such underspecified segments were disallowed in the SPE theory and the representation of 'defective' morphemes must therefore be thought of as anomalous in this theory. Defective morphemes are easier to account for in an autosegmental model, requiring no additional theoretical notions (such as archisegments) apart from those already necessary for 'complete' morphemes.

2.2.4. The independence of autosegmental tiers

The examples we are now about to present have been set apart since they provide the strongest support for the autosegmental model. If tones and segments are really as independent as autosegmental phonology assumes then it should be possible for rules to refer to one tier without affecting the other tier. For example, it is predicted that a rule may delete part of the tonal tier, causing some bearers to be deprived of tones.

The fact that rules may operate on one level disregarding other levels explains why tonal rules often have 'unbounded' effects. Odden (1980) describes a rule in Shona (a Bantu language) that lowers a sequence of high tones in a word possessing a high toned prefix (one out of a limited set):

(10) mbwá   'dog'   né-mbwà   'with dog'
      hóvé   'fish'   né-hòvè   'with fish'
      mbúndúdzí   'army-worm'   né-mbùndùdzì   'with army worm'

Within a multi-tiered model all three words will have the same melody, viz. H:

(11) a. $\begin{bmatrix} H \\ | \\ mbwa \end{bmatrix}$ b. $\begin{bmatrix} H \\ \wedge \\ hove \end{bmatrix}$ c. $\begin{bmatrix} H \\ \diagup|\diagdown \\ mbundudzi \end{bmatrix}$

The dissimilation rule will refer to this single H and change it to L. This means that the change in all three word types is accounted for in terms of a single rule (i.e. not a rule schema) and it is also explained why the rule is unbounded in effect: the number of syllables is completely irrelevant.

An example involving a deletion rule is taken from Elimelech (1976); cf. Clements (1979: 100). In *Etsakọ* the expression 'each N' involves the reduplication of the relevant N:

(12) ówà   'house'   ówǒwà   'each house'

A reasonable derivation of the reduplicated form takes the following underlying form as its starting point. (In section 2.3.4. we will discuss another possible treatment of reduplication.):

(13) $\left[\begin{bmatrix} H \ L \\ | \ | \\ owa \end{bmatrix} \begin{bmatrix} H \ L \\ | \ | \\ owa \end{bmatrix} \right]$

The surface form is derived by deleting the first *a*. The deletion rule refers only to the segmental tier and therefore we expect that the tone that is associated with this *a* will stay. If *Etsakọ* were a language that forbade contour tones on short vowels this would be the end of the story. The floating L tone would remain unassociated, which means that it would not receive a phonetic interpretation. However, *Etsakọ* permits contour tones on short vowels. In this case we need a rule that associates the 'floating' tone to the right. Clements & Ford (1979) have hypothesized

that a tone that is set afloat in this way will always be associated with the
segments that caused the deletion of its original bearer:

(14) $\left[\begin{bmatrix} H & L \\ | & \\ ow & \end{bmatrix} \begin{bmatrix} H & L \\ | & | \\ owa & \end{bmatrix}\right] \rightarrow \left[\begin{bmatrix} H & L \\ | & \diagdown \\ ow & \end{bmatrix} \begin{bmatrix} H & L \\ | & | \\ owa & \end{bmatrix}\right]$

The phenomenon that tones remain when the corresponding tone-bearing segments are deleted is called *stability*.

Stability is also evidenced in the following example. Thai has a word game in which parts of syllables constituting a word may be interchanged. The melody however stays as it was (Leben 1973, Yip 1981):

(15) klúày hɔ́ɔm   klɔ́ɔm hùáy   'banana'
      téǹ r$\bar{\text{a}}\bar{\text{a}}$ táà r$\bar{\text{e}}\bar{\text{n}}$ 'dance'

It is clear that if tonal and segmental features form an integrated whole such phenomena become hard to account for. Though we can represent defective morphemes in the segmental framework (using archisegments) it is more difficult to imagine a rule type that deletes parts of segments or moves such parts around. Note that the reverse is not true. I.e. if one needs rules that refer to tonal and segmental features simultaneously such rules can be formulated in an autosegmental model. Such rules will be more complex than rules that just refer to a single level, and, as Clements and Ford (1979) argue, it is therefore correctly predicted that they are less common. In the next section we will mention a few examples of such rules.

2.2.5. Association principles

The concept of multi-tiered representations was introduced in Leben (1971), where however no details can be found about the way tones are linked to tone bearers. In Williams (1971, published as Williams 1976), a 'mapping rule' is discussed that maps tones onto segments (vowels) from left to right. A similar rule is employed in Leben (1973). Both authors then develop a model in which phonological representations are multi-tiered before the mapping, but one-tiered after the mapping. This makes it possible to distinguish two types of rules in terms of the ordering relation with the mapping rule. We may have rules that apply before the mapping and rules that apply after the mapping. The former can be used for phenomena that bear witness to the independence of autosegmental levels, whereas the latter may be used when we have to refer to tonal and segmental features at the same time.

Examples of the latter kind of rule are provided in Osburne (1979) who discusses the phenomenon that vowels may be lengthened when they are associated with more than one tonal feature. Osburne's point is that such phenomena suggest a more intimate relation between tones and their bearers than is necessary for rules that refer to a single tier.

Recently Odden (1980) has provided new arguments in favor of the Leben-Williams model. He refers to a rule (again in Shona) that has a bounded effect, i.e. in a sequence of high tones only one is changed into a low tone:

(16)   hóvé   'fish'   hóvè húrú   'large fish'

This would be difficult to describe in terms of a dissimilation rule if there is only one tonal segment (i.e. H) to refer to. When we assume that the mapping of tones onto vowels results in a one-tiered representation in which each vowel has its own tonal specification Odden's rule may simply refer to the specification of the relevant vowel.

A major argument against this model comes from contour tones. If tones are merged with segments one cannot account for short vowels that have a contour tone. This simple fact led Goldsmith (1976) to a different interpretation of the mapping relation. Goldsmith proposed that phonological representations are multi-tiered at all levels. The result of the mapping operation is just that we indicate how segments on different tiers are co-articulated. Formally this is done by inserting association lines between the different tiers.

It may now be asked how the examples given in Osburne (1979) and Odden (1980) can be accounted for. It was noted earlier that it is perfectly feasible to write rules that refer to more than one level. Such rules are more complex and this will only be a problem for the autosegmental model if the relevant phenomena turn out not to be as 'marked' as for instance Clements & Ford claim they are. As for Odden's rule, the same facts can be accounted for in terms of a rule that inserts an autosegment (L) associated with the second vowel in *hóvè*.

A compromise between the Leben-Williams model and the Goldsmith model is suggested in Halle & Vergnaud (Part I). They argue that the autosegmental specification of tonal segments at a separate level does not preclude the assignation of *segmental* tone features too. For arguments in favor of this model we must refer to their article. Assuming that the decision of Halle & Vergnaud is well-founded it might be suggested that 'local' phenomena be handled in terms of rules that affect the segmental features, though we must in that case add an extra convention to their theory saying that if a rule changes a segmental value this will imply dissociation with the corresponding tonal autosegment and subsequent reassociation with or creation of another autosegment.

We will now turn to the important question how the association lines come into being and what principles govern the wellformedness of multi-tiered representations. A first approximation to these problems is laid down in the so called Wellformedness Condition (WFC), put forward in Goldsmith (1976):

(17) *Well-formedness Condition*
 1. Each tone is associated with at least one segment
 2. Each segment is associated with at least one tone
 3. Association lines do not cross

As it stands, this convention is both too weak and too strong. It is too weak as an instruction to draw the lines, since in some cases there are several possibilities of satisfying it. Given (18a) as the starting point there are at least three possibilities:

(18) a. $\begin{bmatrix} T & T & T \\ t & t & t & t \end{bmatrix}$ b. $\begin{bmatrix} T & T & T \\ | & | & \backslash \\ t & t & t & t \end{bmatrix}$ c. $\begin{bmatrix} T & T & T \\ | & \backslash & \backslash \\ t & t & t & t \end{bmatrix}$ d. $\begin{bmatrix} T & T & T \\ \backslash & \backslash & \backslash \\ t & t & t & t \end{bmatrix}$

These problems are noted in Haraguchi (1977) and Clements & Ford (1979). These authors then suggest that the Wellformedness Condition should be made more specific. They propose three conventions, the first of which resembles the mapping rule that was already proposed in Williams (1971). This rule states that tones are associated with tone bearers in a one-to-one fashion from left to right until we run out of tones or bearers. The other conventions specify what the following steps should be. According to Goldsmith's WFC we would have to associate the remaining tones with the last bearer (clause 1 in 17) or the remaining bearers with the last tone (clause 2):

(19) a.

Here the WFC is too strong, however. Clements & Ford (1979) as well as Halle & Vergnaud (Part I) argue that tones that remain unassociated after the left-to-right rule has applied (or that become dissociated when their original bearer is deleted) should not be (re)associated as a matter of convention. When nothing is said in a particular grammar such unassociated tones will remain unassociated, which means, as we have said before, that they will not receive a phonetic interpretation. According to Halle & Vergnaud (Part I) the association of more than one tone with a single vowel is a marked phenomenon that requires an extra language specific rule if it occurs. If such a rule is absent from the grammar only one tone per vowel will be permitted. Hence clause 1 of the WFC that requires that each tone must be associated with at least one segment must be abandoned. We refer to Halle & Vergnaud's article, where it is shown that their model may lead to simpler analyses. We have already seen that tones that are set afloat as the result of deletion rules must be reassociated by means of specific rules (cf. our example in (14)). This also implies that there cannot be a general convention governing the association of floating tones.

What is retained from the WFC are clauses (2) and (3). The fact that association lines may not cross (clause 3) is a fundamental aspect of the autosegmental theory that may never be overruled, but clause (2), as it stands, leads to indeterminacy. When an unassociated tone-bearing unit has a tone both to its left and to its right there are two possibilities for association. Clause (2) must therefore be supplemented by additional principles, such as those proposed by Goldsmith himself or replaced by a set of more specific conventions like those of Clements and Ford (1979).

So far we only have considered tone-systems in which the tonal melody is associated with the segmental string from left to right, *starting with the leftmost tone and the leftmost tone-bearing unit.* There are languages in which the association does not begin with the leftmost tone and the leftmost tone-bearing unit. In other words, there are tonal systems in which some other tonal segment than the first must be associated to a particular tone-bearing unit before any other association takes place (according to the universal conventions discussed above). Systems of this type usually have a more limited set of melodies (often just one). The normal convention is to mark with a star ('*') the tonal and the segmental elements whose association precedes all other association.

The most important difference between systems that use stars and those that do not is then in the way the first association line is introduced, connecting in the first case the *leftmost* segments, and in the second the *starred* segments. Once the first line is drawn all other association follows from the same universal conventions. This point was made very explicit in Haraguchi (1977) who proposed that learning the tonal system of a language involves choosing an initial association rule from a limited set of universally available rules. So far we have seen two such initial association rules and it may be that there are no others.

Tonal systems that employ the first choice, i.e. associate the leftmost elements, are usually called (lexical) tone systems: each lexical item is provided with a particular melody in the lexicon. Such systems are opposed to systems that use 'stars' and which are commonly referred to as pitch-accent systems.

In the case of pitch-accent systems the melody may be introduced by a phonological rule. There exists considerable disagreement about a precise definition of pitch-accent or about the question whether tone-systems are fundamentally different from pitch-accent systems. Clements & Ford (1979) suggest for example that 'lexical-tone' languages may be thought of as 'pitch-accent' languages that always have the star on the leftmost position, both on the tonal and the segmental tier.

Goldsmith (1974, 1976: ch. 3, 1981a) has given an analysis of English as a 'tone-language', or, rather as a 'pitch-accent language'. The set of melodies is limited to one: MHL and the starred H tone is associated with the vowel that bears primary accent:

(20) a. $\begin{bmatrix} M & \overset{*}{H} & L \\ & | & \\ & \text{America} & \end{bmatrix}$ b. $\begin{bmatrix} M & \overset{*}{H} & L \\ & & \\ & \text{Kalamazoo} & \end{bmatrix}$ c. $\begin{bmatrix} M & \overset{*}{H} & L \\ & | & \\ & \text{archipelago} & \end{bmatrix}$

Other pitch-accent systems are discussed in Goldsmith (Part I). An extensive analysis of pitch-accent in Japanese can be found in Haraguchi (1977) from whom we have taken the following examples:

(21) a. $\begin{bmatrix} \overset{*}{H} & L \\ | & \\ \text{inoti} \end{bmatrix}$ 'life' b. $\begin{bmatrix} \overset{*}{H} & L \\ & \\ \text{kokoro} \end{bmatrix}$ 'heart' c. $\begin{bmatrix} \overset{*}{H} & L \\ & \\ \text{atama} \end{bmatrix}$ 'head'

The first rule is to associate the starred segments. This is indicated by the closed line. The other association lines follow, in Haraguchi's account, from the WFC. The surface patterns of the present examples show an initial L tone if the first tone-bearer is non-starred. To introduce this L tone Haraguchi formulates a rule that looks like:

(22) $\begin{matrix} & H & & & L & & H \\ & \wedge & & \longrightarrow & | & & | \\ V & C_o & V & & V & C_o & V \end{matrix}$ / # C_o ——

Finally it is necessary to remove the L tone that forms part of the basic melody if its bearer is also associated with the H tone. The final result is:

(23) a. $\begin{bmatrix} H & L \\ | & \wedge \\ \text{inoti} \end{bmatrix}$ b. $\begin{bmatrix} L & H & L \\ | & | & | \\ \text{kokoro} \end{bmatrix}$ c. $\begin{bmatrix} L & H \\ | & \wedge \\ \text{atama} \end{bmatrix}$

It is interesting to note that Halle & Vergnaud would not need the rule that deletes the final L. Their model would not predict association in the first place. Another difference between Haraguchi's treatment and that of Halle and Vergnaud (Part I) follows from the fact that in Halle and Vergnaud's version the universal association conventions apply only to unassociated, i.e. non-starred tones. In example (21c) the starred H cannot spread to the first two tone-bearing units. Segments that remain without a tone receive the unmarked value for tone, but this is not the high tone, at least not in Japanese. Therefore the melody they assume for Japanese is HHL rather than HL.

2.2.6. Tone-bearing segments and 'projections'

There is one important point that must be discussed. How do the tones 'know' where to go? Let us assume, to simplify matters somewhat, that tones are associated with vowels (and not with syllables, or parts of syllables). Consonants then have to be skipped somehow or other. Clements (1976) and Halle and Vergnaud (1981) assume that for each type of autosegmental association a particular set of 'P-bearing units' (tone-bearing units in this case) must be identified. Alternatively, one might make use of the so-called projections that were proposed in Halle & Vergnaud (1978) to take care of a similar problem with regard to vowel harmony. Though Halle and Vergnaud (1981) themselves have rejected to make use of the notion projection for the purpose of association we will indicate what this notion stands for, because it is used in many recent publications. In short, projections are strings of segments that result from omitting segments that do not have a certain property, e.g. the string of vowels, which results from omitting all segments that do not have the property '[+voc]'. Projections, as the notion is used in the literature, do not have to be made up of segments. They can comprise sequences of elements (however defined) of any level of the phonological hierarchy, i.e. we find reference to the rhyme-projection, syllable-projection, foot-projection. One should not think of projections as derivational levels. Different projections including the 'basic' segmental projection (which is itself the segment-projection) constitute simultaneous representations. For some discussion of the notion projection we refer to Anderson (Part II).

2.3. Extensions of the autosegmental theory

We have seen how the autosegmental theory solved a particular problem in the representation of tone. The solution that was proposed entailed certain predictions with regard to the behaviour of tones and tone-bearing units which have turned out to be correct. In this section we show how the autosegmental theory extended its empirical domain to non-tonal phenomena. These display some of the properties that were successfully dealt with in the analysis of tone. First we will look at autosegmental treatments of *sub*segmental phenomena, which remind us of the problem we had with contour tones. Then we will turn to the non-tonal counterparts of *supra*-segmental phenomena such as vowel-harmony and length. A further extension of the autosegmental theory, the treatment of syllable structure, will be discussed in the next section (sect. 4) in order to compare this treatment there with the metrical theory of the syllable.

2.3.1. Complex segments

The representation of complex segments has been discussed over the years in a fair number of articles (see Ewen, Part II for a survey and an analysis of such segments in a dependency framework). Most recently Anderson (1976, 1978) has called our attention to the representation of prenasalized and postnasalized consonants. Anderson rejects the use of features like [prenasal] or [postnasal]. His arguments are completely parallel to the arguments against contour features such as [rising]. For the purpose of rule application a postnasalized consonant behaves like a nasal consonant when it is a left context and like a non-nasal when it is a right context. The similarity to the situation with contour tones is recognized by Anderson. He proposes explaining this behaviour by giving segments sequentially ordered subparts, i.e. ordered opposite specifications for the same feature:

(24) $\qquad$ [b͡m]

syll	−
cons	+
nas	− | +
high	−

Anderson does not make any claims about tiers or association lines but he is aware of the fact that the impact of his proposal is the same as that of the autosegmental theory, although the notation differs: the definition of segments as unordered sets has been abandoned (cf. Anderson 1978: 54). The autosegmental equivalent of (24) would be (25):

(25)

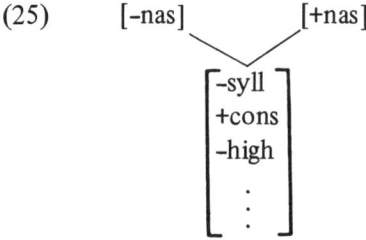

In more recent versions of the autosegmental model one can find a slightly different treatment of complex segments (cf. Clements and Keyser 1981). The basic idea is that a complex segment is characterized in terms of two fully specified segments that are linked to one 'segmental slot':

(26) a.   C   b.   C   c.   V
             / \   / \   / \
            b   m   p   f   i   e
       (postnasalized stop) (affricate)   (short diphthong)

The notion 'segmental slot' will be discussed in sect. 2.3.3. Within this approach complex segments are referred to as *branching segments*.

2.3.2. Harmony

In this section we will discuss how the autosegmental theory has been applied to non-tonal suprasegmental phenomena. The question might be asked whether an autosegmental treatment of harmony phenomena is necessary. Several authors have tried to show that autosegmental treatments run into certain difficulties not present in segmental analyses using iterative rules (cf. Vago 1980, Anderson 1980, Part II). We will not go into their arguments here but refer to Anderson (Part II), who claims that segmental rules can still be used beside autosegmental rules and 'metrical rules' (to be discussed in sect. 4.3.). In fact, Anderson claims that using segmental rules to deal with harmony phenomena solves the overlap problem that exists between autosegmental and metrical theory. Placing vowel harmony outside the range of both theories, he argues, allows one to develop more constrained versions of both, while the power of segmental rules does not have to be increased in any significant way.

2.3.2.1. Vowel harmony. When all vowels in a particular domain (usually the word) have to agree for one or more features we speak of vowel harmony. Clements (1976a) has discussed a number of properties that most vowel harmony systems are claimed to have in common, of which 'unboundedness' and 'bidirectionality' are the essential ones. For a critical discussion of Clements' list we refer to Anderson (1980). Unboundedness refers to the fact that (within a particular domain, in this case the word) a particular feature is assigned to all vowels (regardless of their number), i.e. to the vowel-projection. This 'spreading' resembles the situation with tones, when there are more bearers than tones and tones are spread over several bearers. If harmonizing features are, like tones, autosegments and the same or comparable association principles are applicable then harmonizing features display exactly the behaviour one would expect. The same is true of bidirectionality, which refers to the fact that in most systems both prefixes and suffixes are subject to harmony, i.e. the harmonizing feature of the base spreads in two directions.

The issue of bidirectionality is not uncontroversial. It has been shown that the basic association rule for tones may be directional (i.e. left-to-right) rather than bidirectional, though in particular cases tones may be associated to the left also, e.g. if this is the only way in which a tone-bearer can be associated with a tone (cf. example (21a) in Japanese, where the H tone spreads to the left to become associated with the leftmost tone-bearer). Anderson (1980) claims that directionality statements can not be avoided in autosegmental treatments of harmony. Leaving this matter for further discussion, we will give a simple example of an autosegmental treatment of vowel harmony, taken from Clements (1977a).

In Hungarian vowels agree in their specification for the feature [back]. Lexical entries take one of the two following forms (in the case that they are stems):

(27) a. $\begin{bmatrix} +B \\ tOrOk \end{bmatrix}$ torok 'throat'   b. $\begin{bmatrix} -B \\ tOrOk \end{bmatrix}$ török 'turkish'

('B' stands for the feature [back]; capital letters indicate vowels that are unspecified for the harmonizing feature).

A major difference between tone and vowel harmony is that in the former case one never finds 'melodies', i.e. sequences of unassociated segments at the level of the harmonizing features. In section 2.3.4. we will discuss an extension of the autosegmental model in which tonal melodies do find a counterpart in melodies of vocalic features. It is the fact that there is only one autosegment that makes spreading bidirectional in the case of vowel harmony. Application of the universal association convention will give us:

(28) a. $\begin{bmatrix} +B \\ tOrOk \end{bmatrix}$ b. $\begin{bmatrix} -B \\ tOrOk \end{bmatrix}$

One of the diagnostics for the autosegmentality of a feature that was present in the case of tones was that there may be morphemes in which one of the tiers may be missing from the lexical representation. As is well known, languages with vowel harmony usually have affixes that agree in their vowel specification with the bases they are attached to. Such morphemes can be compared to toneless morphemes in tone languages (cf. sect. 2.2.). An example is the suffix *nAk* 'to (dative)' in Hungarian:

(29) a. $\left[\begin{bmatrix} +B \\ tOrOk \end{bmatrix} nAk\right]$ toroknak b. $\left[\begin{bmatrix} -B \\ tOrOk \end{bmatrix} nAk\right]$ töröknek

A characteristic property of vowel harmony systems is the presence of vowels that in some way interrupt the smooth flow of the spreading feature. Basically these vowels seem to be of two types.

The first type of apparent interruption concerns vowels that are not affected by the harmony process at all. Such segments are called *neutral*. In Hungarian for example the front vowel *i* is not subject to backing harmony. What is curious about neutral segments is that they are transparent for the spreading process. In Hungarian, a back vowel to the left of the neutral vowel /i/ causes backing harmony in a vowel standing to the right of the neutral vowel. Clements' original treatment of neutral vowels runs as follows. First neutral vowels are affected, i.e. associated with the harmonizing feature, then an additional rule ties them to the autosegment −B:

(30) $\left[\begin{bmatrix} +B \\ rAdIk \end{bmatrix} nAk\right] \rightarrow \left[\begin{bmatrix} +B & -B \\ rAdIk \end{bmatrix} \begin{bmatrix} +B \\ nAk \end{bmatrix}\right]$

This treatment is critically discussed in Anderson (1980) and Vago (1980). Another treatment would be to exclude neutral segments from the stipulated set of 'P-bearing' segments.

The second type of interruption concerns segments that, like neutral segments, are not affected by a spreading feature, but that, unlike neutral segments, are not transparent. Such segments block the spreading and they are called *opaque*. The usual treatment of opaque segments is to assume that such segments are lexically associated with 'their' autosegment. An example will be taken from Akan, as analyzed by Clements (1976). In Akan the low vowel /a/ blocks the spreading of the autosegment [Advanced Tongue Root]:

(31) $\left[\begin{matrix} & +A & -A & \\ O & + & bIsA & + & I \end{matrix}\right] \Rightarrow \left[\begin{matrix} & +A & -A & \\ O & + & bIsA & + & I \end{matrix}\right]$

We have assumed here that the universal association conventions apply both to the free [+A] and to the bound [−A]. This is in fact Clements' position.

Another analysis is possible, however. Halle and Vergnaud (1981, Part I) assume that the universal association conventions (both for tonal and non-tonal autosegments) apply only to free autosegments. In their theory then the result of applying the universal conventions in Akan would be (32):

(32) $$\begin{bmatrix} +A & -A \\ \diagup\diagdown & | \\ O + bIsA & + I \end{bmatrix}$$

The final vowel surfaces as [-ATR] and this is explained by assuming that *all* vowels are segmentally specified with the unmarked value (assuming that the unmarked value is [-ATR]). When vowels are linked to an autosegment, the specification of this autosegment overrides the segmental value, but when there is no autosegment the segmental value turns up.

In some cases it is clear that the theory of Halle and Vergnaud must be preferred. One example of this concerns the blocking of rounding harmony in Mongolian by high round vowels (cf. Chinchor 1979). All vowels that follow such vowels are [-round], and this value cannot be explained in terms of spreading from the blocker (cf. Halle and Vergnaud for another example; they analyze Mongolian harmony differently).

However, it is not always the case that vowels surface with the unmarked value when a blocker prevents association with a free autosegment. There are cases (e.g. in Guarani, as discussed in Van der Hulst and Smith, Part II) in which we must assume that the blocker is subject to spreading. This implies that we must distinguish two types of blockers: spreaders and non-spreaders. For the former type Halle and Vergnaud (1981) propose a metrical treatment that will be discussed in sect. 4.2.

For a more detailed account of the autosegmental framework we refer to the publications of Clements. Critical assessments of this type of analysis can be found in Anderson (1980), Vago (1980), Barratt (1981), Battistella (1979) and Halle and Vergnaud (1981).

2.3.2.2. Other types of harmony. Here one example of the autosegmental behaviour of *nasality* will be given, which is interesting since it involves a morpheme that consists only of nasality. This, as the reader will recall was one of the diagnostic features for autosegmental treatment. In Terena, as described in Bendor-Samuel (1960), subjects of verbs and first person possessive pronouns are expressed in terms of a span of nasality that starts from the beginning of the word and spreads to the right as far as the first stop or fricative. This stop or fricative surfaces as a prenasalized obstruent:

(33) e'mo ʔ u   'his word'   ẽ'mõ ʔ ũ   'my word'
      'ayo   'his brother' 'ãỹõ   'my brother'
      'owoku   'his house'   'õw̃õŋgu   'my house'
      'piho   'he went'   'mbiho   'I went'
      a'hya ʔ a ʃ o   'he desires'   ã'nʒa' ʔ a ʃ o 'I desire

One may treat obstruents as *opaque* segments associated with an autosegment [-nas]:

(34) a. [[+nas] [   ]]   b. [[+nas] [-nas]]   c. [[+nas] [-nas]]
         [[ayo]]   [[owuku]]   [[piho]]

(Note that the segments following the opaque segments would also surface as [-nas] if we assumed the theory of Halle and Vergnaud, [-nas] presumably being the unmarked value). It will be assumed here that prenasalized stops in examples like (34b) are the result of a later rule:

(35)   [+nas]   [-nas]
         | |
         V   C

In Van der Hulst and Smith (Part II) other examples of the autosegmental behaviour of nasality will be given. Hyman (Part I) presents an autosegmental analysis of nasality in Gokana, which he compares to 'traditional' segmental analysis.

2.3.3. Three dimensional phonology
There are several questions with regard to the autosegmental theory that have not been dealt with yet. First: what kinds of features show autosegmental behaviour? And second: if several autosegmental tiers are present within the same language (e.g. tonal tier, a harmony tier and a segmental tier) how are they related to each other?

With regard to the first question it may simply be the case that formally each feature can behave independently from all others, but that there are substantial constraints, related to matters of articulation, on the number of tiers present in languages. Interesting proposals in this regard have been made within the framework of dependency phonology (especially Ewen 1980, cf. Ewen Part II), where each segment is seen as an unordered set of 'gestures' each of which is again an unordered set of features in the usual sense:

(36)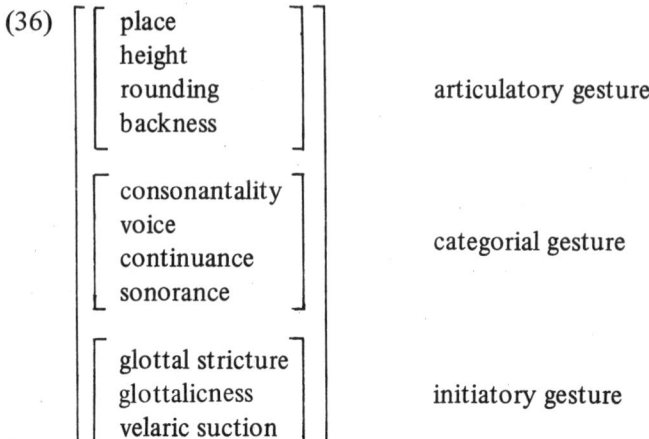

It seems reasonable to assume that a proposal along these lines could account for the relatively independent behaviour of features that belong to different gestures. Something similar is proposed (within an autosegmental analysis of aspiration in Icelandic) in Thrainsson (1978), who sets apart laryngeal and supralaryngeal features.

With regard to the second question - how are different tiers related to each other - one can choose between two alternatives. All the tiers may be piled up, one on top of the other, as it were, or possibly, there is one basic tier with which all other tiers are associated. It is the latter approach (attributed to Halle by Goldsmith 1976) that one finds in recent work.

It is assumed that the basic tier consists of the major class features [consonantal] and [vocalic], with 'C' standing for [+cons, -voc] and 'V' for [-cons,+voc]. The basic tier then takes the form 'CVCVCCVCVCVV...'. In sect. 3 it will be shown that this basic tier corresponds to the terminal nodes of the phonological hierarchy. It is clear that phonological representations take the form of multi-dimensional objects, when the number of tiers that may be associated with the basic tier is only limited by the number of phonological features (or gestures).

2.3.4. Non-concatenative morphology

The possibility of representing different (clusters of) features on different tiers is used in a novel way by McCarthy (1979, 1981, Part I) to deal with certain types of so called non-concatenative morphological operations.

One of McCarthy's most extensive examples concerns the verbal morphology of classical Arabic. McCarthy's framework can be illustrated most clearly by reviewing this example in some detail.

Each verb in Classical Arabic may occur in a number of derivational classes (involving meanings such as habituality, iterativity etc.) and within each such class the verb has a number of inflected forms (indicating tense, voice, finiteness etc.). All the forms in the paradigm of each verb are characterized by a constant element i.e. three or four 'root' consonants that occur in each form. These consonants always occur in the same linear order, but forms of a verb may differ to the extent that different vowel patterns may be interspersed among the consonants in the consonantal pattern. Moreover, one of the consonants may be doubled and occasionally an 'extra' consonant is added:

(37)   perfective   perfective
                Active   Passive

       I   katab   kutib
       II   kattab   kuttib
       III   kaatab   kuutib
       IV   aktab   uktib
       V   takattab   tukuttib
       VI   takaatab   tukuutib
       VII   nkatab   nkutib
       VIII   ktatab   ktutib
       IX   ktabab   ktubib
                            etc.

It can be seen that different derivational classes (numbered I, . . .) are characterized in terms of specific 'CV-skeleta':

(38)   I   CVCVC
       II   CVCCVC
       III   CVVCVC
       IV   CVCCVC
       V   CVCVCCVC
       VI   CVCVVCVC
       VII   CCVCVC
       VIII   CCVCVC
       IX   CCVCVC

Furthermore one will notice that, whereas the skeleta (plus an occasional extra consonant e.g. *t* in V, VI and *n* in Vii) characterize the derivational class uniquely in most cases (with regard to VIII and IX the class is also determined by the way in which the consonantal pattern is 'spread') the vowel melodies characterize tense and voice. McCarthy suggests that the consonantal and vocalic patterns are to be considered as autosegmental levels and that the CV skeleta (familiar in descriptive grammars of Arabic) be given the theoretical status of the basic autosegmental tier we discussed in the previous section.

It has been claimed by McCarthy and others (cf. Goldsmith 1979) that the vocalic and consonantal patterns or 'melodies' form the counterpart of tonal melodies. In section 2.3.2. we noticed that autosegmental levels involving harmonizing features never showed melodies, which, comparing this with tonal phenomena leaves us with a 'gap'. McCarthy's melodies, it is claimed, fill this gap. The reader should be aware of the fact that the motivation for assigning melodies to autosegmental tiers differs crucially in McCarthy's analysis from the analyses that were discussed. McCarthy uses different tiers for different *morphemes*, as well as different (bundles of) features. This means that in McCarthy's theory the same feature may occur on a number of different autosegmental levels. This implies that there is a theoretical difference between autosegmental morphemic melodies and autosegmental harmonizing features, which are usually not independent morphemes (but cf. nasalization in Terena in sect. 2.3.2.2.).

When looking at the example in (39) one will notice that both the vowel and the consonantal melody may 'spread out' in cases where there are more slots than segments:

(39) I a. $\begin{bmatrix} ktb \\ CVCVC \\ a \end{bmatrix}$ II a. $\begin{bmatrix} ktb \\ CVCCVC \\ a \end{bmatrix}$ III a. $\begin{bmatrix} ktb \\ CVVCVC \\ a \end{bmatrix}$

I b. $\begin{bmatrix} ktb \\ CVCVC \\ ui \end{bmatrix}$ II b. $\begin{bmatrix} ktb \\ CVCCVC \\ ui \end{bmatrix}$ III b. $\begin{bmatrix} ktb \\ CVVCVC \\ ui \end{bmatrix}$

One will also notice that in II the consonants and in IIIb the vowels are not associated as expected. It is suggested that in such cases an extra rule is needed that deletes the 'expected' line, after which reassociation takes place; e.g. for IIa:

(40) $\begin{bmatrix} ktb \\ CVCCVC \\ a \end{bmatrix} \rightarrow \begin{bmatrix} ktb \\ CVCCVC \\ a \end{bmatrix} \rightarrow \begin{bmatrix} ktb \\ CVCCVC \\ a \end{bmatrix}$

Other morphological processes that involve 'copying' of some sort can be handled in a similar way. Halle and Vergnaud (1980) analyze plural formation in Hausa, where the stem final consonant is 'copied' in the plural suffix, as follows:

(41) a. dámóo   dámàamée   'land monitor'
          báràa   báròoríi   'servant'

b.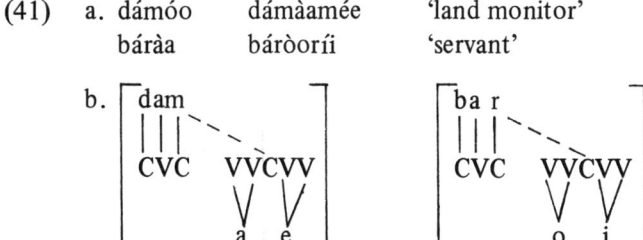

The suffix consists of a CV skeleton that is only partially supplied with a melody. In order to fill the empty C slot the last consonant of the stem melody is associated with it.

Reduplication processes are also ideal candidates for this kind of treatment. Consider reduplication in Gothic. To form the preterite an extra syllable is prefixed to the stem, consisting of a fixed vowel [ɛ] (written as *ai*) preceded by a copy of the first consonant of the stem:

(42) a. i.   fahan   faifah   'to catch'
               slepan   saislep   'to catch'
          ii. aukan   aiauk   'to augment'
          iii. staldan   staistald   'to stand'

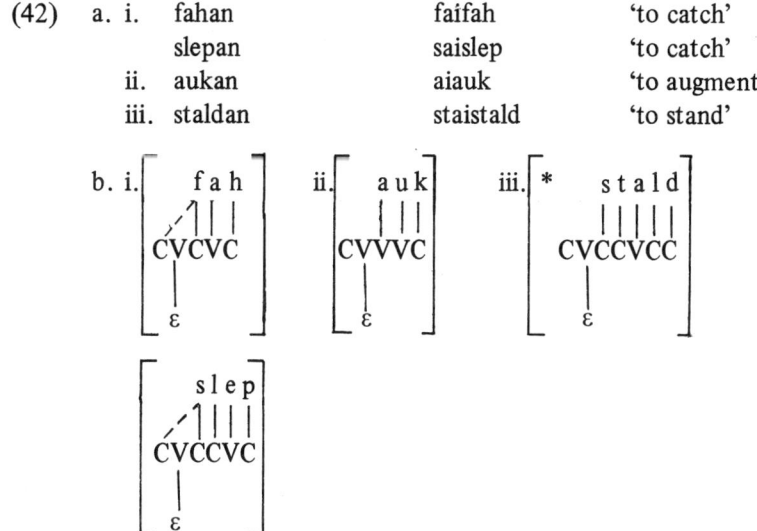

The forms in (42i) illustrate that only the first consonant spreads to the empty Є slot and the form in (42ii) shows that nothing extra need to be stated in those cases where the stem begins with a vowel. Example (42iii) is problematic, however. It appears that when the stem begins with *st, sk* (we may assume also *sp* but an example is lacking in Gothic) both consonants are repeated. This could be accounted for by representing these clusters as single consonants ('complex segments') an idea for which independent motivation exists (cf. sect. 3.3.1. and Ewen Part II). Halle and Vergnaud (1980), quoting Marantz (to appear), mention another possible approach to reduplication that involves having a copy of the whole word melody associated from left to right (or vice versa when the reduplication affix is a suffix). Segments that are 'left over' do not surface by a convention that we are already familiar with (cf. sect. 2.2.5). McCarthy (Part I) also discusses reduplication processes (as well as the special case of echo formations). We refer to his article for further details.

2.3.5. Length

In the previous section the examples show that the autosegmental model, as developed so far accounts for *length* by associating one segment, e.g. of the vocalic melody, with more than one slot in the CV skeleton (cf. the examples in (41)). It is this treatment of length that offers us the possibility of accounting for the cases where long segments exhibit dualistic behaviour — behaving sometimes like a single consonant and sometimes like two consonants. Leben (1980) points out that Hausa long consonants pattern with "single segments in a plural class (...) and yet behave like clusters with respect to syllable structure constraints". The present model explains this dualism, since long consonants will be characterized, at the CV level, in terms of two C slots. This explains why such consonants are clusters with regard to syllable structure, because syllable structure is defined at the CV level. C's and V's correspond, as we said earlier (and will discuss more fully in sect. 4) to the terminal nodes of the syllabic constituent structure:

(43)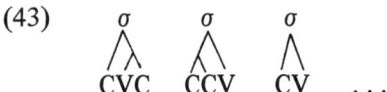

It is also explained why long consonants may behave as single segments since they are in fact represented as such at the autosegmental morphemic level.

Another possibility offered by the model is a means of handling compensatory lengthening. Consider a change that took place in Proto-Germanic where short vowels followed by a nasal consonant and a velar voiceless fricative changed to long vowels with 'simultaneous' loss of the nasal:

(44) a. þaŋxta > þāxta   'I thought'

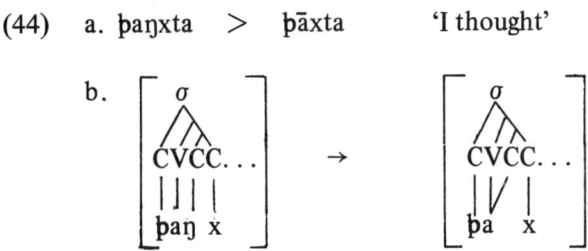

One can account for the lengthening and loss in terms of a single operation: the deletion of the association line between the nasal and its slot. There is one problem, however. Note that the present analysis is only possible if vowels may be associated with C slots (cf. Clements and Keyser 1981). This seems rather awkward and it is perhaps better to alter our conception of the CV skeleton, i.e. we should conceive of this skeleton not as consisting of C's and V's but simply of *segmental positions*. The information which segment constitutes the peak of the syllable is not lost when this move is made, since it can be deduced from the syllable structure that organizes the segmental positions: the position that is exhaustively dominated by nodes labelled with S corresponds to the V, all other positions correspond to C's. (The labelling of nodes will be explained in sect. 3 and, with reference to syllable structure, in sect. 3.3.1.). If this is done, this analysis of compensatory lengthening is virtually identical to that of Ingria (1980), where one can find more examples of this type of analysis. A rather different account of compensatory lengthening using rules that alter the syllable structure itself is offered in De Chene and Anderson (1979).

The fact that segmental slots remain when the associated segment has been cut loose (or deleted) may be regarded as an instance of the phenomenon of *stability* referred to in sect. 2.2.4. This supports the present model in which the relation between the segmental skeleton and the morphemic melodies is indeed one of autosegmental association.

2.4. Recapitulation

In the preceding sections we have discussed how a theory originally designed to 'solve' a tonal problem (i.e. contour tones on short vowels) developed into a general theory of tone. As such the autosegmental model is accepted by most generative phonologists. Then the theory was applied to other phenomena that are traditionally, like tone, considered to belong to the area of suprasegmentals, viz. harmony and length. There also is an autosegmental treatment of syllable structure, but this will be discussed in sect. 3.3.1., where we compare it to the metrical treatment. Finally the idea of linking 'melodies' to a skeleton was used to account for all sorts of non-concatenative morphological processes.

Not all extensions have met with general approval. Some prefer segmental solutions for harmony (Anderson) others have proposed metrical solutions (to be discussed in sect. 4). Other controversial points relate to the possible inventory of autosegmental levels and to the mapping conventions that relate levels to the central skeleton.

3. METRICAL PHONOLOGY

In this section we will discuss the second important development – *metrical phonology*. The theory of metrical phonology was originally developed as a theory of stress, but (and this may sound familiar by now) the domain of this theory was extended to other phenomena exhibiting metrical diagnostic features. As is not surprising the extension of metrical theory has led to a point where it has 'invaded' the territory of autosegmental phonology, which has resulted in the availability of a number of competing theoretical proposals some of which we will discuss in sect. 3. For the moment we will temporarily set aside the idea that phonological representations are multidimensional.

3.1. General remarks

In Fudge (1969) it is argued that there are two types of hierarchical organization imposed on each linguistic expression, both taking segments (or the elements of the segmental skeleton) as their starting point. One is the morpho-syntactic hierarchy in which segments are organized into morphemes, morphemes into words, words into phrases etc. The other is the phonological hierarchy, in which segments are grouped together into syllables, syllables into 'feet', feet into (phonological) words etc. Metrical phonology (in a 'developed' stage) is a theory about the nature of this phonological hierarchy, its internal organization, its role in the application of phonological rules, and its relation to the morpho-syntactic hierarchy. As was said above, metrical theory began as a theory of stress (much as autosegmental theory began as a theory of tone). We will first discuss the metrical approach to stress, and then turn to the extensions, especially with regard to syllable structure.

3.2. The metrical theory of stress

The theory originally proposed in Liberman (1975), further elaborated in Liberman & Prince (1977), Halle & Vergnaud (1978) and Selkirk (1980) will be presented here more or less in the form that it has in Hayes (1981), though a number of details will be omitted.

Within metrical theory the stress pattern of a word (or larger units) is represented in terms of a binary branching constituent structure where sister nodes are labelled 'S' (meaning 'stronger than' or 'dominant') and 'W' ('weaker than' or 'dependent'). The basic building blocks are thus:

(45) a.   b.

The labels S and W are not to be interpreted as phonological features with a fixed phonetic interpretation. They indicate that the node labelled S is *in some way* dominant with respect to the sister node labelled W. The 'stronger-than' relation is binary, asymmetrical and irreflexive, which means that the following structures are excluded from the theory:

(46)   i. Binary   ii. Asymmetrical   iii. Irreflexive

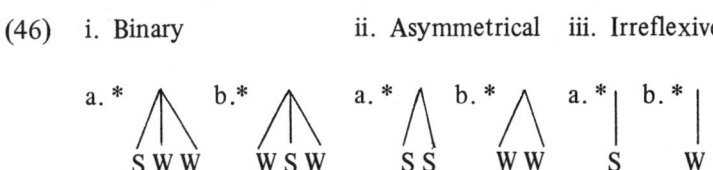

Binary trees, labelled S/W, have one and only one terminal element that is exclusively dominated by nodes labelled S. It is this property which makes them so suitable to express those characteristics of the sound flow that are traditionally called culminative. Stress is one such property (being the peak of a syllable is another). Stress is, however, not only a culminative property — it is also a relative property. This is why the structure under (46 iiia,b) should receive no interpretation in the theory. It makes no sense to say of a single isolated syllable that it is dominant or dependent.

One of the first questions to be answered now is: on what grounds is the precise constituent structure determined for expressions that have more than two syllables. Here one must make a distinction between expressions that do not have a morphological and/or syntactic structure and those that have. In the former case the expression consists of a monomorphemic word. It is generally accepted that in the latter case the prosodic structure can often be built up as a function of the morpho-syntactic structure, though the function in general is not one of isomorphy. We will not discuss here the assignment of metrical structure (also often termed prosodic structure) to syntactic phrases and sentences. We refer to Nespor and Vogel (Part I) and Selkirk (1980). The important point is that the prosodic structure, being only partially determined by the syntactic structure, is not isomorphic with it. This reminds us of the 'readjustment' rules in SPE needed to account for the lack of congruence between syntactic and intonational phrases.

As for morphologically structured words, a major dividing line seems to exist between compounds and derived words. In languages like English or Dutch the prosodic structure of compounds is in the normal case isomorphic with the morphological structure. For some derived words the same can be said, as long as the affixes involved belong to the so-called *neutral* class. In the standard theory it is assumed that neutral affixes are associated with a strong boundary ('#'). Put in metrical terms we may say that such affixes constitute a prosodic unit on their own; they form phonological words, just like their bases. For non-neutral affixes (associated with the boundary symbol '+') the issue is more problematic. The question may be asked whether prosodic structure is built up 'cyclically' or non-cyclically in words derived with non-neutral affixes. Kiparsky (1979, Part I) argues (with regard to English) for the former option. Clearly if prosodic structure is assigned cyclically then the morphological structure determines the resulting structure.

The position defended by Selkirk (1980) is essentially the same as Kiparsky's. The difference is that Selkirk assumes that prosodic structure is a lexical property. In her analysis the cyclic effects follow from the fact that each newly derived word contains the base *with* its prosodic structure. If Selkirk is right, and cyclic effects do not follow from a particular mode in which rules are applied to words, then one is forced to say that prosodic structure will be non-cyclic (i.e. unrelated to morphological structure) in languages in which prosodic structure is not a lexical property (i.e. languages that have completely fixed stress). In these languages the prosodic structure of each derived word must be built up 'without help from the morphology'. In other words, from a prosodic point of view, such words must be treated as if they were underived words. Let us therefore turn to the question how to deal with underived words.

In their original treatment of English stress Liberman & Prince provide the following algorithm for assigning metrical structure. First the English stress rule assigns [+stress] to certain vowels working from right to left. Then every sequence of a single [+stress] vowel followed by a maximal sequence of [–stress] vowels is associated in a left-branching tree labelled S/W (i.e. left node S, right node W). They call the resulting trees *feet*. The feet are then joined into a right-branching structure labelled W/S (with an extra proviso that we will ignore here):

(47) i. stress-assignment: hamamelidanthemum
    + - + - + - -

ii. foot-formation:

```
                    S
          ∧  ∧    ∧
         S W S W S W W
        hamamelidanthemum
         + -  + - +   - -
```

iii. word-tree-formation:

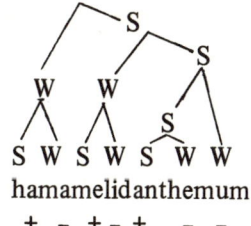
hamamelidanthemum
+ - +- + - -

A structure like (47iii) must be interpreted as follows. Main stress falls on the penultimate vowel, i.e. the vowel that is exhaustively dominated by nodes labelled S. Non-primary stresses fall on the other vowels that are assigned [+stress] by the stress rule. In the SPE notation the vowel bearing the main stress comes out as [1stress], the vowel having the strongest non-primary stress as [2stress], the next strongest as [3stress] etc. These stress values can be deduced from metrical trees by counting the number of nodes dominating the lowest node labelled W (if any) and adding 1 to the resulting integer. This last step (adding 1) is required to achieve descriptive equivalence with the SPE system. (Without this step, main stress would come out as having zero stress.) Since weak syllables in a foot must be interpreted as having no degree of stress at all we will only carry out this procedure for strong syllables (cf. Selkirk 1980):

(48)

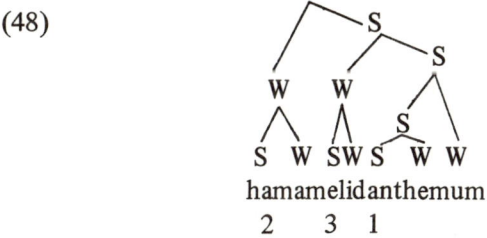
hamamelidanthemum
 2   3 1

In subsequent work (Prince 1976, Selkirk 1980) it has been pointed out that the feature [stress] and the stress assignment rule are superfluous, provided that we make foot assignment sensitive to the same segmental properties that trigger application of the English stress rule. For example: the English stress rule assigns [+stress] to each tensed vowel. Selkirk, in her analysis, forbids the occurrence of tensed vowels in a W position in a foot, which means in effect that syllables containing a tensed vowel will always be the head of a foot, and hence will always have some degree of stress.

The system outlined so far makes use of notions like 'foot' and 'word tree'. In Halle & Vergnaud (1978) an attempt is made to investigate what types of feet and word trees one needs to describe all existing stress systems. Hayes (1981) gives a further elaboration of their proposals and shows that a large variety of stress systems can be elegantly accounted for by stipulating values for a limited number of parameters. We will mention here some of the most important types.

We saw that the assignment of feet in English is sensitive to the make-up of syllables, e.g. whether or not they contain a tensed vowel. Hayes calls such feet *quantity-sensitive* (henceforth Q-sensitive). Q-sensitive feet come in two different types: *bounded* or *unbounded*.

A stress system makes use of bounded feet if there is an upper limit to the number of syllables that may be grouped into a foot. English feet are restricted to an upper limit of three syllables, at least in Selkirk's analysis. Hayes claims that bounded feet are universally limited to disyllabic feet, called binary feet, and monosyllabic feet, called degenerate feet. He has noted that ternary feet only occur at the edge of words, and he argues that in such cases we may assume that the marginal (final or initial) syllable is *extrametrical*. This means that such a syllable is (made) invisible for the foot assignment rules, which can only assign binary and degenerate feet. Afterwards a rule of 'stray syllable adjunction' joins the extrametrical syllable to the final (or initial) foot, thus creating a ternary foot. An argument in favor of the extrametricality device is that in systems using Q-sensitive feet, the quantity of the extrametrical syllable appears to play no role whatsoever. One might ask why the ternary feet are not added to the inventory of possible feet, with the proviso that these ternary feet may only occur at the margins of words. The extrametricality device must also be constrained so as to apply only at the margins of words. However, this issue must be left for future discussion.

An example of *unbounded* Q-sensitive feet is provided in Hayes' analysis of Eastern Cheremis where primary stress falls on the last full vowel of the word and, if there is no full vowel, on the first vowel. The feet are sensitive for the distinction between full and reduced vowels. Every full vowel followed by a maximal sequence of reduced vowels constitutes a separate foot. If a word consists only of reduced vowels, these form a single foot:

(49) a. 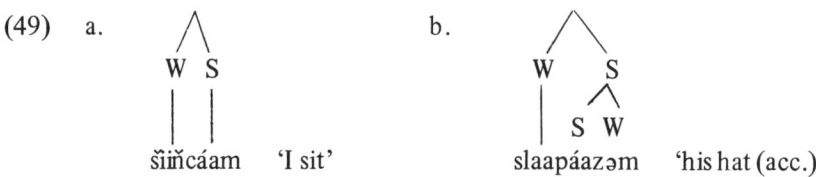 b.

        šińcáam 'I sit'   slaapáazəm 'his hat (acc.)'

c.   d.

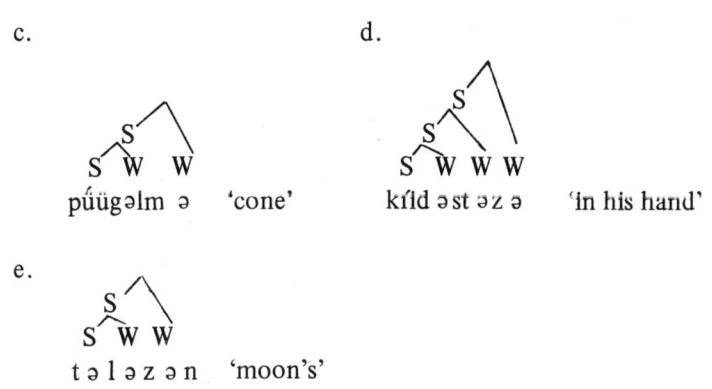

púügəlm ə 'cone'   kíld ə st ə z ə   'in his hand'

e.

```
     S
   / | \
  S  W  W
```
t ə l ə z ə n   'moon's'

Languages may differ in how they interpret quantity distinctions for the purpose of foot construction. The cover terms used are 'light' vs. 'heavy':

(50)
light	heavy
open syllable	closed syllable
lax, short vowel	tensed, long vowel
reduced vowel	full vowel
etc.	

We will see in section 3.3.1. how the light-heavy distinction may be presented metrically (in most cases) as a distinction between non-branching vs. branching nodes.

We will now turn to feet that are Q-*in*sensitive. Here one finds the same distinction of bounded vs. unbounded feet. As an example of bounded Q-insensitive feet Hayes adduces the stress system of Maragungka, where primary stress falls on the initial syllable and a non-primary stress on every second syllable thereafter:

(51) a.   b.   c.

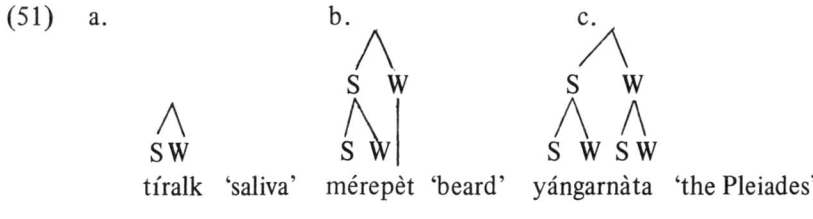

       tíralk 'saliva'   mérepèt 'beard'   yángarnàta 'the Pleiades'

d.

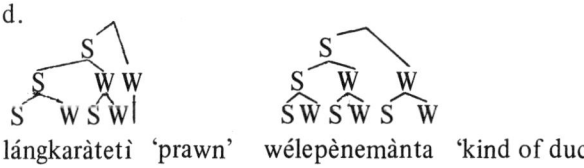

   lángkaràtetì 'prawn'   wélepènemànta 'kind of duck'

When a language has unbounded Q-insensitive feet all syllables of every word will always be grouped together in one foot, meaning that the word tree is always degenerate. Why, one might ask, is it not possible to say that in such languages there is only a word tree, i.e. no foot level. The point is that feet and word trees receive different phonetic interpretations. In a foot all syllables except the head are stressless. So if a language has only one stressed syllable in a word, all other syllables being stressless, one may say that the language has unbounded Q-insensitive feet. But if one is dealing with a language having some degree of stress on each syllable it is necessary to say that the language has only degenerate, monosyllabic feet and dominating them a word tree:

(52) a. b.

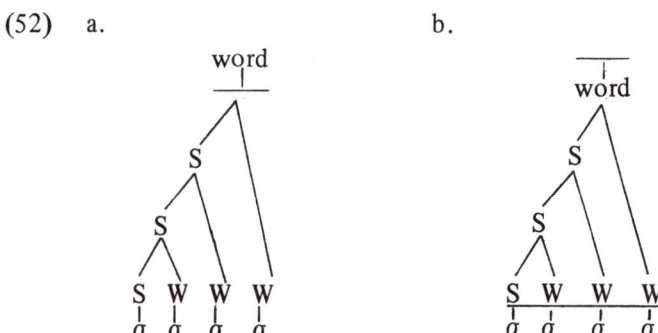

Selkirk suggests that we identify languages of type (52b) as the syllable-timed languages. She mentions French as an example. Stress-timed languages would then be those in which feet may contain sequences of a strong syllable followed by one (if the feet are bounded) or more (if they are unbounded) weak syllables.

The theory of stress as outlined so far has only made use of trees that are uniformly branching *per level*. Furthermore, in all the cases we discussed labelling is predictable on the basis of the direction of branching of the tree (Wheeler 1979 argues that this is always the case). This suggests that the following structures are illformed:

(53) a. b.

Let us assume (simplifying the matter somewhat; cf. Hayes 1981, ch. 4)

that this is indeed the case, and that a child learning his language can only choose trees that are uniformly branching at a particular level, with the labelling being determined by the direction of branching. Learning the stress system of a language now means that the child must find out whether or not there is a foot-level, whether or not feet are bounded and Q-sensitive, what the branching and labelling is at a particular level etc. Having fixed the parameters the stress system will be uniquely determined. We note here that learning the direction of branching and learning the labelling may be considered as one and the same thing if leftbranching trees are always S-W and rightbranching trees always W-S. The redundant nature of the S-W labelling is brought to the surface in recent elaborations of the metrical theory in which the labelling is omitted (Halle, Lectures in Paris, March 1982).

As stated here the metrical theory accounts for the fact that stress is relative and culminative. The success of this approach is also apparent from the fact that certain aspects of the SPE-theory that were especially introduced for the treatment of stress (such as the stress lowering convention) are no longer necessary (cf. Liberman & Prince 1979: 263 and Hayes 1981: ch. 2).

3.3. Extensions

The first extension of the metrical theory we will discuss here concerns syllable structure. In sect. 2.3. we made reference to the fact that there also is an autosegmental theory of the syllable. In the next section we will compare both extensions. After that a proposal to handle downdrift (cf. sect. 2.2.1.) in metrical terms will be looked at. Finally we will review Selkirk's interpretation of the metrical theory as a theory about phonological domains.

3.3.1. Syllable structure

The standard theory makes no use of the notion syllable. It has often been argued that this was an unfortunate attempt to reduce the number of phonological primes. One undesirable consequence was the fact that certain conjunctions had to be constantly repeated in phonological rules, which is the classic indication that a generalization is being missed. Examples are the SPE notion 'weak cluster' and (54a,b) which stand for open and closed syllable, respectively:

(54) a. $\ldots / - \left\{ \begin{array}{c} CV \\ \# \end{array} \right\}$ b. $\ldots / - C \left\{ \begin{array}{c} C \\ \# \end{array} \right\}$

It would be better if the rule could refer to what the conjoined environments have in common. Another motivation for introducing the syllable was that so called phonotactic restrictions (i.e. phonological wellformedness conditions) are most appropriately formulated in terms of the notion wellformed syllable or rather wellformed parts of a syllable. Considerations of this type led to the introduction of *syllable boundaries* which represents the only possible means of accommodating the notion of syllable in a linear theory.

In Kahn (1976) we find the first non-linear approach to the syllable attractive to phonologists working within a generative framework. Kahn's theory is inspired by autosegmental notation. A node labelled 'syllable' is associated by a series of universal and language specific conventions to the segmental string, resulting in structures like:

(55)

One will notice that in certain cases one segment is associated with two syllable nodes. This is allowed by the autosegmental theory. Such segments are termed *ambisyllabic* and they play an important role in Kahn's analysis of allophonic alternations in English.

It has been argued, in particular by Selkirk (Part II) that the formulation of phonotactic restrictions makes a more detailed structuring of the syllable desirable. For example, co-occurence restrictions are not usually applicable to the syllable initial consonant(s) and the following vowel, whereas restrictions between the vowel and its succeeding consonant(s) are extremely common. Such differences are inexplicable if one assumes a Kahn-type structure of the syllable. However, if one assumes that the vowel plus what follows form a constituent within the syllable this difference is given a structural basis:

(56)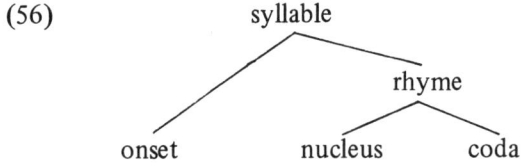

A structure like (56) has been hypothesized by some phonologists for a long time (e.g. Pike & Pike 1948, Fudge 1969). The resulting structure can be given a metrical interpretation. Each syllable has a peak, i.e. the segment that possesses some phonetic feature (e.g. sonority or aperture) to the greatest degree. This is reminiscent of the fact that each word has one syllable bearing main stress. The S/W labelling provides a means of expressing this property of the syllable:

(57)

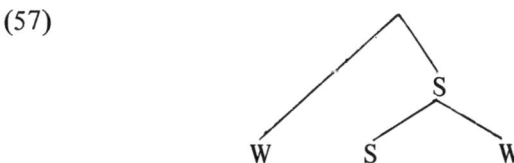

It becomes apparent now why S and W must not receive a fixed phonetic interpretation. Below the syllable level the labels correspond to sonority but above this level to accent (i.e. pitch, duration, loudness).

Kiparsky (1979) contains a proposal concerning the metrical structure of syllables with a more complex structure, i.e. complex onsets, nuclei and/or coda's:

(58)

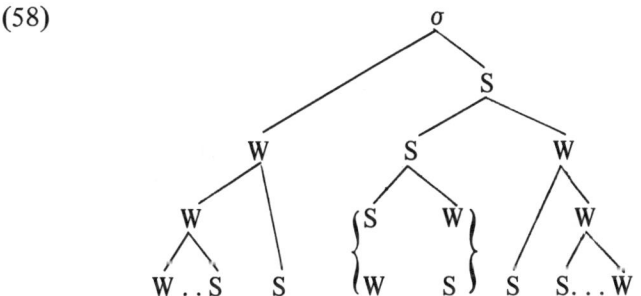

The present structuring of the syllable accounts for the phenomenon that consonants which are nearer to the syllable margin are generally less sonorant than those that are nearer to the peak. Notoriously problematic in this respect are clusters like *sp, st* or *sk*, which, as we have seen in section 2.3.4. are also problematic in other respects. A typical 'metrical' approach is to consider the *s* as being extrametrical in such cases, but it is also possible to regard the clusters as forming one (complex) segment.

It seems clear that ambisyllabicity cannot be accounted for in the metrical theory of the syllable, assuming one interpretation of the formalism used. That is, assuming that the metrical structure forms the output of a phonological grammar that uses rewrite rules. One segment cannot belong to the expansion of two sister nodes. That metrical structure can in fact be seen as the output of a phonological grammar is an essential aspect of the framework of categorial phonology as developed in Wheeler (1981). Cf. also Prince (1980).

In section 3.2. we discussed the distinction between light and heavy syllables, which appeared to play an important role in stress systems possessing Q-sensitive feet. It was noted there that this distinction could be expressed in terms of branching in the metrical theory. It is now possible to show what this means.

When feet assignment rules are sensitive to whether syllables are open or closed one can say that such feet are built on the *rhyme-projection*. If the rhyme node branches this means that the syllable is closed, but if it does not the syllable will be open. It is also possible for feet to be built on the *nucleus projection*. This is the case when the feet are sensitive to the distinction between long and short vowels. Long vowels correspond to a branching nucleus, short vowels to a non-branching nucleus. Apparently feet are never built on the *syllable-projection*, which implies that whether or not a syllable contains an onset is completely irrelevant for stress assignment.

3.3.2. Downdrift
In section 2.2.1. we discussed the phenomenon that the pitch height of tones may gradually decrease toward the end of an utterance. It has been suggested by Clements (1981a) and Huang (1979) that downdrift should be interpreted metrically. They propose the following algorithm:

(59) i. Join each maximal sequence of H's followed by a maximal sequence of L's in a n-ary branching tonal foot
ii. Join tonal feet in a rightbranching structure labelled H/L

When this algorithm is applied to a sequence of H and L tones the result is as follows:

(60)

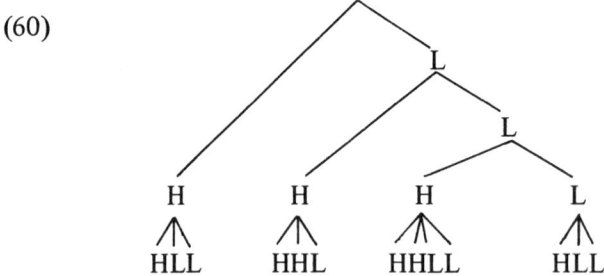

It is clear that one of the central assumptions of metrical structure is abandoned as far as the construction of tonal feet is concerned: the tonal foot is not binary branching. One could attempt to 'save' the fundamental metrical principle of binarity in the following way. In section 2.2.2. we mentioned the so called Obligatory Contour Principle. If in the course of a (morphological) derivation two identical tones come to stand next to each other they will automatically be collapsed into one 'segment'.

The tonal level thus created is then subject to (tonal) foot formation; the tonal feet are binary, containing a H tone as left daughter and a L tone as right daughter. Clause (i) of (61) can now be said to follow from metrical principles. Clause (ii) remains of course necessary:

(61)
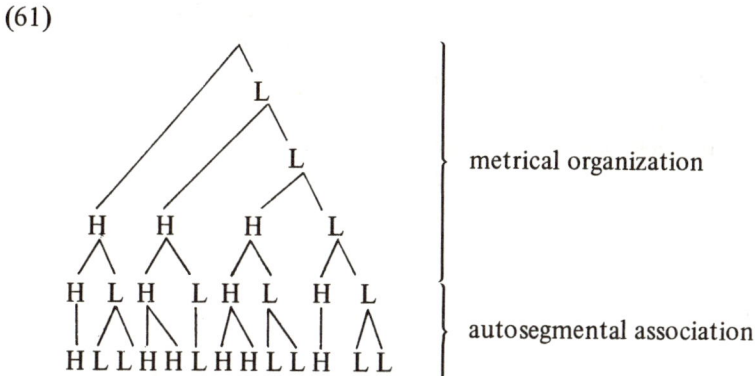

It seems that no empirical consequences are involved, but we believe that the structure in (61) has some conceptual advantages over that in (60).

3.3.3. Phonological domains

Selkirk (1980, 1980a) has pointed out that the metrical theory is not just a theory about 'prominence' (whether in syllables, words or larger units). The constituent structure (with or without the labelling) also serves a clear purpose in the application of phonological rules. It may be the case e.g. that a rule is limited in its application to strings of segments that are dominated by a particular prosodic category, e.g. the foot. The fact that rules may be sensitive to such domains provides independent support for recognizing them as primitives in the theory. According to the domain of application Selkirk distinguishes syllable-span rules, foot-span rules etc. Another way in which phonological domains may be of relevance is that a rule may apply at the edge of a domain or to adjacent segments which stand at the edge of adjacent domains. It is evident that in rules of this latter type reference can be made to the phonological constituent structure, i.e. to the labelled phonological bracketing. This removes the need for so-called phonological boundary markers such as '$' (syllable boundary). In addition many rules that refer to a grammatical boundary can now be reformulated in terms of rules that refer to phonological constituent structure (which is itself partially determined by the grammatical boundaries) (cf. Rotenberg 1978).

4. AUTOSEGMENTAL AND METRICAL THEORY

In section 3.3.1. we discussed two approaches towards syllable structure. The availability of two competing proposals is the result of the fact that both the autosegmental and the metrical theory have extended their empirical domain to this area. There are other areas where the extensions of both theories have also led to the availability of competing analyses, especially with regard to the treatment of harmony processes. In this section we will discuss in more detail this 'clash' of theories and the various ways that have been suggested of achieving a division of labour. First we will return to the treatment of syllable structure and then we will show how an extension of the notion foot has been used to deal with certain types of harmony.

4.1. Syllable structure again

Recently Clements & Keyser (1981) have argued for a return to Kahn's theory of the syllable. They question the arguments that have been put forward for a more complex structure on the general grounds of simplicity: notions like heavy and light syllable can also be expressed structurally in a n-ary tree. One of their more important arguments involves the treatment of ambisyllabicity, which, as we have seen cannot be expressed in the metrical framework.

One might suggest that given the separation of the CV skeleton and the morphemic melodies, which Clements & Keyser have also adopted in their theory, the notion of ambisyllabicity could be expressed in a metrical framework in terms of one consonant that is linked to two C slots of two adjacent syllables:

(62)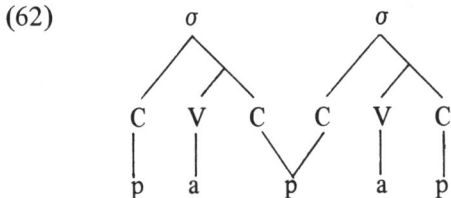

A disadvantage of this approach is that ambisyllabic consonants need not necessarily be long consonants. Earlier (in sect. 2.3.5.) it was shown that segments from the morphemic melody that are associated with two slots at the CV level are interpreted as long in the autosegmental theory. This is perhaps not a real problem, however. It might be suggested (capturing the essence of a proposal advanced in Vogel 1977: 91) that segments, linked to two slots are interpreted as long, *only* if there exists a length contrast in the language in question. Another way out of this problem (suggested by Deirdre Wheeler) would be to make use of the fact that slots may remain unfilled. An ambisyllabic consonant would then be any consonant this is preceded by a 'floating C':

(63)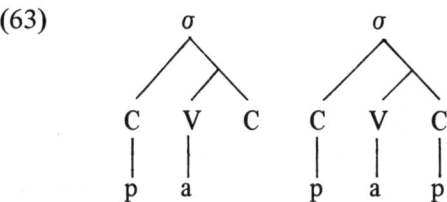

We will leave both proposals for further discussion and turn to another area of overlap.

It has been argued that when tautosyllabic adjacent segments share identical features these features can be assigned to the metrical node dominating those segments. A mechanism called *feature percolation* takes care of the fact that this feature is assigned to each segment dominated by the metrical node (Halle & Vergnaud 1978, Lowenstam 1979). However, assuming the necessity of the autosegmental framework one could also propose that a feature that has all the segments within a metrical constituent in its scope can be handled in terms of an autosegment whose association is tied to this particular domain. In the next section we will see that the *percolation of features* in metrical trees and *autosegmental association* are also competing mechanisms for handling harmony processes.

4.2. Foot structure

One of the most serious attempts to extend metrical theory, or rather the binary branching tree, to areas that were regarded as the exclusive domain of autosegmental theory is the Halle & Vergnaud (1981) treatment of certain types of harmony. They distinguish two types of harmony, viz. directional and non-directional harmony. For the latter type they recommend the autosegmental model, but for the former type they propose using binary branching trees coupled with feature percolation. Directional harmony is characterized by the fact that one can identify designated segments, which trigger the spreading either to the left or to the right up until the next designated segment. There are no opaque segments that are not also triggering segments. For this type of harmony Halle and Vergnaud propose the following treatment. Each sequence of segments terminated to the left (if the direction of the harmony is rightward) by a designated segment (indicated by the arrow in (64) is organized in a binary left-branching tree:

(64)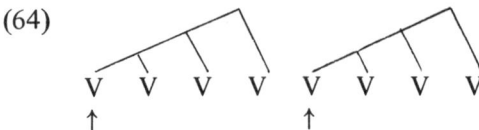

Subsequently the harmonizing feature of the opaque segment is copied onto the top node. The mechanism of feature percolation takes care of the fact that all vowels in a harmony foot receive the appropriate feature. To deal with directional harmony one could also allow for *directional association*. We have seen that the basic association convention for tonal systems is in fact directional, i.e. left-to-right. Anderson (1980) too has pointed out that autosegmental theory cannot escape from directional association. The crucial question is whether there is any reason to prefer binary branching feet over directional association rules. One could argue that, in the absence of arguments in favor of the metrical solution a choice for directional association rules must be made.

The position that even directional harmony must be dealt with autosegmentally does not imply that one denies the relevance of foot structure for particular types of harmony. Such domains are relevant if independently necessary foot structure (i.e. stress feet) specifies the domain within which harmony takes place. An example is reported in Hayes (1981) where it is claimed that stress feet form the domain for vowel harmony in Eastern Cheremis. In Eastern Cheremis the autosegmental association of the harmonizing feature is apparently tied to the domain of the foot. This point will be dealt with in more detail in Van der Hulst & Smith (Part II).

5. CONCLUDING REMARKS

In the preceding section we have discussed a classical problem, viz. the availability of several analyses of one phenomenon, while it is methodologically desirable that the theory be such as to exclude more than one analysis. This seems to be in line with the general state of affairs in generative phonology at present. We have not discussed in detail all the areas where one can find competing analyses. Even with respect to tonal phenomena where the autosegmental theory seems to be best motivated, very challenging metrical alternatives have been proposed, e.g. in Zubizaretta (Part II). There are, in addition, treatments of stress (e.g. in Schane 1979a,b) in which some of the insights of metrical phonology are adopted though *not* the idea that there is a *binary* branching constituent structure (for a discussion of Schane's theory we refer to Haraguchi, Part I and Hayes, Part I).

With respect to the overlap between metrical and autosegmental theory several proposals have been put forward to eliminate this. Anderson (Part II) wants to retain segmental analyses precisely in those cases where the two theories overlap. Halle and Vergnaud (1978, 1981) eliminate the overlap by arguing that there is 'metrical' harmony and 'autosegmental' harmony. Leben (Part I) proposes that the metrical and autosegmental theory can be reduced to one. He mentions a number of similarities between the two systems and proposes stress feet with an autosegmental structure and a metrical labelling. In Van der Hulst & Smith (Part II) yet another way to solve the overlap problem is suggested in which metrical theory is primarily seen as a theory of phonological domains, which set an upper bound to harmony processes. These are then handled in terms of autosegmental association.

We cannot offer the reader a unified theory in this introduction that will meet with general acceptance, but we hope that the present overview has shown that generative phonologists are attacking a variety of theoretical problems and have come up with a number of insightful answers. Not surprisingly this has led to an increase in the descriptive capacity of the theory and also to underdeterminacy. The time has come then to examine critically the devices that are presently available in order to find out which should be preferred.

Accent Systems

John Goldsmith
Indiana University

1. INTRODUCTION

While the study of accent is as old as any of the fields comprising phonology, the nature of accent, and the relation of accent to other phonological phenomena, remain mysterious and obscure.[1] Phonetically, there is little doubt that accent has something to do with loudness, with pitch, and with syllable duration; still, the nature of accent is obscure enough to warrant certain recurrent attempts to defend the reality of accentual distinctions which are allegedly perceived by speakers even in the total absence of specific phonetic cues.[2]

From the point of view of the linguist who wishes to construct a phonological model valid for the description of all human languages, the thorny problems posed by the analysis of languages such as English may be overcome by investigating entirely unrelated languages, and developing descriptive models that are unambiguously necessary for the analysis of these other languages. With this equipment in hand, we may then return to English to see how the accentual system of English looks in the light of a theoretical model motivated elsewhere.

It is in this spirit that I would like to review the essentials of two Bantu languages, Ci-Ruri and Ci-Tonga. Both are, I would like to suggest, accentual languages, yet neither display such characteristics as "accent subordination" or vowel-stress as one might have, wrongly, expected to find in an accent system.

Historically, the Bantu languages of Africa are known to have been tone languages. While there is no simple phonetic criterion that will pinpoint the boundary between accent and tone languages from the sound alone, Ci-Ruri and Ci-Tonga have a special property that distinguishes them from tone languages and that fixes their accentual character: at a certain point in the phonological derivations in both languages, the tonal representations consists strictly of an integral number of copies of a fixed, language-specific Basic Tone Melody (Low-High-Low for Ci-Ruri, High-Low for Ci-Tonga).

This sort of characterization makes particular sense when viewed within the framework of autosegmental phonology.[3] Phonological representations permit words and phrases to be composed of parallel rows, or tiers, of segments which are organized with respect to one another by association lines that connect segments on facing tiers, as in (1).

(1) CV   CV   CV
      \ / \ /
       H   L

The case at hand is that in which the features specifying tone — and thus, ultimately, pitch or fundamental frequency — are on a tier separate from the segments specifying the consonants and vowels, much as in (1).

The specific properties of the rules and phonological representations in the strictly autosegmental part of the derivation (see (2)) have been studied in some detail. There is, however, relatively greater uncertainty at this point concerning the range of mechanisms possible in assigning the tones to their respective syllables at the beginning of the autosegmental derivation.

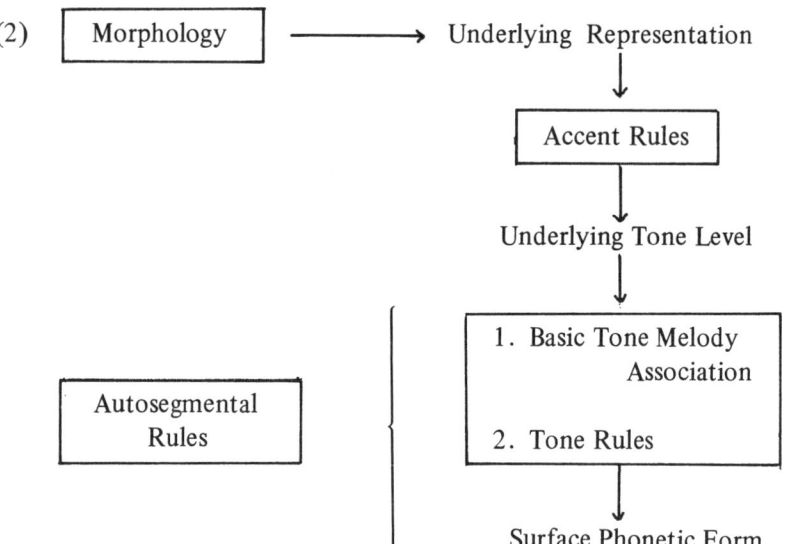

There is less uncertainty regarding the *source* of the underlying tone melodies, however, and it is here that the fundamental notion of an accentual system enters the picture. Since an underlying tone pattern appears in a specific position in a sentence, it follows that the choice of a specific pattern may be a governed by (a) lexical considerations; (b) grammatical factors; (c) both (a) and (b); or (d) neither (a) nor (b). Cases (a) through (c) are typical of tone languages; (d) represents the accentual case. In

Accent Systems

the first case, the lexical entry present in a given structure includes (or, conceivably, consists simply of) a complete tonal melody, much as the Igbo word *m̀mà* 'knife' contains underlyingly not only vowel and consonant specifications, but also the tonal sequence High-Low. In the second case, the syntactic structure or syntactic features on constituents can give rise to segments on the tonal tier, as argued, for example, in Clark (1979). These two types of information can work in tandem to produce a tone melody, as in Igbo (Goldsmith (1976)) or Kikuyu (Clements (1982)), that is, case (c). When none of these factors come into play, there can be only one pattern that is used throughout the language in question (case (d)); and that is precisely the case of an accent language, with one Basic Tone Melody.

In accent languages, then, Basic Accent Melodies are inserted, one per (derived) accent at the Underlying Tone Level.[4] This is achieved by the general Accent Association Rule (3). From that point on, the derivation in such languages is virtually indistinguishable from that of tone languages (see McCawley (1978)), except that, in principle, reference to the accented syllables is still possible in the formulation and application of autosegmental rules.

(3)

At this point, some elements on each tier are associated, while others are unassociated. In earlier work on autosegmental phonology, it was assumed that the Well-formedness Condition came into effect immediately, inserting association lines as necessary (see Goldsmith (1976)).

(4) *Well-formedness Condition* (WFC)
   1. All vowels are associated with at least one toneme.
   2. All tonemes are associated with at least one vowel.
   3. Association lines do not cross.

Subsequent work over the last five years has suggested an elaboration of this picture in two directions. The original proposal for the Well-formedness Condition (Goldsmith (1974)) separated the definition of the well-formed autosegmental state, as in (4), from the principles used by the theory (or each language) to insure maximal meeting of those conditions. That is, it is possible in theory that all languages would share (4) as a well-formedness condition, yet differ as to how they chose to meet the condition. One language might decide to delete all offending vowels; another might insert Low tones for any unassociated vowels; and yet a third might automatically and immediately add association lines as necessary. It was originally proposed (in Goldsmith (1974, 1976)) that only the third option was available.

As Odden (1982) points out, however, such a claim makes unavailable a type of rule-formulation which, intuitively, seems entirely in keeping with the spirit of the theory and which, more importantly, is well-motivated in natural languages. We would like to make reference to elements — vowels or tonemes — which are "free", or unassociated; but if the WFC applies immediately, there will, under almost all conditions, *be* no free elements. Viewed from a slightly different perspective, the function that the WFC plays in autosegmental theory, that of associating otherwise unassociated elements, can be pre-empted by language-specific rules whose formulation requires reference to the notion of a "free" element. In fact, if we permit autosegmental rules to refer to free elements (as suggested in Goldsmith (1976, p. 104)), and if we take Kiparsky's Elsewhere Condition (Kiparsky, 1973a) to be a regulative principle of grammars' operation, then the Well-formedness Condition and such a rule would be in the appropriate Elsewhere relationship, and the rule, being more specific, would have precedence over the application of the WFC.

Thus the immediate application of the WFC should be taken in this more complex sense. In another area, concerning how a language elects to meet the WFC, subsequent research has indicated that a language may specify the direction of association of a free element. Thus while the WFC is itself symmetric and adirectional, the algorithm chosen by a language to meet the WFC may give directional precedence.

We turn, now, to the problem of accent within the autosegmental framework.

2.   CI-RURI

Ci-Ruri, or Ruri, is a Bantu language spoken in northwestern Tanzania.[5] The morphology of Ruri is like that of most Bantu languages: nouns normally consist of a monosyllabic class prefix on a monomorphemic stem, although an additional pre-prefix is present in Ruri as well. Verbs have a more intricate structure, with anywhere from three to seven morphemes, most of which can vary independently.

To give us an idea of how the surface tonal patterns arise, let us consider first the perfect tense. We observe that all verbs behave either like *gur* ("unaccented") or like *kam* ("accented"). Here as elsewhere, the acute accent (´) represents High tone; no mark indicates Low tone. Rising tone is represented "ˇ"; Falling tone is represented "ˆ".

Accent Systems

(5)

a.	na	a	gur	ir e	'I bought'	ca	a	gur	ir e	'we bought'
	wa	a	gur	ir e	'you bought'	mwa	a	gur	ir e	'you (pl) bought'
	a	a	gur	ir e	'(s)he bought'	be	a	gur	ir e	'they bought'
b.	na	a	kam	ír e	'I milked'	ca	a	kam	ír e	'we milked'
	wa	a	kam	ír e	etc.	mwa	a	kam	ír e	etc.
	a	a	kam	ír e		ba	a	kam	ír e	

The structure of these forms is as in (6):

(6)   na   a   kam   ir   e

   Subject   tense$_1$ verb   tense$_2$ Final
   marker   stem   Vowel

Thus we see that while the verb stem has been changed in (5a,b), the tonal difference appears on the tense suffix, which has otherwise remained unchanged. This "tonal displacement", a common phenomenon in one form or another throughout the Bantu languages, is one part of the following informal generalization that we can make about Ruri morphemes, once we recognize that all syllables can be divided into two categories, the inert or *unaccented* syllables that contribute no High tones, and the *accented* syllables, which contribute to the tonal pattern as follows:

(7)   a. An accent on the *final syllable* of a phrase is realized as a Rise-Fall contour over the last two syllables.
       b. An accent on the *penultimate* syllable of a word is realized as a High tone on that syllable.
       c. Elsewhere, an accent is realized as a High tone on the following syllable.

In (5), we have seen several examples of case (c). If we consider the infinitival form of the verbs in (5), the verb stem will be in penultimate position, and the accent will be realized as a High on its own syllable (7b). See (8).

(8)   o-ku-gur-a   'to buy'
       o-ku-kám-a   'to milk'

Finally, if we observe an accented verb stem which ends in a vowel, the verb stem will form a single syllable with the Final Vowel, and the accent will then be in word-final position. In isolation, then, we will find a

52   *John Goldsmith*

tone pattern as in (9).

(9)   o-ku-li-a → o-kŭ-lyâ   'to eat'   (from -*li*- 'eat')

It is worth noticing at this point that in an accentual language, like Ruri, resyllabification rules apply before the Underlying Tone Level (see (2)).[6]

Statement (7) has no theoretical status as it stands. Case (b), I would like to suggest, actually represents the simplest case. When accent, represented henceforth as an asterisk (*), falls on the penult, it does not move, and the Basic Tone Melody, L H̆ L, is assigned, as in (10).

(10)   o ku kǎm a
                    |
                    |
                    *
             L   H   L

No further rules apply in this derivation; the Well-Formedness Condition produces the correct output.

Case (a) of (7) is derived in similar fashion; there is, however, a tonological rule (11) that adds an association line so as to make a simple phrase-final Fall into a Rise-Fall.

(11)

In (11), the dotted association line indicates the structural change of the rule.

Case (c) of (7) represents the most interesting part. In pre-penultimate position, and also word-finally when the word is not phrase-final, an accent is shifted over one syllable to the right. At this point it would be useful to introduce the basic elements Pre-accent and Post-accent represented "←" and "→", respectively. These elements, on a par with accent, "*", have the properties indicated in (12). That is, a Post-accent immediately and automatically hops over one syllable to the right, leaving nothing behind. These principles of the Accent Component have the same status as the Well-formedness Condition: they apply immediately at any point in the derivation where they can.

(12)   a. V⃗ C V → V C V̊*

       b. V C V⃖ → V̊* C V

Case (7c), then, illustrates the late accentual rule in Ruri which turns accents into Post-accents, (13).

(13) *Accent Hop*

$$\overset{*}{\underset{\downarrow}{V}} \left\{ \begin{matrix} V \\ \#\# \end{matrix} \right\} V \quad \begin{matrix} (a) \\ (b) \end{matrix}$$

$$\vec{V}$$

(13a) is illustrated in (14); we have not yet seen the effects of (13b).

(14) na a kắm ir e   Underlying representation
      na a kam ïr e   (13a): Underlying Tone Level
      na a kam ïr e   Basic Tone Melody Association
                │
             L H L

Let us turn now to a slightly more complex structure, differing from the perfect tense form in (5) by the presence of an object prefix preceding the verb stem, as in (15).

(15) a. *Unaccented Verb Stem*

      na   a i gúr ir e   ca   i gúr ir e
      wa   a i gúr ir e   mwa i gúr ir e
      a   a i gúr ir e   ba   i gúr ir e

   b. *Accented Verb Stem*

      na   a i kám ir e   ca   i kám ir e
      wa   a i kám ir e   mwa i kám ir e
      a   a i kám ir e   ba   i kám ir e

We observe two effects in (15): first, a High tone appears even though the stem (*gur*) is itself unaccented; clearly the source is the new prefix, $\overset{*}{i}$, which is accented. Secondly, in (15b), $k\overset{*}{a}m$, though underlyingly accented, no longer acts as if it were accented — that is, it no longer contributes a surface High tone to the following syllable. While the first effect follows directly from the accented character of this object prefix (and all object prefixes in Ruri are accented), the second is the result of an accent rule in Ruri which is, in one form or another, apparently wide-spread in accentual Bantu languages. Because of the prominence of a similar rule in Meeussen's (1963) analysis of Tonga, I shall call this rule (16) "Meeussen's Rule" (see Goldsmith (1982)).

(16) V̊* V̊* → V̊* V

(17) na a i̊ k*am ir e   Underlying form
      na a i̊ kam ir e   Meeussen's Rule (16)
      na a i k*am ir e   Accent Hop (13)
      na a i kam ir e   Basic Tone Melody Assignment
           L   H* L

It is possible to have an indirect object prefix on the verb in Ruri as well. An "applicative" suffix -ir- then appears following the verb. The applicative is unaccented in the perfect, although, as we shall see, it is accented in the present continuous. When the applicative and the perfect — both marked by -ir- — come together, they are replaced by -ii(y)-, as we see in (18).

(18) a. na a   gur   iiy   e
        I-tense-*buy*-applic/tense   FV
        'I have bought for someone'
     b. na a   ku   gúr   iiy   e
        I-tense-*you buy*-applic/tense   FV
        'I have bought for you'

We can, as noted, have two object prefixes, one marking the direct, the other the indirect, object. Observe this case in (19), where the two objects -*ku-i*- appear. In (19a), a Rise-Fall pattern emerges, signalling an accent on the Final Vowel; in (19b), the appearance of a High Tone on the -*ci*- prefix of the object *ecitébe* 'chair' similarly signals the earlier presence of an accent on the FV of the verb which merged with the pre-prefix *e*- of the Object, and then shifted over one syllable by rule (13).

(19) a. /na a ků* i̊* gur iiy e/ → [na a ku í gur ǐiy ê]
        'I bought   it   for you'

     b. /na a ků* i̊* gur iiy e e ci te̊*be/ →
        [na a ku í gur iiy ȩ e cí tébe]
        'I bought (it) for you the chair'

We would find the same surface pattern had we chosen an accented verb stem. The curious aspect of (19) is that a new accent has arisen on the Final Vowel, an accent that subsequently shifts in (19b). This rule-created accent arises whenever two accents precede the verb stem; see (20).

Accent Systems 55

(20) 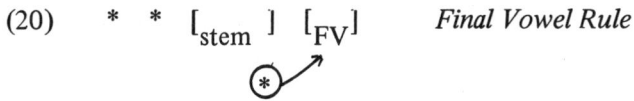 *Final Vowel Rule*

These rules apply as in (21). Note that if Meeussen's Rule applied before (20) Final Vowel Rule, (20) would be bled.

(21) na a kú í gur iiy e   Underlying Form
      na a kú í gur iiy é   Final Vowel Rule (20)
      na a kú i gur iiy é   Meeussen's Rule (16)
      na a ku í gur iiy é   Accent Hop (13)
      na a ku í gur iiy é   Basic Tone Melody Assignment
           L H L   LH L

      na a ku í gur iiy é   High Flop (11)
         L H L L H L

Let us turn now to another tense, the present continuous. Consider the simple verbs in (22a), based on the unaccented stem *gur* and the same verbs with a low-toned noun (*omusimu* 'arrow') as object in (22b).

a. e ni gúr â   'I am buying'
    o u gúr â   'You are buying'
    ka a gǔr â   '(S)he is buying'

b. e ni gúr á ómúsimu 'I am buying an arrow'
    o u gúr á ómúsimu   'You are buying an arrow'
    ka a gùr á omúsimu '(S)he is buying an arrow'

The first two syllables in these verbs (*eni*, etc.) represent the subject marker in each case.

(22a) shows that the first and second person subject markers are accented (*ení*, *oú*, but *kaa*). Furthermore, the Final Vowel is underlyingly accented in this tense. Thus *enigura* is derived as in (23).

(23) e ní gur á   Underlying Form
     D.N.A.   Meeussen's Rule
     e ni gúr á   Accent Hop
     e ni gúr á   Basic Tone Melody
       L H L HL

56   John Goldsmith

However, we see that the circled L tones in (23) do not associate, but are rather deleted. In fact, when accents are *either* adjacent, as in (23), or distanced from each other by a single syllable, the intervening Low tones delete. Before formulating the rule necessary for (23), let us consider the generality of the scope of its application. Consider the derivation for the first form in (22b).

(24) e ni̍ gur a̍ omusimu   Underlying Form

      e ni̍ gur o̍ - omusimu   Vowel Merger

      e ni gu̍r o - omu̍simu   Accent Hop

      e ni gu̍r o - omu̍simu   Basic Tone Melody
       \ | /\ | \/
        L H   L L H L

Once again, the fact is that the circled Low tones delete, rather than associate with the pre-prefix vowel *o*. The rule necessary to handle the case in (24) is clearly (25), Double L Deletion.

(25) *Double L Deletion*

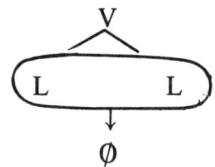

(25) says that any two L tones associated with a single vowel delete. We may now observe that this rule is sufficient to handle the case in (23) above as well. The initial association of the Basic Tone Melody works outward from the accent (see Haraguchi (1977)), Clements and Ford (1979)); whatever the left-right precedence of the two basic melodies, both Ls must eventually associate with either *gur* or *a*. At that point, (25) will delete both. On the assumption that *gur*'s melody is associated first, the derivation will procede as in (26).

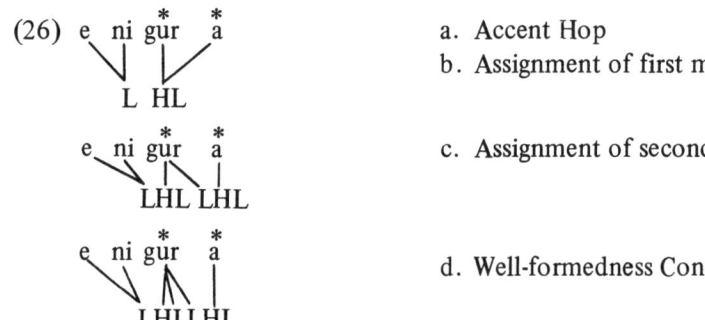

a. Accent Hop
b. Assignment of first melody

c. Assignment of second melody

d. Well-formedness Condition

Accent Systems 57

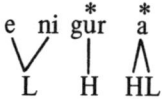

e. Double L Deletion (25)

In (26c), the assignment of the first L of the second melody to *gur* — radiating outward, so to speak, from the accent on the Final Vowel — has cut the association line produced in (26b), and the Well-formedness Condition has deleted that line (see Goldsmith (1976) for a discussion of this function of the WFC). The Well-formedness Condition then reassociates that L with the only available vowel, which is in *gur*, producing (26d), input of Double L Deletion. Note that Vowel Merger applies before Tone Assignment, as we expect in an accent language. In a true tone language, such as Kikuyu, Tone Assignment occurs before rules like Vowel Merger (see Clements (1982)).

Let us compare now the case of the unaccented verb stem, as in (22), with the accented verb stem, (27).

(27) a. e ni tém a   'I am cutting'
       o u tém a   'You are cutting'
       ka a tém a   '(S)he is cutting'
    b. e ni tém a omusimu   'I am cutting the arrow'
       o u tém a omusimu   'You are cutting the arrow'
       ka a tém a omusimu   '(S)he is cutting the arrow'

The contrast with (22) is striking. In (27), I have indicated the underlying accents with "*", and the surface High tone. While there are more accents in (27) than in (22), since here the verb stem *tem* is accented, Meeussen's Rule deletes all but the first in a string of consecutive accents. Thus, in this case, the more underlying accents, the fewer High tones on the surface — a striking but unsurprising result, given this view of accent, but an occurrence that would not arise in a true tone language. The derivation of *enitéma* is given in (28).

(28)
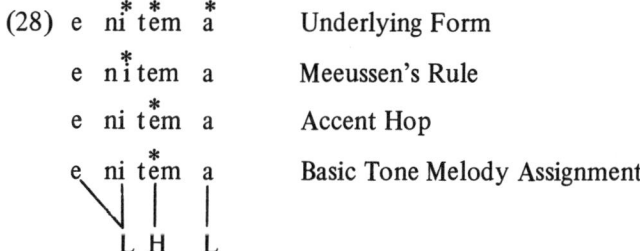

If we consider the Present Continuous tense with an applicative extension -*ir*/-*er* we find similar results: the unaccented stems produce more High tones than the accented ones, because they escape some of the effects of Meeussen's Rule.

(29) a. e ní tém ⓔ̃r ⓐ   [e ni tém er a]
       o ú tẽm ⓔ̃r ⓐ   [o u tém er a]
       ka a tẽm ⓔ̃r ⓐ   [ka a tem ér a]
    b. e ní gur ír ⓐ   [e ni gúr ír a]
       o ú gur ír ⓐ   [o u gúr ír a]
       ka a gur ír ⓐ   [ka a gur ír a]

In (29), I have circled those underlying accents which are deleted by Meeussen's Rule.

In (20), the Final Vowel Rule, we found a rule that placed an accent on the FV when two accents precede the stem. In the Present Continuous, this rule comes into play even though the FV is underlyingly accented. Since the subject (except in the third person singular) is accented, only one object prefix need be present to trigger the FV Rule (20). Observe the tones in (30).

(30) a. e ní cí gur á   [e ni cí gǔr â]
     b. e ní cí tẽm á   [e ni cí těm â]

While (30a) is expected, (30b) is surprising in the light of either (28) or (29). Why did the FV accent not delete? The answer is that it did, in fact; it was, however, reinstated by the FV Rule.

Still, it is not immediately obvious how the FV Rule and Meeussen's Rule can interact to permit the correct result in (30b). If the FV Rule were to apply *before* Meeussen's Rule, its application would be vacuous, for the FV would not yet have lost its accent. If Meeussen's Rule applies first, however, $c\overset{*}{i}$ will lose its accent under the influence of the preceding subject accent, and the structural description of the FV Rule, which requires two accents before the stem, will never be satisfied. Neither order appears to work correctly.

A cyclic approach, however, has precisely the right effect. The derivation is given in (31).

Accent Systems   59

(31) e nǐ cǐ gur ȧ   e nǐ cǐ tem ȧ
           gur ȧ   I: M's Rule   tėm a
        cǐ gur ȧ   II: M's Rule   cǐ tem a
  e n̄ǐ cǐ gur ȧ   III: FV Rule   e nǐ cǐ tem ȧ
  e nǐ ci gur ȧ   M's Rule   e nǐ ci tem ȧ
  e ni cǐ gur ȧ   Accent Hop e ni cǐ tem ȧ

Note that Accent Hop applies post-cyclically.

The cyclic approach is strikingly confirmed when we consider the contrast between the forms in (32), with surface forms *e ni mú gu gur ír a* and *e ni mú gu tem ěr â*. These derive from a pre-Accent Hop form *e nǐ mu gu gur ir a* and *e nǐ mu gu tem er a*.

(32)
e nǐ mu gu gur ir a   e nǐ mu gu tem er a
        gur ir a   I: M's Rule   tėm er a
     gu̇ gur ir a   II: M's Rule   gu̇ tem er a
  mu̇ gu̇ gur ir a   III: FV Rule   mu̇ gu̇ tem er a
  mu̇ gu gur ir a   M's Rule   mu̇ gu tem er a
e nǐ mu gu gur ir a   IV: FV Rule   e nǐ mu gu tem er a
e nǐ mu gu gur ir a   M's Rule   e nǐ mu gu tem er a

3. CI-TONGA

Ci-Tonga, or Tonga, is a major language spoken in Zambia. My primary source of data is published material by Hazel Carter, though I have benefited from discussions with Jerome Hachipola, a linguist and native speaker of Tonga at Indiana University.[7]

Tonga's accentual system is remarkably similar to that of Ruri, but the Basic Tone Melody in Tonga is HL̇. Thus instead of an underlying accent being realized as a High tone on the following syllable, it is realized as a Low tone on the vowel in question preceded by an indefinite string of High tones. This contrast is illustrated in (33).

(33) a. Tonga: b. Ruri:

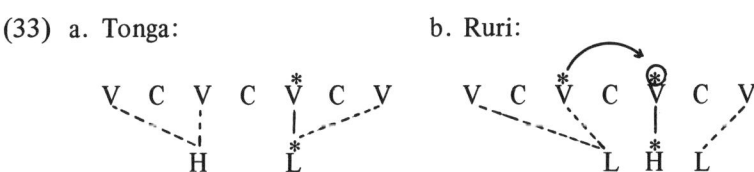

Along with this difference in Basic Tone Melody, Tonga and Ruri differ in virtually all respects in their strictly tonal components. There is no analog in Tonga to Double L Deletion; rather, a single low-tone vowel between two Highs, much as in (24) above, dissociates and leaves its effect as a downstep.

Nonetheless, the two languages share certain accentual properties. Quite striking is an etymological connection; that is, etymons by and large agree in underlying accent placement in the two languages.

Even more striking is the effect of Meeussen's Rule in Tonga and its parallels to Ruri. For the reasons that we have already observed, the area where Meeussen's Rule operates is primarily in the verb, where successive accents can rise. The verb is also the locus of a simple tone rule whose effects obscure the basic Tonga HL tone melody. This rule, (34), deletes initial H in a verb. A verb with only a single accent, then, will be all L, as we see in (35). It will thus be identical to a totally unaccented word.

(34) H → ∅ / # [$\overline{\text{verb}}$

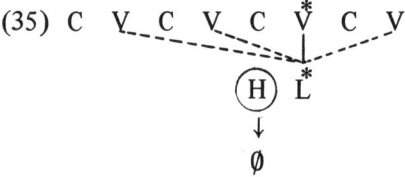

These principles, along with the observation that unaccented words are all Low, account for a typical verb pattern, the Present Indicative, as in (36). While the default condition of all Low is common among tonal systems when no tones are provided (see Pulleyblank (1981), for example, in his study of Tiv), it is not universal (Ki-Langi provides an H tone that spreads, for example; see Goldsmith (in preparation)).

(36) a. *lang* 'look'

	No object	Type 1 prefix	Type 2 prefix
'we'	tu-la-lang-a	tu-la-mu-lang-a	tu-la-ba-lang-a
'they'	ba-la-lang-a	ba-la-mu-lang-a	ba-lá-ba-lang-a

b. *bon* 'see'

	No object	Type 1 prefix	Type 2 prefix
'we'	tu-la-bon-a	tu-la-mu-bon-a	tu-la-ba-bon-a
'they'	ba-lá-bon-a	ba-lá-mú-bon-a	ba-lá-ba-bon-a

Accent Systems

The accented morphemes here are *ba-* 'they', *-ba-* 'them', and *bon* 'see'. In (36a), we see that the only H syllable is precisely the one flanked by two accented morphemes, as in (37a).

(37)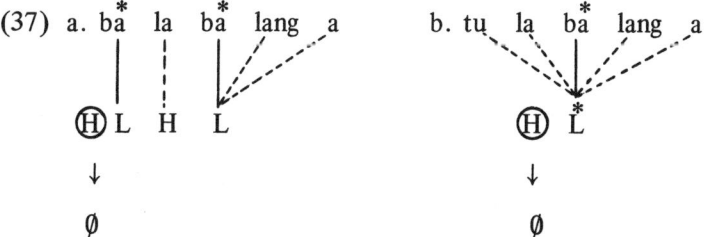

As the contrast in (37a,b) shows, two accents are necessary in order to preserve one of the H tonemes in the basic tone melody from deletion by rule (34).

It should be pointed out that the accent utilized in Tonga has only tonal reflexes phonetically. In a recent phonetic study, Luce (1981) showed that there was no influence on length caused by the accent in Tonga. There is also no perceptible loudness effect of the tonal accent.

We see in (36b) that *bon* is clearly accented (cf. *ba-lá-mú-bon-a*, for example; *bon* must be accented to induce the H tones to its left). How do we account, then, for *ba-lá-ba-bon-a*? See (38).

(38)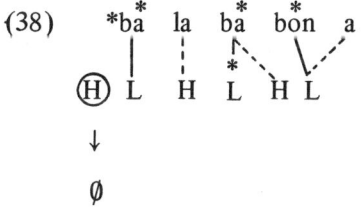

We would expect an extra H tone — in between *ba* and *bon* — to appear, and to associate by the Well-formedness Condition. However, there is no such H tone. What is operating, in fact, is Meeussen's Rule, (16), just as in Ruri; *bŏn* loses its accent under the influence of the immediately preceding *bă*.

As in Ruri, Meeussen's Rule can operate to delete an indefinite number of consecutive accents. In the Weak Recent Past, for example, *bá a bá bón a* simplifies to *bá a ba bon a*, and then is realized as *bàbàbònà*. (In Tonga, there is no evidence for a cycle, however, and the Strong Recent Past would be difficult to generate in cyclic fashion; see Goldsmith (1982).)

It has been suggested (Morris Halle, personal communication) that the lack of association in (38) might indicate that a constraint was ope-

62   *John Goldsmith*

rative in Tonga that blocked association of more than one toneme per vowel, a condition that would supersede the Well-formedness Condition. Under such an interpretation, Meeussen's Rule would not be necessary; the Low tone on *bon*, in particular, would be the realization of the Low tone corresponding to its inherent accent, not the reassociation rightward of the Low tone that is part of *ba*'s Basic Melody.

Such an attempt to eliminate Meeussen's Rule in Tonga is not possible, however. A phrase-level tonal phenomenon demonstrates that *bon* has no tone of its own, not even a Low tone. Under certain conditions of object-focus (what Carter calls the "Weak" pattern), a High tone from the object associates leftward, into the verb stem, as far as possible. This leftward spreading occurs up to, but not including, an accented (and thus Low-toned) vowel in the verb. Since the Well-formedness Condition gives precedence in reassociation to unaccented tones, what is happening is that the tone melody from the object spreads into the verb at the point of initial Basic Tone Melody association. It follows that verb-object cliticization precedes Basic Tone Melody association; this is consistent with the more general principle that Basic Tone Melody Association is always post-cyclic in accent languages.

In the crucial case at hand, those parallel to (38), we find that in the Weak forms, the object's H-tone spreads all the way leftward onto *bon*, and onto any vowel whose accent is lost (under the analysis proposed here) by Meeussen's Rule. Hence we conclude that Tonga does retain Meeussen's Rule.

(39)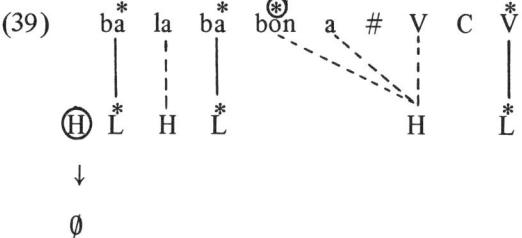

4. CONCLUSION

The accentual and tonal systems of Ci-Ruri and Ci-Tonga support a view according to which accent is not a local property of a segment, nor a relational property of relative prominence; it is, rather, a simple formal device for relating parallel autosegmental tiers. The notion of accent appears to have no influence on syllabic loudness or, more significantly, syllabic length, or rhythm, in the broadest sense. True accent languages operate with accent, but no tone, at the cyclic and word level, and become tone language-like, only at the post-cyclic (that is, phrasal) level.

At this point, it appears to be the case in the Bantu languages that tonal and accentual systems can be studied largely independently of the rules governing vowel length and other rhythmic effects. If this is in fact correct, then it suggests that the various levels of "stress" in a language such as English may well still be more clearly understood when factored into tonological and rhythmic components. The notion of a single dimension of relative stress — either numerologically, or through trees or grids of relative prominence — as presently conceived would furthermore be inappropriate. Be this as it may, the study of Bantu accentual languages will continue to serve as a testing ground for theories concerning the diachronic development of accentual systems out of pure tonal systems. It is in that spirit that the present studies are offered.

FOOTNOTES

1.   I am grateful to Nick Clements and Morris Halle for many discussions of the issues in this paper. I am especially indebted to David Massamba, a Bantu scholar, foremost expert on Ci-Ruri, and colleague, without whom section 2 could not be. Except for the fact that he has a different analysis of the facts (for which, see Massamba (1982) and Massamba (to appear)), section 2 might better be co-authored by the two of us.
2.   See, for example, Chomsky and Halle (1968), p. 26, or Ladd (1980), pp. 41ff.
3.   This framework is developed in Goldsmith (1974, 1976); a series of detailed autosegmental studies of tone and accent in the Bantu languages can be found in Clements and Goldsmith (1982).
4.   It is not logically necessary, clearly, that the principle at play at the Underlying Tone Level be as simple as I have indicated. Hyman (1981), for example, has argued that there is a specific rule of some complexity, but also of some elegance, in Luganda; Laughren (1982) makes a similar claim for Zulu.
5.   The material described in this section derives from work done jointly with David Massamba. Other sources on the language are Becker and Massamba (1980), Massamba (1982), and Massamba (in preparation). The careful reader will note that some simplification in the derivations can be achieved if (20) is viewed not as a copying rule but rather, as Massamba suggests, as a movement rule.
6.   We will suggest below that all cyclic phonology in accentual languages precedes the Underlying Tone Level.
7.   This section is based primarily on Goldsmith (1982).

On the Framework of Autosegmental Phonology*

Morris Halle and Jean Roger Vergnaud
M.I.T. and C.N.R.S., ERA 247

One of the most productive developments in phonology of the last decade has been the emergence of autosegmental phonology. The major insight lying at the base of autosegmental phonology is that the phonological representation is composed not of a single sequence of entities roughly resembling a line of type, but rather that the phonological representation is made up of several parallel sequences of entities, resembling thus more a score for a musical ensemble than a single line of type. This type of representation was, of course, not invented during the last decade. Multi-line phonological representations have standardly been used in notating the tonal characteristics of utterances, and in such representations the tones of an utterance have frequently been written on a separate line above the speech sounds that compose the utterance. However, it has usually been thought that much like the neumes used in the notation of the Gregorian chant or of the Massoretic text of the Hebrew bible the tones are diacritic features of the syllables or vowels. What has been novel in autosegmental phonology is that the tones of an utterance are not viewed as diacritics of vowels or syllables; rather the tones are viewed as constituting an autonomous sequence of entities, separate from and equal to the sequence of consonants and vowels that make up what we shall call here the phonemic core of the utterance.

Once the phonological representation is viewed as consisting of several independent sequences (or tiers) of entities — one sequence composed of tones, another of phonemes — there immediately arises the question as to how the entities on different tiers are synchronized, since ultimately the various tiers are actualized in a single acoustic signal emanating from the speaker's vocal tract. The precise statement of how entities on one tier are linked to those on another tier has, therefore, been an important topic in autosegmental phonology, and the fact of having focussed atten-

---

* The material in this study is to be included in a longer study *Three Dimensional Phonology* now in preparation. The authors are grateful to J. Goldsmith and P. Kiparsky for help and advice. This work was supported in part by the National Institutes of Mental Health Grant #5 PO1 MH13990-15.

tion on this issue is perhaps one of the most significant contributions to be credited to autosegmental phonology, for it is only when tones and phonemes are viewed as constituting autonomous sequences that the question of their synchronization can arise.

As one examines the different autosegmental studies that have appeared during the last decade there appear two rather different conceptions as to how autosegments on different tiers are to be linked. For reasons that are not altogether clear to us these quite fundamental differences have not previously been brought out in the open and debated, and we believe that this has affected negatively the progress that has been made in this area. We shall, therefore, state what we perceive to be the salient differences between the two approaches and then contrast the two approaches in order to bring out some of their respective advantages and drawbacks.

The most important difference between the two approaches concerns we believe the way in which the links between entities on different tiers are established. In one of the two approaches a critical role in establishing the links is played by the so-called Well Formedness Condition. As is well known, the Well Formedness Condition has been central in the studies of John Goldsmith. We have reproduced in (1) the Well Formedness Condition in the form it is given in Goldsmith's recent paper (February 1981) on Tonga:

(1)   i.   All tones must be associated with (at least) one syllabic element.
       ii.   All syllabic elements must be associated with (at least) one tone.
       iii.   Association lines do not cross.

Goldsmith explains that "the Well Formedness Condition functions not to rule out, or eliminate derivations which violate any of its conditions, but rather to add or delete association lines in order to maximally meet its specifications." In addition Goldsmith postulates the existence of a diacritic mark — the accent — which serves to synchronize the different autosegmental tiers. Specifically, in their lexical representations morphemes may have any number — including zero — of accented tone bearing phonemes (which, unless noted otherwise, will be taken to be vowels). Accented vowels are linked to specific (accented) tones on the tonal tier. Once the accented autosegments are linked, the Well Formedness Condition comes into play adding "association lines in order to maximally meet its specification."

It was pointed out by Clements and Ford (1979) that in certain cases the Well Formedness Condition can be satisfied in several ways as shown in (2).

On Autosegmental Phonology

(2)

Not all of these alternatives are made equal use of in the languages of the world. As remarked by Clements and Ford, it appears rather that in the languages that have been studied to this point the second alternative given in (2) is preferred. To deal with this fact Goldsmith supplements the Well Formedness Condition with a special tone linking rule that has the effect of associating tones and vowels one to one and from left to right.

In the approach that we want to contrast with that of Goldsmith, tone linking is accomplished by a similar left-to-right rule. But here the left-to-right rule produces the correct output without requiring recourse to the Well Formedness Condition or its equivalent. We find this approach in Williams' (1971) paper, in Haraguchi's (1977) book on Japanese, and in a number of other studies. Williams describes his Tone Mapping Rule, as follows (p. 469):

(3)   i.   It maps from left to right a sequence of tones onto a sequence of syllables.
        ii.   It assigns one tone per syllable, until it runs out of tones,
        iii. then, it assigns the last tone that was specified to the remaining untoned syllables on the right, ...
        iv. until it encounters the next syllable to the right belonging to a morpheme with specified tone.

It is obvious that the type of linkings established by this rule are rather different from those envisaged by the Well Formedness Condition. In particular, there is no requirement that each tone be linked to at least one vowel. While the last tone is normally linked to several vowels when the number of vowels exceeds the number of tones, the converse is not normally the case when the number of tones exceeds the number of vowels. Williams is quite specific on the fact that the linking of more than one tone to a given syllable is a marked phenomenon for which special provision must be made in the grammar of the language. He writes: "An idiosyncratic fact about the rule in Margi is that if there are two tones and only one syllable then both tones may be assigned to that syllable." To make this explicit we add to the Mapping Rule (3), the provision (3v)

(3)   v.   If the procedure above runs out of vowels (syllabic elements or syllables), more than one tone may be assigned to the last vowel only if the grammar of the language includes a stipulation to that effect.

Having established some differences between the two approaches we now attempt to find evidence which might decide between the two approaches. Consider first the facts in Etung in (4a), which are taken from Goldsmith's dissertation (1976; we reproduce here the 1979 version published by Garland Publishing, Inc.).

(4) a.

kpá	'first'	kpè	'even'	nâ	'it is'	nǒ	'how'
ńsé	'father'	ègù	'evening'	ódà	'platform'	èkát	'leg'
ékúé	'forest'	èyùrì	'dress'	ákpùgà	'money'	bìsóné	'spoon'

As shown by the monosyllabic words in the first row, Etung is one of those languages which, like Margi, are subject to the special stipulation allowing two tones to be linked to a single vowel. The absence of contour tones in polysyllabic words is then accounted for by the fact that we are running out of vowels only in the case of monosyllabic words. Thus, it would seem that Etung has melodies consisting of at most two tones; consequently we run out of vowels to assign tones to only in monosyllables. This, however, cannot be the entire story, as shown by the examples in (4b)

(4) b.

| érôp | 'spear' | èbĭn | 'farm' | ábǒ | 'they' | òbô | 'arm' |
| ésébè | 'sand' | òròbé | 'beam' | édìmbá | 'pot' | m̀bútà | 'rain' |

The trisyllabic forms in (4b) show that there are three-tone melodies in Etung; specifically HHL, LLH, HLH and LHL and since with such melodies we run out of vowels in the case of bisyllabic words, we find – as predicted by (3iv) – contour tones on the second syllable, and we do not find the tone contours in (4c).

(4) c. âbó   ǒbó

There is still more to this story. We recall that unlike the Well Formedness Condition the Mapping Rule (3) does not require that each tone be linked to a vowel. The question may then be asked what happens to such tones that remain unlinked at the end of the derivation. The simplest assumption is that in (5).

(5) Only tones linked to segments in the phonemic core are phonetically actualized.

Hence tones remaining unlinked cannot surface and forever remain in a phonetic limbo condemned never to see the bright daylight of phonetic reality. Condition (5) allows us to propose a very simple analysis of the Etung facts presented above. Note that we have encountered eight tone patterns on polysyllabic words; i.e., 2^3 or precisely the number of all possible sequences of the two tones, High and Low, taken three at a time. Given the stipulation that Etung allows at most two tones to be linked to a single vowel the Mapping Rules (3) and Condition (5) directly account for the tonal contours of the monosyllabic words in (4a).

The situation is less straightforward if the Well Formedness Condition were to be applied here. In that case, the Well Formedness condition would have to be supplemented by a special rule deleting all but the two leftmost tones linked to a single vowel; i.e., a rule of the form (6)

(6)
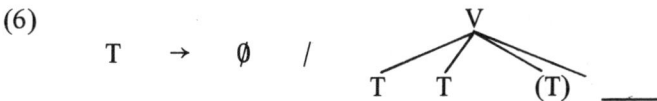

Since rule (6) is far from intuitive a solution without such a rule is to be preferred over one requiring this rule. Thus, the facts of Etung provide some evidence favoring the Mapping Rule over the Well Formedness Condition.

The intricate tonology of Tonga, a Bantu language spoken in Zambia has long attracted the attention of scholars, and much fascinating data on Tonga has been published by H. Carter (1962) (1971) (1972), Meeussen (1963) McCawley (1973), and M. Cohen (1974). Goldsmith early recognized the importance of the Tonga facts. He discussed some of them in his dissertation and has recently devoted to them two articles, of which the second, published by the Indiana University Linguistics Club, is to be recommended especially because of the large body of data covered and the clarity of its exposition. Our remarks below are heavily influenced by Goldsmith's study.

Tonga has both accented and unaccented morphemes. There are several kinds of accented morphemes in the language. The simplest kind of accented morpheme illustrated in (6a) has a single accented vowel. The accented vowel always has a Low tone and all preceding vowels have High tones. We follow Goldsmith in postulating that each accented vowel is supplied with the melody High-Low of which the Low tone is linked to the accented vowel whereas the High tone is unassociated as shown in (7a)

(7)a. í – bú – s ì   "smoke"   í – mú – súnè   "ox"
           | |
           H L   H L

As illustrated in (7a) unaccented morphemes — as expected — have no inherent tone. As a result the H tone of the accented morpheme spreads on to these morphemes.

Tonga also has morphemes with several accented syllables. As illustrated in (7b) these are readily dealt with in the same way as morphemes with a single accented vowel.

(7) b.

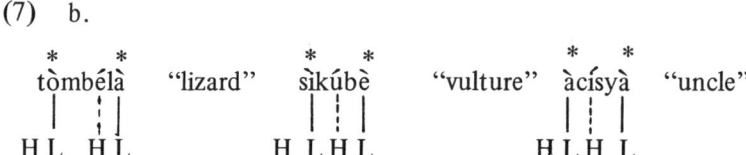

If we adopt the Mapping Rule (3) nothing further needs to be said since Tonga is one of the many tone languages that does not admit contour tones. Formally this means that in the grammar of Tonga there is no special stipulation allowing us to link more than one tone to a given vowel. In view of this the word initial H tone in (7b) cannot be linked to any vowel and, pursuant to (5) above, does not surface. The solution is not quite as simple if the Well Formedness Condition is employed. We have reproduced in (7c) the passage from Goldsmith's paper (1981, p.7) dealing with the multiple accent words above.

7) c. (15)

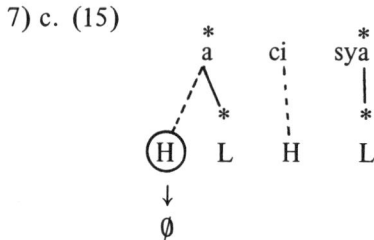

By the Well-Formedness Condition (2), the initial H will be associated with the first vowel of the word, even in a case like (15), thus producing in effect a falling tone. The surface L tone is the effect of the tone-simplification rule (16), which simplifies HL to L (compare with (11b)).

(16)

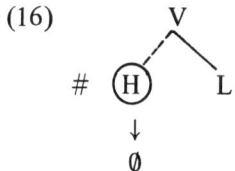

On Autosegmental Phonology 71

We note that because of the way the Well Formedness Condition operates, a special tone-simplification rule (rule (16) in the passage quoted in (7c)) is required. No such rule is required if the Tone Mapping Rule (3) is employed.

This brings us to words consisting exclusively of unaccented morphemes which are illustrated in (7d)

(7)d. ì – bù – sù   'flour'   ì – mù – ntù   'person'
     ì – bà – sànkwà   'men'

The obvious way to deal with such words is to assign to them no tone whatever — for as we have already seen in (7a), this gives the correct results in the case of unaccented prefixes. The problem with this solution is that we would then have no way of accounting for the fact that accentless words are composed exclusively of Low tones. Since no tones are linked to the vowels in these words it would seem that our theory predicts that such words should be toneless.

Faced with this dilemma we have two options. Our first option is to add some rules to the description of Tonga so as to insure that a Low tone will be linked to all vowels in unaccented words. This is the procedure followed by Goldsmith in the passage reproduced in (7e) which directly follows the material quoted in (7c):

(7) e. Rule (16), independently needed, suggests an analysis for Class C, the unaccented class of stems, as Bill Poser has pointed out to me. As has been noted both in Slavic and Japanese accentual systems, a rule of recessive accent placement may place an accent on the initial vowel of an otherwise unaccented word, as in (17).

(17)

$$V \rightarrow \overset{*}{V} \ / \ \#\# \ C \underline{\quad} \ X \ \#\# \qquad \text{Cond: } X \neq ....\overset{*}{V}....$$

This rule will apply to (Class C) unaccented forms, then, as in (18).

(18) a. i + bu + su   →   b. $\overset{*}{\text{i}}$ + bu + su   →
                              |
                              $\overset{*}{}$
                              H L

c. $\overset{*}{\text{i}}$ + bu + su   →   d. $\overset{*}{\text{i}}$ + bu + su
   H L   (H) L
                                 ↓
                                 ∅ (16)

We conclude this survey of the basic nominal types by noting that the basic tone melody is HL; but that all words are accented, either by the accent or accents contributed by their component morphemes (stems, in the cases considered so far), or by the recessive accent rule (17).

While this solution produces the correct output, it is not altogether unproblematic, for it leads to the rather strange conclusion that "all words are accented", even though we know that some words are not accented. There is thus reason to explore another alternative.

The alternative solution starts out by questioning the implication of the theory as developed to this point that vowels — or tone bearing phonemes — which are not linked to an autosegmental tone should surface as toneless. This implication presupposes that if a feature is specified on an autosegmental tier, it may not also be specified in the phonemic core. This proposition is surely the one to be adopted in view of Occam's razor, which enjoins us not to multiply entities without necessity. We note, however, that Occam's razor does not prevent us from multiplying entities when this is made necessary by the facts. In the present instance we believe that we can indeed justify such a multiplication of entities. We, therefore, postulate condition (8)

(8)   The fact that a feature is specified on a separate autosegmental tier does not preclude it from also being specified in the phonemic core. Whenever a given phoneme is linked to an autosegment, the autosegmental feature specification supersedes the specification in the core.

We shall assume that in Tonga all vowels are redundantly specified in the phonemic core as being [+Low tone]. At the present time we do not know whether this can be made a universal principle; i.e., whether all vowels in all languages must be redundantly specified as [+Low tone]. If so, then nothing further needs to be said about accentless words in Tonga. If the redundant assignment of Low tone to vowels is not universal, a redundancy rule to this effect will have to be added to the grammar of Tonga.

The preceding has an interesting consequence for the treatment of Tonga words with nonfinal accents. As shown in (9a) in such words the vowels following the last accented vowel have Low tone.

(9) a. í – cí – tòngà   "the Tonga language"

bá – sìlùwè   "leopards"

We now have two ways of achieving this result. We can either allow the linked Low tone to spread to the right. Alternatively, we can assume that the Low tone on postaccentual vowels is the redundantly specified tone that was discussed above.

On Autosegmental Phonology

We would like to propose that the latter rather than the former is the correct resolution, and to implement this proposal formally we suggest that the Tone Mapping Rules (3) are subject to the restriction:

(9) b. The Tone Mapping Rules (3) apply only to floating (= unlinked) tones.

Given condition (9b) the Low tones on the postaccentual vowels in (9a) can only be redundantly specified since the linked Low tone cannot spread to these vowels.

We must now justify this restriction, and Tonga provides crucial evidence. It was observed by Meeussen that all morphemes of the language can be divided into two classes "according to whether ... they are constantly low (or lowered high [i.e. downstepped H]) or not." He next proposes to mark the former class of elements and leave the latter class unmarked. He then observes that

(9) c. "unmarked" elements are high between "marked" elements (Meeussen (1963), p. 73)

It is important to observe that (9c) is not a rule in our sense; it is rather an observationally correct statement about tonal contours of Tonga words, which falls out as a consequence of the rules and principles that we have developed to this point. To see this consider the forms illustrated in (9d)

(9) d.
i) bà — lí — si(y) — ìde
   with tones H L H L H L

ii) bà — lí — bá — si(y) ìde
    H L H L H L H L

iii) bà — lí — láng — ìde
     H L   H   L

iv) bà — lí — bá — láng — ìde
    H L H L   H   L

(from Meeussen p. 73).

These forms consist of the verbal stems /siy/ "leave" and /lang/ "look for", the word initial prefix /ba/ 'they", the word medial prefixes /ba/ "them" and /li/, which has affirmative meaning, and the suffix /ide/ which signals the perfective aspect. We observe that (with the exception of the last form) once the melodies are assigned to the accented morphemes the tonal contours of the words are derived by the Tone Mapping Rule (3).

Given the rules developed to this point the last form in (9d) should surface with the tone contour LHLHL, whereas its actual contour is LH!HHL. It has been observed by Goldsmith (p. 5) that when a prefix is attached to the stems in (7b) their tone contours are modified as shown in (9e)

(9) e.

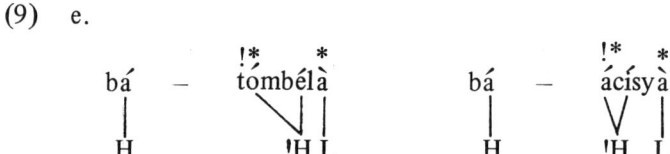

As Goldsmith notes in Tonga, as in many other tone languages, the downstepped High tone is the standard implementation of a High tone immediately preceded by a floating Low tone. There is no difficulty in the present instance to account for the presence of a Low tone in the required position, for the underlying representations of the forms in (9e) are

9) f.

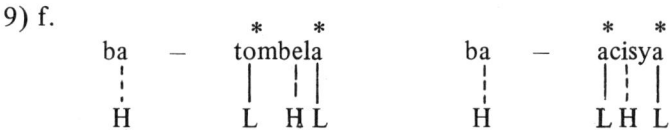

All that we need, as Goldsmith has already shown, is a rule that links the High tone to the left vowel if preceded by two vowels, linked respectively to a High and Low tone as given in (9g)

9) g.

In view of the fact that in Tonga multiple associations of tones with a single vowel are not admitted, we shall assume that an automatic side effect of the rule is to float the Low tone, thereby triggering downstep in the High tone on the right. (We provide further justification for this assumption in the discussion of condition (12d) below). It is obvious that the Downstep Rule (9g) accounts for the deviant tone contour of the last example in (9d). As noted above, all other facts in (9d) directly follow from the underlying representation, the Mapping Rule (3) and other conventions developed here.

This straightforward and therefore desirable result cannot be obtained by the Well Formedness Condition as simply. To produce it the Condition must be supplemented by additional rules. In discussing forms with consecutive accented morphemes such as the present indicative

(9) h. *   *   *
       ba – la – ba – bon – a   "they see them"

which correspond tonally to the example (9d-ii) Goldsmith remarks (p. 14) that the string in (9h) would produce the tone contour in (9i-1) with a rising tone on the second /ba/ and that the correct tone contour with Low tone on the /ba/ would require the string in (9i-2):

(9) i.

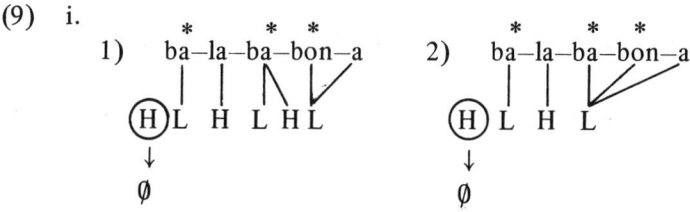

In order to obtain the required string Goldsmith postulates that a special rule applies which deletes all but the first of several accents appearing on consecutive vowels. This rule, which is referred to as Meeussen's rule, is reproduced in (9j)

(9) j. *   0   *
        V   →   V   /   VC ____

Since Meeussen's Rule "must apply before the insertion of the basic tone melodies," the required string (9i-2) is derived from (9h). [It will have been observed that in (9i) the word initial H-tone is deleted. We discuss this deletion directly below, see rule (11c).]

We note that if instead of the Well Formedness Condition the Tone Mapping Rule (3) is applied to the underlying string (9h) the correct tone contour is produced without recourse to any additional rules or principles. We show this in (9k).

9) k.   *   *   *
         ba   – la   – ba   – bon   – a
         | ⋮ | |
         H L   H   L   H L

We conclude, therefore, that the application of Meeussen's Rule in the derivation of this form is yet another example where the Well Formedness Condition generates incorrect outputs which must be fixed up by other rules.

The present instance, however, differs somewhat from the examples of misgeneration discussed above. Whereas in the above example the grammar had to be complicated by the addition of an otherwise unnecessary rule (cf. (6) (7c) and (7e)), Meeussen's Rule (9j) is a fully motivated rule of Tonga phonology. It functions, however, not in all words but only in weak forms of the verb about which a few words need to be said here. Each Tonga verb can appear either in a "strong" form or in a "weak" form. The weak form induces an accent on the first (or only) syllable of an immediately following nominal or particle, with which it stands in a close syntactic relation. Thus, a verb like *tola* "take" can appear in either of the two forms (10a):

(10)a. i)   ndà–ká–tòlà   nyàmà   "I TOOK meat" (strong)

   ii)   ndà–ká–tólá   nyàmà   "I took MEAT" (weak)

As the translations indicate, the two forms have different interpretations. In (10ai), the focus is on the verb, whereas in (10aii) the focus is on the complement of the verb. Carter notes that "the strong series require no support and may stand at the end of an utterance; the weak series require the support of a following item, usually nominal or particle." The fact that the weak form cannot be final is implicit in the phonological characterization given above, which places an accent on the following syllable. The formation of a weak form might be viewed as a sort of cliticization.

As shown in (10b) the effect of this process is as predicted by the rules developed to this point. Since each accented vowel is linked to the melody High-Low the High tone, which is floating, is spread to the unlinked vowels at the end of the verbal form, which in the strong forms surface with Low tone. We illustrate this in (10b) where the letter O represents the accented syllable of the following word; the word initial prefix represents the l.sg.subject "I". [The prefix which has the underlying form /ndi/ loses its vowel if followed by a vowel; see (12a) below.]

(10) b.   strong   weak

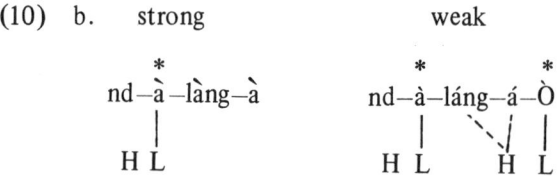

On Autosegmental Phonology

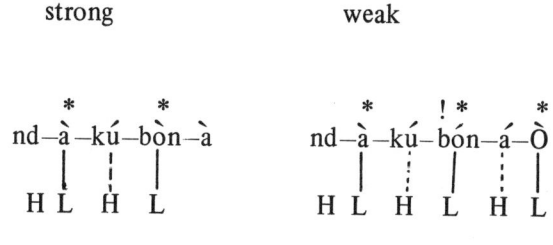

(Examples from Meeussen p. 82, 83 – Tenses 15, 16)

It will be noted that in the last form of (10b) a downstepped H tone appears on the stem vowel *bon* in place of the L tone which is linked to it by the Mapping Rule. This is, of course, to be expected since the string produced by the Tone Mapping Rule undergoes the Downstep Rule (9g). Not all weak forms of the Tonga verb are derived as straight-forwardly. We illustrate some problematical forms in (10c)

(10) c. i)   nd–à–bón–á–Ò   (Tense 16 - Meeussen p. 83)
             | \ \/
             H L HL HL

ii) nd–à–bá–bón–á–Ò   (Tense 16 – Meeussen p. 83)
     | | | | |
     H L HL HL H L

iii) nd–à–ká–bá–bón–á–Ò   (Tense 19 – Meeussen p. 83)
     | \ \ | | |
     H L   HL HL H L

As shown above, the Mapping Rule produces incorrect outputs in all these examples. In particular it assigns a Low tone to the stem *bon* in (10c-i) instead of the attested High tone; and in (10c-ii,iii) it makes incorrect tone assignments both to the stem *bon* and to the object prefix *ba*. These incorrect tone assignments will not arise if Meeussen's Rule (9j) is applied to these forms, for then the stem *bon* will lose its accent in all forms, as will the object prefix *ba* in (10cii), yielding the representations in (10d)

(10)d.

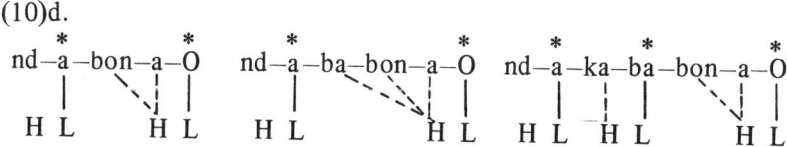

In the first two examples nothing further needs to be said; in the third example the Downstep rule (9g) will apply yielding the tone contour shown in (10c-iii).

The application of Meeussen's Rule in the weak forms is natural, since accent loss commonly accompanies cliticization of one form onto another. Accordingly, it is to be expected that Meeussen's Rule would not apply to the strong forms. And indeed, as we have seen above, Meeussen's Rule was not needed in the generation of the correct contour of any strong form of the verb.

We now shall attempt to show that when applied to strong forms in the way in which phonological rules are normally applied, Meeussen's Rule produces incorrect results whenever there are more than two consecutive accented vowels. Examples of this kind have led Goldsmith to propose conditions on rule application of a very unorthodox kind. As the facts involved are of some complexity, they require a brief digression into certain other aspects of Tonga tonology.

As we have seen above in (9d), like nominal stems, verbal stems may be accented or unaccented, and this leads to surface contrasts such as those in the infinitive forms in (11a)

(11) a. ì–kù–làng–à   "to look for"   í–kú–bòn–à   "to see"

                                                          H   L

In finite forms of the verb, however, the tonal contrast is neutralized as shown in (11b)

(11) b. tù–mù–làng–à   "we look for"   tù–mù–bòn–à   "we see"

                                                              H   L

To obtain the correct output in such cases we follow Goldsmith in postulating a rule which deletes the first H tonal autosegment in finite verbal forms

(11) c.   H → ∅ / $_{Vb}$ [___

It might be noted here parenthetically that H-Tone Deletion (11c) applies also in the derivations of the forms in (9d), but this has no effect on the output. Moreover, in finite verbal forms with accented suffix, rule (11c) does not apply; e.g., it fails to apply in the 1.sg. pres. perf. ind. aff. forms

On Autosegmental Phonology

$$\underset{H\quad L}{ndí\text{–}lí\text{–}láng\text{–}\overset{*}{\grave{\imath}d\grave{e}}}$$

which otherwise would have surfaced with a uniformly Low tone contour. Neither of these facts, however, affects anything that is at issue here.

Consider now the strong forms of the recent past of which a few are given in (12a) with the surface representation on the left and the underlying representation on the right.

(12) a.

$$\underset{}{nd\text{–}\grave{a}\text{–}bá\text{–}b\grave{o}n\text{–}\grave{a}} \quad \underset{H\ \ L\ HL\ \ HL}{\overset{*\ \ *\ \ *}{ndi\text{–}a\text{–}ba\text{–}bon\text{–}a}} \quad \text{'I saw them''}$$

$$\underset{}{nd\text{–}\grave{a}\text{–}bá\text{–}l\grave{a}ng\text{–}\grave{a}} \quad \underset{H\ \ L\ HL}{\overset{*\ \ *}{ndi\text{–}a\text{–}ba\text{–}lang\text{–}a}} \quad \text{"I looked for them"}$$

$$\underset{}{w\text{–}á\text{–}b\grave{a}\text{–}b\grave{o}n\text{–}\grave{a}} \quad \underset{H\ \ LHL\ HL\ \ HL}{\overset{*\ \ *\ \ *\ \ *}{u\text{–}a\text{–}ba\text{–}bon\text{–}a}} \quad \text{"he/she saw them"}$$

$$\underset{}{w\text{–}á\text{–}b\grave{a}\text{–}l\grave{a}ng\text{–}\grave{a}} \quad \underset{H\ \ LHL\ HL}{\overset{*\ \ *\ \ *}{u\text{–}a\text{–}ba\text{–}lang\text{–}a}} \quad \text{"he/she looked for them"}$$

It is immediately obvious that the subject prefixes /ndi/ "I" and /u/ "he/she" undergo phonetic changes in position before the vowel: /ndi/ loses its vowel and /u/ becomes a glide prevocalically. We shall assume that this is the result of two separate rules: Vowel Deletion and Glide Formation. If we now make the plausible assumption that these two rules and H-Tone Deletion (11c) apply to the forms in (11a) we get the representations in (12b)

(12) b.

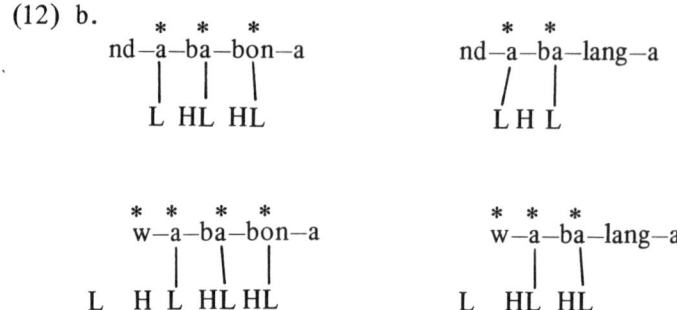

It is not difficult to get the correct output from the forms in (12b). All that is required is a rule that links the first H of the melody to the nearest accessible vowel on its right. The rule which is required has the form (12c)

(12) c.   SD: [C V̇ C V̇   SC: link H to nearest accessible vowel on its right
               [L H   L

Although (12c) has the form of a transformational rule it can be narrowly constrained so as not to require any of the extra power of transformational rules. We suggest, moreover, that the application of rules is subject to the condition (12d)

(12d) If the application of a rule results in a violation of the conditions — either universal or language-specific — which must be met by well-formed representations in the language in question, the violation is removed by deleting links between autosegments and core phonemes established by earlier rules or conventions.

Condition (12d) has the effect of deleting the link to the Low tone in vowels to which a High tone is linked by rule (12c). It must be noted that in its structural description rule (12c) requires two consecutive accented vowels. It is this requirement which will correctly prevent rule (12c) from applying to such forms as

(12) e.

   w – à – làngà   "I was looking for"   u̇ – ȧ – lang – a
                                          | |
                                          H L H   L

provided, of course, that rule (12c) applies after Glide Formation as was proposed above.

Much more important for the topic under discussion than the preceding is the fact that the account that was just proposed grossly violates the requirement of the Well Formedness Condition that each tone be linked to at least one tone bearing segment. We are thus presented with very clear alternatives: the Well Formedness Condition and the proposed account cannot both be right — one or the other must be wrong.

Some evidence has been given above which suggests that the Well Formedness Condition should be abandoned. To complete our case we shall examine the solution of the facts in (12a) that is given in Goldsmith's paper of which the Well-Formedness Condition is one of the cornerstones.

Recall that Meeussen's Rule, which must be allowed to apply in the strong forms if the account is to be based on the Well Formedness Condition, deletes all but the first of several accents appearing on consecutive vowels. If Meeussen's Rule were to apply to the form in (12a) it would produce incorrect results in all cases since it would delete all but the first accent in all words. To handle these problems Goldsmith proposes the rule of Accent Shift given in (13a)

(13) a.   a. $-\overset{*}{a} - \overset{*}{V}\ V \rightarrow \overset{*}{a} - V\ \overset{*}{V}$ or

         b. $\overset{*}{a} - \overset{*}{V} \rightarrow \overset{*}{a} - V$

This, however, does not resolve the difficulty completely, for in order to obtain the correct results it is necessary that the rule of Accent Shift interact with Meeussen's Rule in a fashion that is quite unprecedented in the literature. Specifically, it is necessary that the two rules apply disjunctively. However, the disjunctivity required is not the traditional one but, to quote Goldsmith, rather "one according to which the more GENERAL rule can be precluded from applying not only by the ACTUAL application of the more specific rule, but [by] the PRESENCE of the more specific rule — that is, by its potential application later in the derivation" (p. 24). These are far-reaching modifications in the algorithm for rule application and they are not to be welcomed since they render the rules extremely powerful, for now whether or not a given rule applies to a given string no longer depends purely on the form of the string, but may also depend on what other rules might apply to the input string.

This undesirable increase in the power of the rules is unnecessary in the alternative account, for as we have tried to show above the strong forms of the Tonga verb can be accounted for without recourse to either Meeussen's Rule or Accent Shift, and in that case, there is also no need for the significant increase in the power of the rules. This desirable result, however, can be achieved only if the Well Formedness Condition is replaced by the Tone Mapping Rules (3) and other conventions presented here.

On Schane's Linear Theory of English Stress and Rhythm*

Shosuke Haraguchi
The University of Tsukuba

0. INTRODUCTION

In his epoch-making study of English stress and linguistic rhythm, Liberman proposes a new theory, which he calls a metrical theory. Based on the proposals of Liberman (1975), Liberman and Prince (1977) (henceforth LP) elaborates the metrical theory, which has triggered an explosion of interest in stress, rhythm, syllable, foot, length, and metrics. Since the appearance of LP's article, the theory has received considerable modification due to the work of Kiparsky (1979), McCarthy (1979), Halle-Vergnaud (1978), Selkirk (1980), Hayes (1981), and many others.

Notwithstanding the amazingly rapid changes in theoretical frameworks, there is, however, a central and unchanged core which is shared by almost all the metrical theorists: the relative prominence of English stress is represented in terms of (i) binary node labels 's' (for 'strong') and 'w' (for 'weak') and in terms of (ii) hierarchical structures. Thus the word "America" is considered to be represented as follows:

(1)
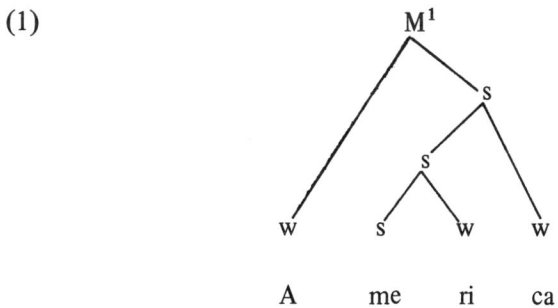

* I have profited greatly from presentation of large parts of the material contained in this article at the monthly meeting of the Circle of Linguistic Theory and Information Processing, at the University of Tsukuba. In addition, I am grateful to G. N. Clements, H. v.d. Hulst and N. J. Teele for valuable comments and suggestions on an earlier draft. Being pressed on time, I cannot incorporate some of them in this article.

Various versions of the metrical theory which incorporate this core make it possible to yield a number of interesting generalizations and to account for various phenomena concerning stress, rhythm, syllable, etc. For ease of reference, I will call the metrical theory which incorporates (i) and (ii) the hierarchical theory (HT).

Schane, on the other hand, has challenged these two widely accepted conceptions. In his two provocative articles, Schane (1979a,b) maintains that the basic foot in English is SWW, and that "lexical stress requires no more than LINEAR ORDERING." [p.599] He thus proposes an alternative theory of linguistic rhythm, which I will call the linear theory (LT), and he claims that his theory is superior to LP's theory.

Schane's approach deserves careful scrutiny, because if his claim can be upheld, it will have much impact on the metrical theory. Thus, in the ensuing discussion, I will, after a brief review of LT, examine the validity of his proposals, and argue that his proposals run into serious difficulties and fail to account for a number of important generalizations. It will thus be concluded that LT is, contrary to Schane's assertion, inferior to HT and cannot therefore be counted as a genuine alternative to HT.

1. BELIEFS OF LT

Although I believe that the reader is already familiar with Schane's approach, I will begin with a brief summary of his LT, in order to make the discussion below easier to follow. Schane assumes that accented syllables should be separated by one or more unaccented ones and thus claims that there are no contiguous accented syllables in English. Based on this assumption, he proposes that the basic rhythmic pattern of English is a ternary SWW and that English has the following system of rules and constraints. He then tries to argue against metrical theorists' claim that "rhythmic units are hierarchically ordered at the word level and they are binary-branching in structure." [p. 599]

(2)   S-placement[2]
        (a) Final Rule (FR):
            $X \to S / \underline{} \,]$
        (b) Antepenultimate Rule (APR):
            $X \to S / \underline{} XX\,]$
        (c) Penultimate Rule (PR):
            $X \to S / \underline{} X\,]$

(3)   Rhythmic Constraints
        (a) Weakening Convention (WC):

Schane's Linear Theory

The assignment of S's causes a CONTIGUOUS (previously) assigned S to be converted to W.

(b) Heavy Constraint (HC):
The first W of a WW sequence becomes S if it is heavy.

(c) Initial Constraint (IC):
If a word begins with two W's, the first one must be changed to S.

(4) (a) "Detail" Rule (for SPE) (DR):
$$S \rightarrow \begin{cases} [\text{1 stress}] \ / \ \underline{\hspace{1em}} \ldots ((X)(y))\#^3 \\ [\text{3 stress}] \end{cases}$$

(b) Rhythm Rule:
(i) $3 \ldots 3 \ldots 1 \rightarrow 3 \ldots 4 \ldots 1$
(ii) Rhythm Rule for Phrases:
$2 \ldots 1 \ldots 1 \rightarrow 1 \ldots 2 \ldots 1$

(c) Non-reduction Rule:
$$\begin{bmatrix} W^4 \\ -\text{reduced} \end{bmatrix} \rightarrow \begin{cases} [\text{4 stress}] \ / \ [\text{3 stress}] \\ [\text{3 stress}] \end{cases}$$

To illustrate how this LT works, consider the following derivations:

(5)

	(a) Monongahela]	(b) Winnepesaūkee]
	W W W WW	W W W W W
APR	↓	↓
	W W S WW	W W S W W
HC	↓	↓
	W W S SW	W W S S W
WC	↓	↓
	W W W S W	W W W S W
IC	↓	↓
	S W W S W	S W W S W
HC	↓	———
	S S W S W	
WC	↓	———
	W S W S W	
DR	3 1	3 1(?3)

(c) compensate] ory]

```
            W   W W
FR              ↓
            W   W S
APR         ↓
(? or IC)   S   W S   W(W)
FR                    ↓
            S   W S   S(W)
WC              ↓
            S   W W   S(W)
HC          ↓
            S   S W   S(W)
WC          ↓
            W   S W   S(W)
DR              1  3
```

In (5a) and (5b), the APR assigns S to the antepenultimate syllable. The first W of these derived SWW sequences is then changed to S by the HC, and the antepenultimate S automatically becomes W by the WC. The IC then assigns the initial S, giving each case the SWWSW sequence.[5] The second syllable of 'Monongahela', being heavy, is changed to S by the HC, thereby causing the initial S to be turned to W by the WC. Since the second syllable of 'Winnepesaukee' is light, it remains as it is. Finally, the "Detail" rule (DR) operates on the derived rhythmic structures to provide each of them with the 3 1 pattern.

In (c), S is first assigned to the last syllable of the verb 'compensate' by the FR and then to the antepenultimate syllable by the APR.[6] Because the final 'y' of the suffix '-ory' is assumed to be extrametrical, the FR assigns the S to the initial syllable of the suffix. The S previously assigned to the syllable 'ate' then becomes W by the WC. The second syllable of 'compensatory', which is heavy, is changed to S by the HC, thus triggering the initial S to become W by the WC. Finally, the 1 3 pattern is provided by the DR, since the righthand S, which is on the final syllable, cannot be provided with [1 stress].

This concludes our brief summary of Schane's LT. Now that we have established a sufficient foundation, let us hasten to proceed to the next step.

2. ON SOME EMPIRICAL INADEQUACIES OF LT

Although Schane's approach as summarized above looks elegant and ap-

Schane's Linear Theory 87

pealing at first glance, closer examination shows that it involves a number of difficulties. Notice first that Schane's Non-reduction rule (4c), which is introduced to derive the stress patterns of SPE, would assign [3 stress] to the final syllable of 'Winnepesaukee'. However, this is clearly incompatible with SPE's stress pattern.

It should incidentally be emphasized that this is by no means an exceptional case, since English has a fairly large number of words with a final tense vowel such as 'ChicagO', 'tomatO', etc. and with a word-medial non-reduced vowel such as 'crapUlous', 'IndIana', 'incongrUence', 'monadIc', etc. (Notice that the non-initial capital letters stand for non-reduced vowels in question.)

To prevent the Non-reduction rule from assigning the incorrect [3 stress] to these cases, it would be necessary to modify the system a little in some way. Though a number of possible solutions come to mind, I will not delve further into the matter here, and leave the matter open, since this is a relatively minor insufficiency.

Let us next examine one by one Schane's rhythmic constraints, which constitute the core of his LT. He proposes a possible universal convention, the WC, whose function is to convert any contiguous (previously) assigned S to W. This convention serves to eliminate the non-permissible sequences of S's, as illustrated in (6):

(6)   telegraph] y]   solid] ity]
        S W S   S W
WC   ↓   ↓   ↓
        W S W   W   W S W W

This convention is interesting in that it can cover a wide range of destressing phenomena, thus making unnecessary special auxiliary reduction rules as in SPE.

It cannot, however, be free from some inadequacies. To see this, consider the following cases of English compounds:

(7)   a. high-principled   b. Japan Current[7]
            good-natured   return ticket
            self-interested   police station
            well-favored   police justice

It seems that the compounds in (7a) have the following rhythmic pattern:

(8)   a. high-principled   b. self-interested
            good-natured   S S W W W
            well-favored
            S S W W

These patterns typically appear when a strong stress immediately follows, and they are correctly expressible in any version of HT, since these compounds are represented as having the following hierarchical structures:

(9)   a.   b.

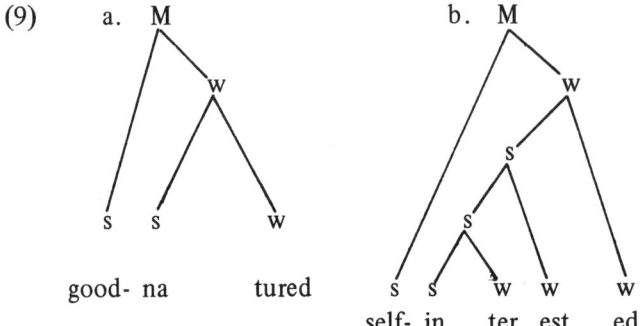

However, in LT the SSWW(W) pattern of (8) would be underivable as well as impermissible. Suppose for the sake of argument that the SSWW (W) patterns be somehow assigned to cases (8). Then, within Schane's framework the WC would apply to them to convert the patterns to SWWW(W):

(10)   good-natured   self-interested
             S S W   S S W W W
    WC   ↓   ↓
             S W W   S W W W W

Furthermore, the HC (3b) would incorrectly apply to these outputs to convert all SWWW(W)'s to WSWW(W)'s, since the initial syllable of the second member of these compounds is heavy. To exclude this undesirable derivation, it would be necessary to somehow restrict the applicability of these rhythmic constraints, which suggests that these constraints are not as general as they appear to be.

Consider now the more serious cases in (7b). Their stress patterns should be something like (11):

(11)   Japan Current   police station
          W S   S W   W S   S W

The WC would predict that the second S be turned to W, thereby producing the WSWW pattern:

(12)   a.   Japan Current   b.   police station
             W S   S W   W S   S W
    WC   ↓   ↓
             W S   W W   W S   W W

Schane's Linear Theory

Notice however that in the case of (12b) the HC would now operate to derive the incorrect pattern of WWSW, which would ultimately be converted to the non-existent SWSW pattern by the IC. These defects of the IC would be difficult to overcome, without introducing hierarchical structures, in the case of compound words.

Now turn to the IC, which has the function of converting the two word-initial W's to SW. This constraint works as illustrated in (13):

(13)   attest] ation]
        W S
WC   ↓
        W W S W
IC   ↓
        S W S W

It is already noted in footnote 1 that Schane (1979b) slightly modified the theory, thus opening a way to do without the IC even within the framework of LT. This very fact suggests that the IC is rather unstable and therefore the theoretical importance of the constraint is virtually nil. But even if it turned out to be necessary to introduce this constraint in LT, it should be restricted to apply at the word level only (excluding of course the cases of compounds). This should be done, because there are many well-formed cases at the phrasal level which begin with the initial sequence of W's. By way of illustration, observe the following:

(14)   a. in America
            W W S W W
        b. to the initial syllable
            W W W S W S W W

It is clear that the IC should not operate in these phrases. Since initial sequences of W's are common in English phrases, it is inappropriate to claim that this constraint works at a certain phrasal level.

Consider, in connection with this observation, the following cases in which Schane suggests that the two constraints discussed above can account for stress shifts not only in morphologically related words (e.g., 'solid', 'solidity') but also certain phrasal stress shifts:

(15)   thirteen students
        W S   S W
WC   ↓
        W W   S W
IC   ↓
        S W   S W

I believe that this suggestion is not justifiable because, for one thing, the very existence of the IC is, as suggested above, rather shaky and, for another, there is some evidence to show that the IC, if it were to be proven to be necessary, should be restricted to lexical items. Furthermore, as we will see later, it is a false generalization to handle phrases such as 'thirteen men' in a way parallel only with words such as 'attestation', while excluding other phrases such as 'anaphoric reference'. Taking all of these into consideration, we can safely conclude that the IC should be eliminated from the theory of rhythm. This further entails that Schane's assertion to the effect that the system of constraints of LT can be extended to a certain phrasal stress is ill-founded.

Let us now turn to Schane's final rhythmic constraint, the HC. This constraint, which is intended to "capture the observation that the first W of a WW sequence becomes S if it is heavy". Notice that this constraint is indispensable only under the assumption that the basic foot in English is SWW. Thus, if the basic foot in English and other languages turns out to be binary branching SW, then the SWW pattern will lose its raison d'être.

Furthermore, this constraint is also unable to handle a large number of cases of compound words. To show this, consider the following cases:

(16) a. blackboard eraser   b. compound formation
          S   W   W S W   S   W   W S W

Each of these compounds has a SWWSW sequence, which is the legitimate rhythmic pattern of these phrases.

Suppose that the HC be applicable to any sequence, phrasal or lexical. Then, by the interaction of the HC and the IC, the well-formed SWWSW pattern in (16) would be converted to the ill-formed WSWSW pattern:

(17)   blackboard eraser
              S   W   W S W
       HC   ↓
              S   S   W S W
       WC   ↓
             *W   S   W S W

To prevent this kind of undesirable derivation, it would be necessary to put some restriction on the HC, thus excluding the compounds from its range of application. This line of argument seems to suggest that within the framework of LT, the compounds be, strangely enough, excluded from the domain of the rhythmic constraints. This in turn implies that we need some special constraints for compounds, which indicates that LT fails to capture the generalization which is captured within metrical theorists' HT.

Schane's Linear Theory

To put it another way, HT can handle the compounds in exactly the same way as other lexical items, and therefore needs no special constraints for compounds, while Schane's LT requires some special mechanism to handle the cases of the compounds. This observation indicates that something important is missing in LT, which makes the theory rather dubious.

3. ON STRESS SHIFTS AND RHYTHM RULES

Let us now reconsider cases of phrasal stress shift. It should be recalled that Schane asserts that the phrasal stress shift of 'thirteen students' be accounted for in terms of the WC and the IC. We have already seen that this assertion is not justifiable. Here it will be argued that a somewhat different consideration of the phenomena in question also confirms the conclusions reached above.

As Schane himself admits, the WC and the IC cannot be used to account for stress shifts found in phrases such as 'anaphoric reference', 'Artificial Intelligence', etc., because these phrases, as illustrated in (18), have an alternating rhythm:

(18)   anaphoric reference
        S W S W S W W

To handle this kind of phrasal stress shift, Schane is, it seems to me, forced to introduce the following Rhythm rule for phrases:

(19)   Rhythm Rule for Phrases:
        $2 \ldots 1 \ldots 1 \rightarrow 1 \ldots 2 \ldots 1$

Furthermore, Schane maintains that the stress contour of 3 4 1 on 'attestation' should be handled by the following rhythm rule:

(20)   Rhythm Rule:
        $3 \ldots 3 \ldots 1 \rightarrow 3 \ldots 4 \ldots 1$

This implies that Schane is claiming that all of these three processes should be handled differently.

However, all of these seem to be closely related in that all of them derive alternating rhythms. In Schane's system, this relation cannot be directly expressed, which means that the mutual relations under consideration cannot be correctly captured in his LT.

Now it should be noted that within the framework of HT, all of these cases are handled in exactly the same way, i.e., in terms of the following rhythm rule:

(21)   Rhythm Rule in Metrical Theory:

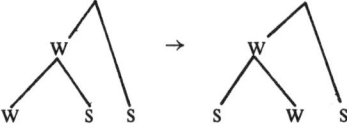

We will not be concerned with the details of this rule at this time. For some related observations, see LP, Kiparsky (1979), etc. Notice that this rhythm rule eliminates the stress clash and derives the desired alternating rhythm.

In HT, these three processes (i.e., 'thirteen men', 'anaphoric reference', and 'attestation') have the following hierarchical metrical trees at a certain level of their derivations:

(22)   a. R   b. M

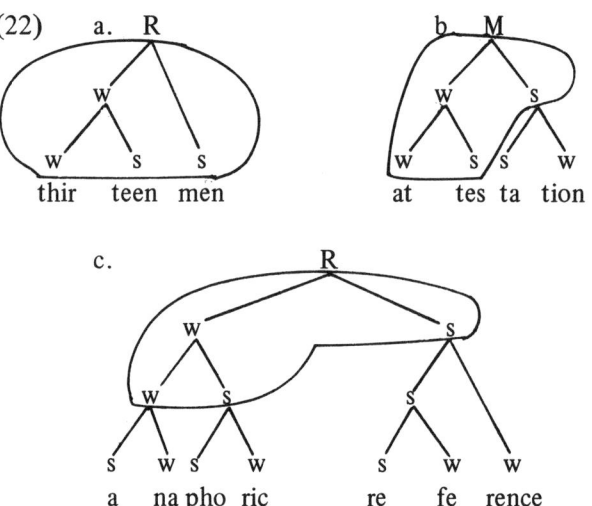

c.

To these structures, the Rhythm rule in (21) applies, thus converting them to the following structures:

(23)   a. R   b. M

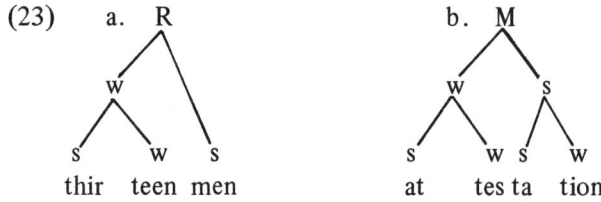

c.

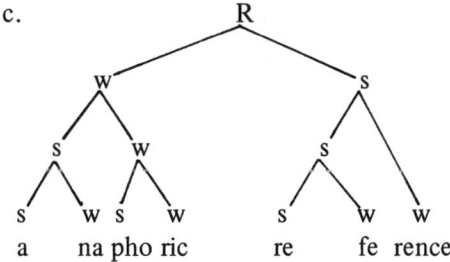

a na pho ric   re fe rence

These metrical trees are basically correct representations which reflect the alternating rhythmic patterns under consideration. Thus the observation above suggests that HT can capture the generalization concerning the alternating patterns in a straightforward fashion. Based on these considerations, I conclude that metrical theorists' HT analysis is superior to the revisions suggested by Schane.

4. MORE ON STRESS SHIFTS

We will now turn to another aspect of phrasal stress shifts, which is discussed in Haraguchi et al. (1980). As supporting evidence for metrical theorists' HT over Schane's LT, observe the following examples:

(24) a. automatic recognition
      b. retroactive confirmation
         S W SW S W S W

According to our informant, these phrases sometimes show the rhythmic pattern of 2 4 3 1 as well as the predicted 3 2 3 1 pattern. The latter will be heard mainly in a slow and careful speech. In contrast, the former will be heard more often in faster speech, and the faster the pronunciation of the phrase in question becomes, the more natural the former sound.

It is clear that neither of Schane's rhythm rules can handle this type of stress shift. Thus, it will be necessary to supply his LT with another rhythm rule which applies to this case.

In metrical theorists' HT, however, the 2 4 3 1 pattern will be accounted for by the independently necessary rhytm rule (21). To see how this pattern is derived, consider the following metrical tree:

(25)
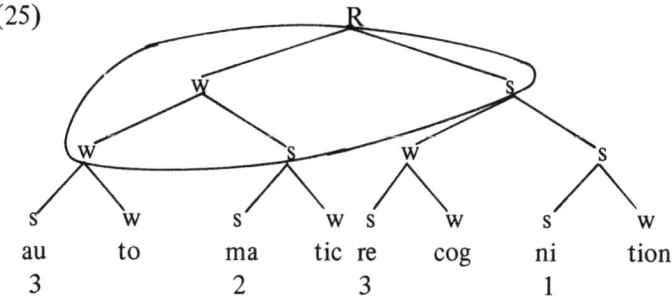

au to ma tic re cog ni tion
3   2   3   1

This metrical tree seems to be an appropriate representation of the 3 2 3 1 pattern. As indicated in (25), this tree has the 'wss' structure which satisfies the structural description of the rhythm rule in (21). Thus, the rule works here and turns structure (25) to (26):

(26)
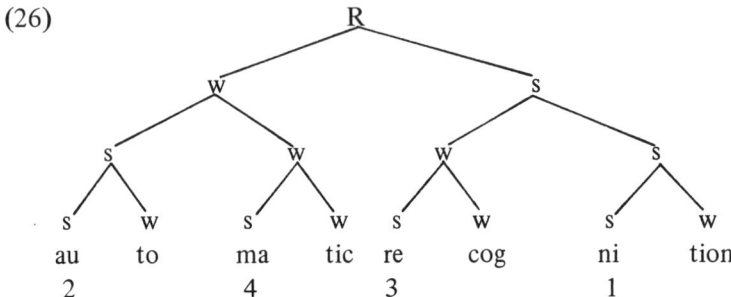

It will be obvious that this structure correctly represents the 2 4 3 1 pattern. This observation will suffice to show how to derive the 2 4 3 1 pattern within the metrical theory. The very fact that the independently necessary rhythm rule (21) in the metrical theory can handle this type of stress shift shows again that HT is superior to LT.

Notice by the way that the optionality of the rhythm rule (21) in this case, as compared with the obligatoriness in (22), is not so difficult to explain. It will be immediately clear that the latter contains the stress clash 'w s s' at the level of either the syllable or the metrical foot, while the former has no such clash at either level. In fact, the clash appears at a higher phrasal level in (25). The optionality of the rhythm rule in the cases of 'automatic recognition', 'retroactive confirmation', etc. seems to be due to this difference in the levels at which stress clash occurs.

5. CONCLUSION

The present critical survey of Schane's LT shows that the theory has a number of defects and that metrical theorists' HT is superior to Schane's alternatives. In his concluding remarks, Schane claims that his "rhythmic constraints provide much of economy. They handle stress shifts in the derivational morphology" as well as certain phrasal stress shifts (e.g., (15)). As we have seen above, neither of these claims is justifiable.

We have argued in particular that (i) all of his rhythmic constraints are problematic in that they cannot handle stress facts of compounds; (ii) his rhythmic constraints cannot, contrary to his claim, be extended to handle phrasal stress shifts; (iii) his system of rules misses certain generalizations that can be easily covered by HT.

Taking all of these into consideration, we now conclude that Schane's LT cannot be regarded as a genuine alternative to metrical theorists' HT. This conclusion is extremely important in that it opens a way to reduce the number of theoretically possible rhythmic theories, and thus contributes towards more narrowly restricting the number of possible grammars.

NOTES

1. Here and elsewhere, the special symbol 'M' stands for 'mot (i.e., word)'.
2. In these rules, the symbol X stands for a syllable. Schane uses the capital letters 'S' and 'W' to represent what he calls 'accented' and 'unaccented', respectively. Thus, these are slightly different from the metrical theorists' 's' and 'w'. For further discussion, see Schane (1979a, b).

Notice incidentally that Schane (1979b), which is apparently an abridged and slightly revised version of Schane (1979a), modifies the S-placement rules as follows:

(i) $X \rightarrow S / \underline{\quad} \left\{ \begin{array}{ll}] & \text{Final S-placement} \\ (X) X \left\{ \begin{array}{l}] \\ S \end{array} \right\} & \begin{array}{l} \text{Prefinal S-placement (a)} \\ \text{Prefinal S-placement (b)} \end{array} \end{array} \right\}$

This revision makes it possible to dispense with the IC in (3c) even within the framework of Schane's LT. It will later be shown that the version which incorporates the IC poses a number of difficulties and that thus the IC should be abandoned. However, Schane admits that it is difficult to choose between these two alternative solutions and leaves the matter open.

3. Schane (1979b) adds to this rule a condition to the effect that "where ... contains no S." This stipulation can be shown to be unnecessary, but we will not go into detail here since it is irrelevant to the present discussion.
4. Although Schane (1979b) replaces W with V, the change seems to be only notational, and will thus be disregarded below.
5. It should be noted that in Schane (1979b), the initial S is considered to be assigned not by the IC but by the "Prefinal" S-placement rule (b) (See footnote 1 above). Whether the initial S is assigned by the IC or by the "Prefinal" S-placement rule (b) will not substantially affect the present discussion.
6. It is unclear why the APR, but not the IC, applies here. In this connection, it is interesting to note that the IC, but not the APR, is used in the derivation of 'devotee' and 'investee'. For further discussion, see Schane (1979a, p. 577).
7. I owe examples (7b) to M. Watanabe.

Metrical Structure as the Organizing Principle of Yidin^y Phonology

Bruce Hayes
UCLA

1 .INTRODUCTION

The study of phonological systems often turns up rules that are in some sense interrelated — that is, rules which clearly represent different processes, but nonetheless apply in similar environments. Consider, for example, the following three rules of English, all of which apply both before # and before stressless vowels:

(1) $\emptyset \rightarrow t\ /\ n \_\_ s \begin{Bmatrix} \# \\ \breve{V} \end{Bmatrix}$

   prínce, píncĕr vs. cónsòrt

(2) $t \rightarrow [\text{+lax}]\ /\ [\text{-cons}] \_\_ \begin{Bmatrix} \# \\ \breve{V} \end{Bmatrix}$

   hít, híttĕr vs. Híttìte

(3) $n \rightarrow \eta\ /\ \_\_ k \begin{Bmatrix} \# \\ \breve{V} \end{Bmatrix}$

   hónk, cónquĕr vs. cóncòurse

The recurrent, mysterious disjunction found in these rules has been clarified by Kiparsky (1979), who suggested that they be restricted to apply *within the metrical foot*, where feet can be defined independently on the basis of the English stress system (cf. Selkirk 1980). For example, in *prince* and *pincer*, the [n] and [s] are within the same foot, thus permitting [t] insertion, whereas in *consort* the intervening foot boundary blocks the rule:

(4)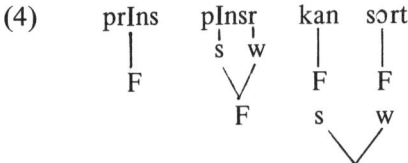

Kiparsky showed that many other rules of English respect foot structure; for example the devoicing of /l/ after /s/, the mutual assimilation of /k/ and /r/, and the reduction of vowels to schwa. This insight raises the possibility of a new mode of phonological description: we can now capture generalizations about a language that go *across* phonological rules, by showing how the rules all refer to the same prosodic constituent structure. In this sense, metrical structure serves as an organizing principle for much of English phonology.

In Dixon (1977a, hereafter PRY), the phonology of Yidin^y, an Australian language, is described with clarity and insight. This article is an attempt to show that there is a pervasive link among virtually all the phonological rules of Yidin^y, similar to that among the rules of English, and that the metrical theory of stress is both sufficient and necessary to provide a formal account of this link. As a further benefit, we will find that many of Dixon's rules are considerably simplified under a metrical analysis.

2. DATA

The central feature of Yidin^y phonology is the interaction of vowel length, syllable count, and stress. According to Dixon, most of the long vowels of Yidin^y result from one of the following three rules:

(4)   Penultimate Lengthening (PRY 6)

In every word with an odd number of syllables, the penultimate vowel is lengthened.

cf. barganda-d^{y}i-n^{y}u → bargandad^{y}i:n^{y}u   'pass by-antipassive-past'

gudaga → guda:ga   'dog'

magi-ri-ŋal-da-n^{y}u-nda → magiriŋaldan^{y}u:nda

'climb up-going-comitative-coming-subordinate-dative'

(5) Pre-Suffix Lengthening (PRY 16)

$$V \rightarrow V: / \underline{} (C) + \begin{Bmatrix} -d^y i \\ -li/-ri/-ri \\ -da \end{Bmatrix}$$

That is, lengthen a vowel before the antipassive suffix $-d^y i$, the "going" aspect $-li/-ri/-ri$, and the "coming" aspect $-da$.

cf. barganda-d^{y}i:-n^{y}u → barganda:-d^{y}i:-n^{y}u

magi-ri-ŋal-da-n^{y}u:-nda → magi:-ri-ŋa:l-da-n^{y}u:-nda

(6) Pre-Yotic Lengthening (PRY 22)

$$i \rightarrow i: / \underline{} y \# \quad ^1$$

cf. galbiy → galbi:y (→ galbi:) 'catfish'
gurilíy → guri:liy → guri:li:y (→ guri:li:)
'black nose wallaby'

The remaining long vowels are underlying, occurring in just a handful of morphemes such as *durgu:* 'mopoke owl', *wara:buga* 'white apple tree', and *-d^{y}ulu:* 'durative'.

Not all of these long vowels reach the surface, as some of them are liable to shortening by a rule that Dixon states as follows:

(7) Illicit Length Elimination (PRY 18)

If a long vowel ... occurs in an odd-numbered syllable of an odd-syllabled word ... then it is shortened.

This rule converts *barganda:-d^{y}i:-n^{y}u* to *barganda-d^{y}i:-n^{y}u* and *guri:li:* to *guri:li*, but leaves *guda:ga* intact, as the long vowel is in an even syllable. *wuŋaba:-d^{y}i-ŋ* 'hunt-antipassive-present' is similarly left alone, as it contains an even number of syllables.

The long vowels that remain then determine the placement of stress by the following rule:

(8) Stress Assignment (PRY 3)

Stress is assigned to the first syllable involving a long vowel. If there is no long vowel, it is assigned to the first syllable of the word. Further stresses are then assigned (recursively) to the syllable next but one before, and the next but one after, a stressed syllable.

cf. galbí:
gudá:ga
yad^{y}í:-ri-ŋá-l
bargándad^{y}í:n^{y}u   'walk about-going-comit.-pres.'
wú ŋabá:-d^{y}i-ŋ
magí:riŋ á:ldan^{y}ú:nda
gúygal   'bandicoot'
gúdagá- ŋgu   'dog-ergative'
mád^{y}indá-ŋal-n^{y}ú-nda   'walk up-comitative-subordinate-dative'

A striking aspect of these rules is that three of them refer to an alternating count of syllables: Stress Assignment, Penultimate Lengthening, and Illicit Length Elimination. The "alternating count" in the latter two is implicit in any procedure that determines whether a word has an odd or even number of syllables — an odd syllabled word, after all, is just a word in which a syllable is left over after syllables have been counted off in pairs. Further facts reinforce our suspicion that a generalization is being missed: reference to an alternating syllable count seems to be pervasive in Yidin^y phonology. An obvious case is Dixon's rule of Final Syllable Deletion (PRY 15):

(9)   Final Syllable Deletion

$$(C)V_i \rightarrow \emptyset \ / \ \# \ X \ V \ <+>_a \begin{bmatrix} C \\ +son \\ -round \end{bmatrix} \underline{} \ \#^2$$

Conditions:
A. The input form is odd syllabled.
B. Either

(i)   a is present; or
(ii) V_i is a "morphophoneme"; i.e. occurs in a restricted set of roots.

cf. bama-yi → bama:-yi → bama:-y   'person-comitative'

barganda-d^{y}i:-n^{y}u → bargandad^{y}i:n^y

gindanu → ginda:nu → ginda:n   'moon'
[+Rule 9]

And five more rules that respect an alternating syllable count may be culled from Dixon's *Grammar of Yidin^y* (1977b, hereafter GY):

(10) a. Rhotic Dropping (GY 127, 129)

$$r, \underset{.}{r} \rightarrow \emptyset \;/\; \# \; X \; \underline{\quad} \; d$$

obligatory if X is even syllabled
optional if X is odd syllabled

b. y Deletion (GY 130)

$$y \rightarrow \emptyset \;/\; \# \; X \; \underline{\quad} \; \text{-nda [Dative]}$$

where Xy is odd syllabled

c. Nasal Cluster Simplification (GY 132-133)

$$n^y m \rightarrow n^y \text{ or } ym \;/\; \# \; X \; \underline{\quad}$$

where Xn^y is odd syllabled

d. n Drop (GY 135)

$$n \rightarrow \emptyset \;/\; \# \; X \; m \; \underline{\quad}$$

where Xm is even syllabled
(optional, coastal dialect only)

e. Genitive i Backing (GY 135-136)

$$i \rightarrow u \;/\; \# \; X \; V \; + \; n \; \underline{\quad} \; +$$

where XV is even syllabled[3]

The point here is that rules which delete or modify segments based on an odd-even syllable count are not especially common — it would be a colossal coincidence to find eight of them in a single language if all applied on an independent basis, particularly when the language in question has an alternating stress pattern. Clearly, there must be some common basis or organizing principle for all of these Yidin^y rules. Dixon partially recognizes this (cf. PRY 1,4), but fails to provide a formal account of the problem. An adequate treatment is possible under metrical theory.

3. A METRICAL ANALYSIS

It is straightforward to determine the proper metrical structure for Yidin^y. The feet obviously must be disyllabic; and they must be assigned from left to right across the word. The evidence for the latter claim is as follows. (a) All of the rules that count off syllables from one end of the word (those of (10)) count off from the beginning, not the end. (b) The rules that simply refer to the length of the word (i.e. Penultimate Lengthening and Final Syllable Deletion) have their effects at or near the right edge. These rules can refer to a local property (whether the word ends with a left over syllable or not), and thus avoid the use of variables, provided that we assign the feet from left to right instead of right to left. (c) Yidin^y has a late, optional rule of Stress Fronting (PRY 5), which may shift stress from the second syllable to the first, as in *galí:-na* → *gáli:na* 'go-purposive'. This rule can be formulated as a very simple relabelling, provided that the first two syllables of a word always constitute a foot; cf. (11)a:

(11) a. galí:na → gáli:na   b. galí:na ??

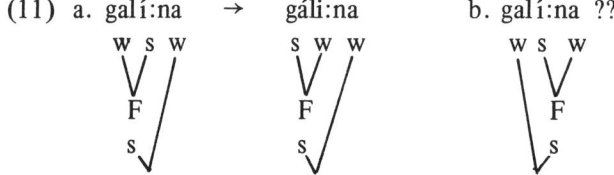

In contrast, if we posit right to left construction (as in (11)b), there is no simple formal operation that will both place stress on the first syllable and remove it from the second.[4]

The only difficulty here concerns how the feet are to be labelled. As we shall see shortly, labelling depends on the distribution of long vowels in the word, including long vowels induced by Penultimate Lengthening. But Penultimate Lengthening itself refers to the odd-even distinction, and thus by hypothesis is sensitive to metrical structure. The way around the problem is to construct the trees first, let Penultimate Lengthening refer to them, and only then provide them with their final labelling. We are of course free to assign a preliminary labelling and change it later; this strategy has minor advantages which are shown below.

On the basis of this reasoning, I would offer the following specific analysis:

Metrical Structure in Yidin^y

(12) Tree Construction

Going from left to right across the word, group syllables into binary feet, labelled w s.

cf. a. guygal

b. mad^yindaŋaln^yunda

c. bargandad^yin^yu

I assume that any syllable not affected by (12) is adjoined as a weak member of the adjacent foot by a universal Stray Syllable Adjunction convention, discussed in Hayes (1981, 73). After the convention has applied, (12)c would appear as follows:

(13)   bargandad^yin^yu
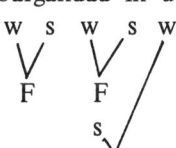

The feet constructed by (12) form the basis on which the other rules apply — instead of counting the syllables of the word over again for each rule, we can have the rules refer to local properties of the metrical structure, just like the rules of English outlined above. For example, Penultimate Lengthening can now be formulated to lengthen metrically strong penultimate vowels, as under (14):

(14) Penultimate Lengthening (metrical version)

$$V \rightarrow V: / \underline{\quad} \overset{s}{|} \, (C) \, X \, \# \quad \text{where X is a syllable}$$

cf. a. gudaga → guda:ga

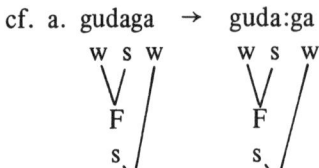

b. bargandad^yin^yu

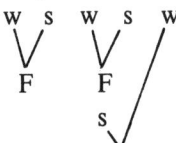

→ bargandad^yi:n^yu

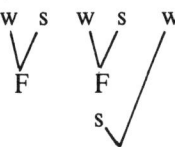

but c. mad^yindaŋaln^yunda   no change

Similarly, the rule of Final Syllable Deletion can be reformulated to delete syllables in weak metrical position:

(15) Final Syllable Deletion (metrical version)

$$(C)V \rightarrow \emptyset \ / \ V \begin{bmatrix} C \\ +son \\ -round \end{bmatrix} \overset{w}{\_\_} \ \#$$

The rationale for assigning a preliminary labelling to the metrical feet can now be seen to be phonetic naturalness: it is the norm for stressless vowels to be deleted and stressed vowels to be lengthened. Notice, however, that the preliminary labelling is not crucial, as the rules in question could just as well refer to position within the foot rather than metrical labelling.

Similar reanalyses of the syllable counting rules under (10) can be made. The lesson of these rules is the same as before: by making them refer to prosodic structure, we can show how they fit into the overall phonological pattern of Yidin^y, rather then treating them as isolated phenomena.

The placement of stress in its correct surface position can be carried out by the following rule:

(16) Stress Shift

> Relabel all sister nodes s w, unless there is a strong node dominating a long vowel.

cf. a. guygal → guygal

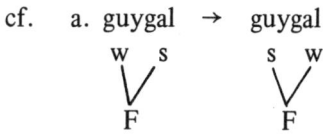

b. mad^{y}inda ŋaln^{y}unda → mad^{y}inda ŋaln^{y}unda

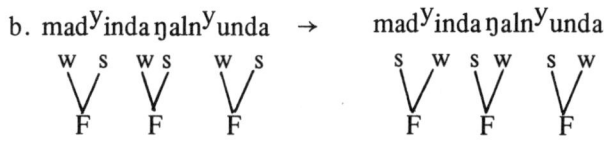

c. wuŋaba:d^{y}iŋ → wuŋaba:d^{y}iŋ

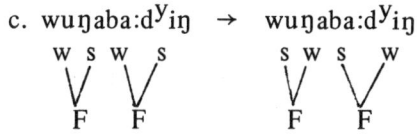

but d. guda:ga no change

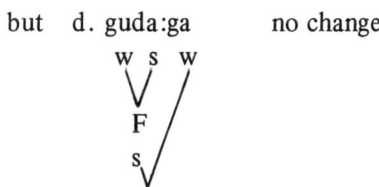

e. barganda:d^{y}i:n^y no change

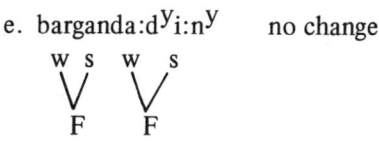

The "unless" clause of Stress Shift is highly reminiscent of the "right nodes strong iff branching" convention from other metrical analyses (cf. Liberman and Prince 1977, Hayes 1981).[5] This similarity can be made explicit, given the appropriate formal devices, i.e. a projection of vowels and geminate representation of length. What is unusual about the rule is that it postulates *labelling harmony*: if one foot of the word receives w s labelling by the "unless" clause, the others must follow suit. Note, however, that this is not a necessary ingredient of the analysis, as a more localistic (though slightly more complex) version can be formulated.

106 Bruce Hayes

After stress has been settled in the right place, we can apply a metrical version of Illicit Length Elimination:

(17) Illicit Length Elimination (metrical version)

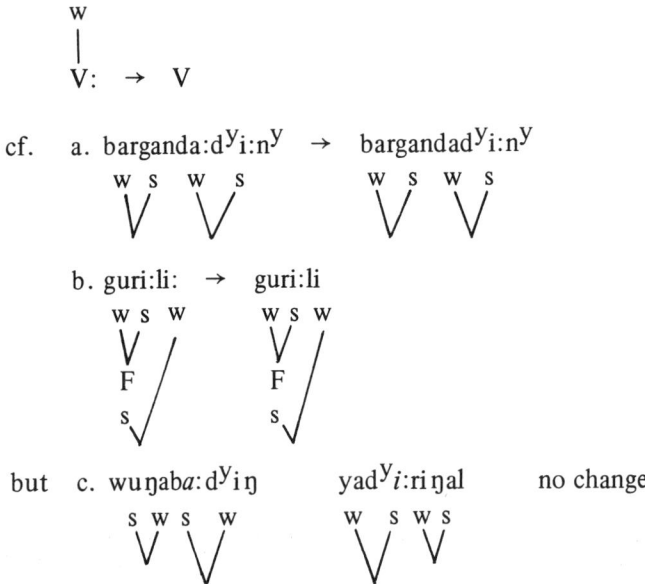

cf. a. barganda:d^{y}i:n^y → bargandad^{y}i:n^y

  b. guri:li: → guri:li

but c. wuŋaba:d^{y}iŋ   yad^{y}i:riŋal   no change

Notice that the new rule is a fair improvement over Dixon's: it is intuitively simpler; it no longer has to refer directly to syllable count; and it is phonetically natural, in that it shortens stressless vowels.

The metrical versions of Stress Assignment and Illicit Length Elimination are formulated quite differently from Dixon's rules, and are reversed in their ordering, but nevertheless have the same effects. To see this, consider first words that have an underlyingly odd number of syllables. Here Penultimate Lengthening will apply, inducing iambic labelling of the feet. The odd numbered vowels will therefore be weak and subject to shortening, while the even numbered vowels will receive stress. With the even syllabled words, it is easy to see that the two analyses agree *unless* there are long vowels in both odd and even syllables: for example $V\ V\ V:\ V:$ would surface as $V\ \acute{V}\ V\ \acute{V}:$ under the metrical theory and $\acute{V}\ V\ \acute{V}:\ V:$ under Dixon's. However, such cases simply never arise: Penultimate Lengthening does not apply to even syllabled words, and a widespread conspiracy in Yidin^y morphology (cf. PRY 30-34, GY 74-76, 227-232) insures that none of the other sources of vowel length can create a length clash. The predictions of the streamlined analysis are thus exactly the same as those of Dixon's.

4. COMPARISON WITH OTHER THEORIES

I have tried to show that metrical structure provides an adequate basis for characterizing a general pattern of Yidin^y, by which numerous rules refer to an alternating count of syllables going from left to right. We turn now to the other half of the argument, which is to show that metrical structure is *necessary* as well as sufficient. All of the phenomena presented so far might also be handled by rival theories of stress, for example a theory holding that stress is a feature, or the system proposed in Schane (1979a, b). We will argue against these theories by presenting further facts about Yidin^y which can be explained only under the basic assumptions of metrical theory — that is, that stress is to be represented as relative prominence defined on prosodic constituent structure.

In a system in which stress is a feature, the obvious analysis of the Yidin^y facts is to create an intermediate level of representation in which all even-numbered syllables are marked [+stress]:

(18) Initial Stress Assignment (featural version)

$$V \rightarrow [\text{+stress}] \;/\; \left\{ \begin{array}{c} \# \\ [\text{+stress}] \end{array} \right\} C_0 \; V \; C_0 \; \underline{}$$

(left to right iterative)

The output of (18) would naturally parallel the representations created by the metrical rule (12), allowing us to capture the unity of all the rules referring to odd-even syllable count — they would simply refer to the value of [stress] in the relevant syllable rather than to metrical position. The problem arises when we attempt to place the stresses in their correct surface position. This would necessitate a rule of the following form:

(19) Stress Shift (featural version)

$$C_0 \; V \; C_0 \; \begin{bmatrix} V \\ \text{+stress} \\ \text{-long} \end{bmatrix} \rightarrow \quad [\text{+stress}] \quad [\text{-stress}]$$

$$1 \quad 2 \quad 3 \quad\quad 4 \quad\quad\quad 1 \quad 2 \quad 3 \quad 4$$

$$/ \; \# \, (C_0 VC_0 \begin{bmatrix} V \\ \text{-long} \end{bmatrix})_0 \; \underline{} \; (C_0 VC_0 \begin{bmatrix} V \\ \text{-long} \end{bmatrix})_0 \; C_0 \; \#$$

Aside from its complexity, (19) misses an obvious generalization: it doesn't explain why the placement of stress on the odd numbered vowels happens to be accompanied by the removal of stress from the even numbered vowels. Notice that any rule that involved one of these operations in the absence of the other would be quite unlikely. The metrical theory offers a better account: it represents stress as *relative* prominence among syllables, so that the linking of the two operations follows automatically.[6]

The framework of Schane (1979a, b) offers an improvement over a purely segmental system. The basis of Schane's system is a binary opposition between accented (S) and unaccented (W) syllables, crucially augmented by the following convention:

(20) Weakening Convention (Schane 1979b, 487)

> The assignment of S causes any *contiguous* (previously assigned) S to be converted to W.

The Weakening Convention embodies the claim, correct for Yidin^y, that languages avoid stresses on adjacent syllables. It also allows us to meet the objection raised against the account using a stress feature. We would first posit an Initial Stress Assignment rule, entirely parallel to the segmental rule (18):

(21) Initial Stress Assignment (Schane's system)

$$X \rightarrow S \;/\; \left\{ \begin{matrix} \# \\ S \end{matrix} \right\} \; X \; \underline{\quad} \qquad \text{(iterative, X is a syllable)}$$

The odd-even syllable count rules could then refer to the distinction between S and W, just as they referred to [+,-stress] in the featural analysis. Stress Shift can then be formulated as in (22):

(22) Stress Shift (Schane's system)

$$X \rightarrow S \;/\; \underline{\quad} \; X \; \left\{ \begin{matrix} \# \\ S \end{matrix} \right\} \qquad \text{(right to left iterative)}$$

> Condition: may not apply if a long vowel would be weakened to W by (20).[7]

Rule (22) need not contain a separate provision to destress the formerly accented syllables, as this follows automatically from the Weakening Convention, as shown below:

(23) mad^y indaŋaln^{y}unda
```
 w   s   w   s   w   s
             s              Stress Shift
         w           w      Weakening Convention
     s                      Stress Shift
 w                          Weakening Convention
 s   w   s   w   s   w      Stress Shift
```

The Schanian analysis is thus not subject to the objection leveled against the featural account. However, there are other arguments that favor the metrical theory over Schane's. The metrical theory claims that Yidin^y words are organized into a constituent structure, which can have effects beyond just that of organizing the phonological rules. Consider, for example, the following performance effect noted in GY (p. 41):

(24) When (informant) Dick Moses recorded a Yidin^y song, he missed exactly one (word initial) disyllabic unit every time he took breath — this was either a complete word (the first *buŋgu* of *búŋgu búŋgu yíŋal*), or else the first two syllables of a trisyllabic word (*bugu* from *bugú:ba d^{y}úndulúbi d^{y}ánaŋ*).

The metrical analysis provides a straightforward account of what is going on here: Moses was apparently omitting a single metrical foot. However, under the account based on Schane's framework, the material deleted is an arbitrary sequence, unrelated to the phonological structure of the language. A similar argument can be made from reduplication in Yidin^y, the normal mode of which is to copy and prepose the first two syllables of a word, as in (25):

(25) a. mulari   'initiated man'
     mulamulari   'initiated men'

   b. gindalba   'lizard species'
     gindalgindalba   'lizards'

Again, the metrical account provides a formal insight into the phenomenon which is lacking under Schane's framework: reduplication is simply copying of the stem initial foot. Notice that in neither of the two cases here will reference to the output of rule (21) under Schane's framework be at all helpful.

To summarize, we have seen that other representations for stress could also serve as an organizing principle for the Yidin^y phonological rules in the sense we have described. But the metrical theory is better suited to the inherent nature of stress: the facts of Yidin^y support the notion that stress is represented as relative prominence, within a prosodic constituent structure.

NOTES

1 Dixon attempts to collapse this rule with another rule which deletes syllable final /y/. His rules appear as follows (PRY 22):

(i)   iy → i : / __ #

(ii) i<:>y → i<:> / __ C

However, the ostensibly deleted /y/ shows up before a vowel initial clitic, as in *galbi:y#ala* 'catfish—now'. This suggests that the deletion of syllable final /y/ is a separate process, with syllabification allowed across at least internal word boundaries.

2 It might be imagined that the odd syllable condition could be eliminated from the structural description of Final Syllable Deletion by requiring that the vowel preceding the syllable to be deleted be long. Since such vowels will only occur by virtue of Penultimate Lengthening, the odd syllable requirement would then follow from the similar restriction which was placed on the Penultimate Lengthening rule. However, Dixon points out that the ablative suffix *-mu* idiosyncratically blocks Penultimate Lengthening on the vowel that precedes it. In such cases, Final Syllable Deletion nonetheless applies, as in (i):

(i) bun^{y}a-mu → bun^{y}a-m   'woman-ablative'

The odd syllable restriction on Final Syllable Deletion is thus still necessary.

3 As with Final Syllable Deletion, some of these rules might be formulated so as to refer to the long vowel induced by Penultimate Lengthening, rather than syllable count. However, in the case of n Drop a rule based on vowel length would produce the wrong results: if the deletion of /n/ depended on the presence of a long vowel in the preceding syllable, we should erroneously predict that /n/ could not be dropped in forms like *mud^{y}am-nu-ŋgu* 'mother-genitive-ergative', where the addition of a further suffix after *-ni* has blocked Penultimate Lengthening. For rules (10)a, b, c, e, it is impossible to determine whether the conditioning factor is vowel length or syllable count. However, given the pattern displayed by all the clear cases, we would expect the latter to be the relevant factor.

4 This constitutes one of the counterarguments to the reanalysis of Nash (1979), who posits right to left foot construction. For full details see Hayes (1981, 137-142).

5 Under the slightly more abstract framework of Hayes (1981), the Yidin^y labelling rule would fall under the convention "dominant nodes strong iff branching," with right nodes marked as dominant by the initial foot construction rule (12). This has the advantage of automatically assigning a preliminary w s labelling early in the phonology, as under the theory the default labelling convention is "dominant nodes strong."

6 Yidin^y is of course not the only language in which this sort of argument can be made. In general, "rhythm rules" such as those found in English and other languages can be expressed as a single operation under metrical theory, but require two operations when expressed using a stress feature.

7 The condition attached to rule (22) is needed to block shifting in words like *durgu:, yad^{y}i:riŋal*. It plays the same role as the "unless" condition placed on the
      w s   w s w s
metrical rule. (16).

The Representation of Nasality in Gokana

Larry M. Hyman
University of California

0. INTRODUCTION

With the exception of certain Coastal Salishan languages (Hockett 1955: 119), all languages exploit the feature of nasality within their respective sound systems. However, despite the near universality of the nasal-oral opposition, languages vary considerably in the ways in which they allow nasality to be manifested. These variations are attributable to two separate "choices" languages must make: (a) they must situate nasality *paradigmatically* and designate a set of features which may cooccur with the specification [+nasal]; and (b) they must situate nasality *syntagmatically* and establish a sequential domain within which a single [+nasal] specification may reside. The term "nasality bearing unit" (henceforth NBU) is chosen as an instantiation of Clements' (1981) notion of "P-bearing units". Certain segments (i.e. feature complexes) will be specified as allowing an opposition in nasality, where the term nasality covers both nasal and nasalized articulations. In many languages a [+nasal] specification is restricted to noncontinuant sonorant consonants, e.g. the only nasal or nasalized segments in such a language may be /m/, /n/ and /ŋ/. Other languages allow the nasal-oral opposition on vowels or continuant sonorants, e.g. /ã/, /ĩ/ and /w̃/. Still others, although fewer, are reported to have nasalized fricatives, as in Owerri Igbo (Green and Igwe 1963). The NBU will thus have to be specified for each language. We expect, however, that the range of possible NBU's will be seriously constrained by universal considerations — considerations which in reality limit the choice to a relatively small class of feature complexes.

The range of nasal domains varies more dramatically. In many languages the domain of nasality coincides with the NBU. Thus, in many varieties of English, the NBU is defined minimally as [+son, -cont], and the domain of a [+nasal] specification is, except for certain superficial assimilations, the nasal segment itself.[2] On the other hand the domain can be different from the NBU. First, it can be *subsegmental*, in which case the language in question allows either or both prenasalized and postnasalized consonants, e.g. /^{m}b/ and /b^m/. In this case the [+nasal] specification captures only part of the NBU (read: segment), as discussed by Anderson (1976). Second, the domain can be *suprasegmental*, in which case the language in question allows nasal "prosodies" as in, for example, Terena (Bendor-Samuel 1960), Desano (Kaye 1971) and Guaraní (Lunt 1973). In these languages a [+nasal] specification covers a spread larger than the segment. It is such languages which provide the greatest challenge to the formal analysis of nasality, and it is one such language whose suprasegmental nasality I would like to address in this paper.

The language in question is Gokana, an Ogoni language (Benue-Congo branch of Niger-Kordofanian) spoken in Eastern Nigeria.[3] In this language it will be demonstrated that any segment which is [+voice] can be an NBU (provided certain conditions are met) and that the domain of a single [+nasal] specification may encompass several segments and several morphemes. I shall begin in section 1 with a brief sketch of the surface phonology of the language. In section 2 I discuss the distribution of nasality within (lexical) morphemes, followed in section 3, with a discussion of nasal alternations in grammatical suffixes. Section 4 presents a segmental analysis of nasality of Gokana followed by discussion in Section 5. In section 6 I present an autosegmental analysis of the same facts and argue that it is superior to the segmental account.

1. PRELIMINARIES

The surface sound segments encountered in Gokana are given in (1):

(1) a. *Vowels:*   i   u   ĩ   ũ   m̩   N̩
                   e   o
                   ε   ɔ   ε̃   ɔ̃
                       a   ã

b. *Consonants:* p   t   k^y k   kp   ʔ
                  b   d   g^y g   gb
                       f   s
                       v   z
                            l   r
                  m   m̥   n   ɲ   ŋ

c. *Tones:*   V́ (high)   V̄ or V (mid)   V̀ (low)

Gokana distinguishes seven oral and five nasalized vowels. The nasalized vowels /ẽ/ and /õ/ do not occur. Long vowels occur phonetically, but they are always analyzed and transcribed as a sequence of like vowels, e.g. bɛ́ɛ́ 'cheek', súú 'seed', etc.[4] The nasalized vowels /ĩ/ and /ũ/ are pronounced lax (i.e. as [ɪ̃] and [ʊ̃]), which property may be responsible for the failure of /e/ vs. /ɛ/ and /o/ vs. /ɔ/ to contrast when nasalized (cf. Hyman 1972, Williamson 1973).

The surface consonant system is relatively simple, although several comments are in order. First, /k^y/ and /g^y/ are palatal stops pronounced with a palatal offglide, while /kp/ and /gb/ are labiovelar stops. The symbol ɱ represents a labiodental nasal consonant, which Brosnahan (1964) and the Ibadan studies (note 3) transcribe as a nasalized approximant, [ṽ]. (just as they transcribe my ɲ as the nasalized approximant [ỹ]). We shall address the unusual consonant ɱ below.

The glottal stop is considered as a "juncture phoneme" in some of the earlier studies, since it is found predictably (a) before a word-initial vowel, and (b) after a pre-pausal short vowel (e.g. utterance-finally): ʔéb 'pumpkin', téʔ 'tree', ʔúʔ 'death'. These words can thus be analyzed /éb/, /té/ and /ú/, respectively. A few words such as niʔei 'today' and sɔ̃ɔ̃ʔea 'yesterday' have an internal glottal stop, but are almost certainly of complex morphological origin.

There are three level tones in Gokana: high, mid and low. In general there is one tone per syllabic unit, which can be either a vowel or a syllabic nasal. In the rare (and grammatically predictable) cases where more than one tone is realized on a single vowel, or on a vowel + consonant, the two tones are combined (a macron substituting for ∅ in the case of mid tone), e.g. m ɛ̄ǹ nɔm 'the neck of the animal'. The syllabic nasal is either a bilabial or is homorganic to the following consonant, e.g. nɛ̃m̄ 'give (it) to me!', ŋ̀gà 'needle'.

The canonical shapes of lexical morphemes (i.e. stems) are summarized in the following formula:[5]

(2)   + C$_1$ V$_1$ (V) (C$_2$ (V)) +

That is, we have the following possibilities:

(3)   CV : tɔ   'house'   CVVC : bĩɔ̃m   'fingernail'
      CVV : vái   'bed'   CVCV : kigi   'axe'
      CVC : zib   'thief'   CVVCV : fɔ́ɔ́rɔ́   'wind'

Of these, only CVVC is rare. While any of these shapes may also be morphologically complex (except CV), any other structure *necessarily* contain more than one morpheme (or are ideophones), e.g. CVVV, CVCCV etc. The major constraint on lexical morphemes is that they must begin with a consonant. This follows from the fact that Gokana is a suffixing language and the above stems in (3), which can stand independently as words, occur directly after a ## boundary. Lexical morphemes which underlyingly begin with a vowel will receive a glottal stop as we have already demonstrated. Thus, the initial C in (2) can be filled by the predictable word-initial ʔ.

Consonant sequences are rare, but can occur at a # or ## boundary in Gokana. On the other hand, vowel sequences are rampant (cf. note 4). Of the consonants listed in (1b), all except [r] and [ŋ] occur as C_1 in (2). More serious restrictions are placed on the C_2 slot, which can be filled only by one of the following segments: [b, l, g, m, n, ŋ]. This fact will be important for our analysis. What is important to note at this point is the alternations which C_2 consonants undergo. First, in word final position, [b] and [g] are unreleased and can be at least partially devoiced. We shall, however, follow the earlier Gokana studies and always transcribe these segments as voiced, e.g., *zib* 'thief', *lóg* 'story', etc. Second, in intervocalic position, [b] alternations with [v] and [l] alternates with [r], as seen in (4).

(4) a. zib   'thief'   ziv-í   'this thief'
    b. bɔ́l   'goat'   bɔ́r-í   'this goat'

The alternation in (4a) is obligatory, while the l~r phoneme is characterized by considerable variation dependent upon the village, tempo, speaker preference etc. The rule(s) responsible for these alternations affect only a C_2 consonant, e.g. *nà bí* 'my excrement' does not become **nà ví*.

2. NASALITY IN LEXICAL MORPHEMES

We have seen that Gokana contrasts seven oral vowels with five nasalized vowels, and that it has five surface nasal consonants. In this section we shall examine the distributional constraints on phonetic nasal and nasalized segments *within lexical morphemes*. We begin by considering the relationship in nasality between the C_1 and any following segments:

Constraint #1: If the C_1 is [+nasal], then all successive segments must also be [+nasal].

This agreement in nasality between a [+nasal] C_1 and the remaining segments of a lexical morpheme accounts for the following acceptable vs. unacceptable forms:

(5) NṼ   : nũ   'thing'   *nu
    NṼṼ   : nãã   'gun'   *nãa, *naa
    NṼN   : nɔ̃m   'animal'   *nɔm, nɔ̃b, *nɔb
    NṼNṼ   : mɛ̃nɛ̃   'chief'   *mɛnɛ, *mɛ̃nɛ, *mɛ̃lɛ, etc;
    NVVNV : nãã nã 'snake'   *naana, *nãã na, *nãã la, etc.

Thus, if the C_1 is [+nasal] there can be no [-nasal] segment within the same lexical morpheme.

The second distributional constraint concerns the relationship in nasality between a [+nasal] C_2 and its adjacent vowels:

> *Constraint #2*: If the C_2 is [+nasal], then any and all preceding *and* following vowels must also be [+nasal].

This agreement in nasality between a [+nasal] C_2 and preceding and following vowels accounts for the acceptability vs. unacceptability of the following forms:

(6) C$\tilde{\text{V}}$N   : dɛ̃́m̃   'tongue'   *dɛm
    C$\tilde{\text{V}}$N$\tilde{\text{V}}$: fĩnĩ   'monkey'   *finĩ, *fĩni
    C$\tilde{\text{V}}\tilde{\text{V}}N\tilde{\text{V}}$: kũũnĩ   'cooking stone' *kuũnĩ, *kuunĩ, *kũũni

When both the C_1 and C_2 are [+nasal], then the intervening one or two vowels will have to be [+nasal] by either Constraint #1 or #2. In addition, since there is a necessary [+nasal] agreement between a vowel or vowels and either a preceding or following [+nasal] consonant, and since [ẽ] and [õ] do not occur in the language, it follows that there are no morphemes of the phonetic shape *Nẽ, *Nõ, *Nẽẽ, *Nõõ, *CẽN, *CõN, etc. Nor do the vowels [e] and [o] occur in these environments as unnasalized.

The above two constraints have to do with restrictions on the nasality of vowels due to an adjacent [+nasal] consonant. A third constraint states that all segments following a [+nasal] vowel must also be [+nasal]:

> *Constraint #3*: If a vowel or vowel sequence is [+nasal], then all successive segments must also be [+nasal].

This constraint thus allows the forms for 'tongue', 'monkey' and 'cooking stone' in (6), but disallows lexical morphemes of the shapes *dɛ̃b, *fĩli, and *kũũli, among others. Note, however, that Constraint #3 is almost identical to Constraint #1. The only difference, in fact, is that the conditioning [+nasal] segment in the earlier constraint is the C_1, while in Constraint #3 it is the V_1. While the point at which a [+nasal] specification begins in a morpheme cannot always be predicted, its segment represents the point to the right of which all remaining segments must also be [+nasal]. In effect, this defines three kinds of morphemes with respect to nasality: (a) morphemes consisting entirely of [-nasal] segments (e.g. bɔ́l 'goat'), (b) morphemes consisting entirely of [+nasal] segments (e.g. nɔ̃m 'animal'), and (c) morphemes consisting of a [-nasal] C_1 followed by all [+nasal] segments (e.g. dḿ̃ 'tongue'). Thus, the above three constraints can be replaced by the following if-then sequential constraint:

(7)   + C_1 $[+seg]_1^n$ +
            ⇓   ⇓
       $\begin{Bmatrix} [\alpha\text{nasal}] & [\alpha\text{nasal}] \\ [-\text{nasal}] & [+\text{nasal}] \end{Bmatrix}$

That is, either all segments in a morpheme will agree in nasality, or there will be a [-nasal] C_1 followed by segments which are all [+nasal].

The final observation to be made in this section concerns the identity of [-nasal] C_1 consonants. As seen in the following constraint, [+cont, +voice, -nasal] C_1 consonants can only be followed by [-nasal] segments:

Constraint #4: If the C_1 is /v/, /l/ or /z/, then all successive segments must be [-nasal].

This constraint accounts for the following acceptable vs. unacceptable forms:

(8) a. vV   : va   'wife'   *vã
        lV   : lí   'root'   *lĩ́
        zV   : zɔ̀   'pain'   *zɔ̃
     b. zVC   : zib   'thief'   *zĩm, *zim
        zVCV : zárí   'buy'   *zãni, *zanĩ, etc.
        zVVCV : zaari 'scatter'   *zããni, *zaanĩ, etc.

Any other oral consonant (including glottal stop) may occur before a nasalized vowel with or without a following nasal consonant. That is, C_1 voiceless and voiced stops and voiceless fricatives show a nasalization opposition on a following vowel:

(9) tɔ   'house'   tɔ̃́   'ear'
     bá   'arm, hand'   bã́   'pot'
     sí   'go, visit'   sĩ   'face'

Although it has not been separately stated, it should be clear that vowel sequences differing in nasality are disallowed, i.e. '*ṼV and *VṼ

3. ALTERNATIONS IN NASALITY

The data presented in the preceding section demonstrate the severe constraints on the distribution of nasality within lexical morphemes. Not surprisingly, some of these constraints are in effect across morpheme boundaries. Gokana is a suffixing language, and most suffixes agree in nasality with the preceding lexical morpheme (or stem). For example, the demonstrative suffixes for 'this' and 'that', which occur on nouns, fall into this category:

(10) bɔ́l 'goat' bɔ́r-í 'this goat' bɔ́r-á 'that goat'
dɛ̃́m 'tongue' dɛ̃́m-ĩ́ 'this tongue' dɛ̃́m-ã̂ 'that tongue'

As seen in (10), the demonstrative suffixes are pronounced orally after an oral segment (here, a consonant), but nasally after a nasal segment. Although the forms in the middle and right hand columns have two morphemes each, it is clear that the sequential constraint in (7) is responsible also for this distribution of nasality.

It is especially in verbs, however, that alternations in nasality are common. Verb forms have the following structure:

(11)

	(a)		(b)		(c)		(d)	
##	Verbal Base	+	Grade Sfx	+	Pers Sfx	#	Obj Pro	##
	CV		V		V		VV	
	CVV		CV		(C)VV		CV	
	CVC						m̩	
	CVVC							

In the above schema only the verbal base (VB) is obligatory. Thus, a verb form can consist of a VB and optionally a grade suffix (GS), a person suffix (PS), and an object pronoun (OP). The different syllable structures contributed by each "slot" are indicated beneath each position. A complete discussion of the above morphological analysis is beyond the scope of this paper. However, the following brief definitions will clarify subsequent discussion:

(a) The verbal base (or "root") consists of the initial CV(V)(C) of a lexical verb stem. Thus, the only cases where the VB will be different from the corresponding verb stem is in the case of lexical verbs of the shapes CVCV and CVVCV, i.e. underlying bisyllabic verb forms. Examples are *bṹnũ* 'break (by snapping)' and *zaari* 'scatter'. The VB's are *bṹn-* and *zaar-*, respectively, and the final vowels *-u* and *-i*, although meaningless, are considered "grade suffixes".

(b) The grade suffixes, except for the preceding, have mostly to do with transitivity. Below we shall see examples of intransitive and transitive suffixes as well as an instrumental suffix.

(c) The person suffixes include a second person plural subject suffix and a logophoric suffix (see Hyman and Comrie 1981).

(d) The object pronouns are enclitics, but they must be separated from the preceding verb form by a # boundary since they do not receive their tone from the overall melody of the verb, but rather have their own inherent (mid) tone.

The important generalization concerning the above analysis is that no verb form has more than one filler in any given slot.

We can now begin to investigate alternations in nasality in verb forms. We begin with the outermost position, object pronouns:

(12) mm̀ dìv-ee   'I hit him/her'   (dìv 'hit')
      mm̀ mɔ̃̂n-ɛ̃ɛ̃   'I saw him/her'   (mɔ̃n 'see')
      mm̀ sà-ɛ   'I chose him/her'   (sà 'choose')
      mm̀ nɛ̃̂-ɛ̃   'I gave him/her (it)' (nɛ̃ 'give')

The third person singular object pronoun (which is double after a consonant, but single after a vowel) is oral after an oral consonant or vowel, but nasalized after a nasal consonant or nasalized vowel. The examples in (13) show the same distribution with the second person plural suffix -ii (which belongs to slot (11c)):

(13) oò divi í-e,   'you pl. hit him/her'
      oò mɔ̃n ĩ ĩ-ɛ̃   'you pl. saw him/her'
      oò saí-ɛ   'you pl. chose him/her'
      oò nɛ̃ ĩ́-ɛ̃   'you pl. gave him/her (it)'

This suffix takes an alveolar sonorant epenthetic consonant after VB's with a sequence of like vowels, e.g.

(14) oò s i i r i í-e   'you pl. caught him/her' (sí i 'catch')
      oò ʔĩ ĩ n ĩ í-e   'you pl. stung him/her'   (ʔĩ ĩ 'sting')

In both (13) and (14) the nasal/oral agreement applies to both suffixes. (We shall return to the alternation between [r] and [n] below.)

The final cases of alternations to be discussed concern the grade suffixes. First, as seen in (15),

(15) a. aè kʸɔ́   'he spoiled (it)'   aè kʸɔ́ à   'it spoiled'
       aè ʔig̀   'he twisted (it)'   aè ʔigà   'it twisted'
    b. aè gɔ̃́   'he hid (it)'   aè gɔ̃́ ã̀   'he hid (himself)'
       aè mɔ̃́n   'he saw (it)'   baè mɔ̃́nã̀   'they met (e.o.)'

the intransitive suffix -a/-ã is oral after an oral vowel or consonant (15a), but nasalized after a nasalized vowel or consonant (15b). In addition, two transitive suffixes have the shape -CE, where the consonant varies between nasal and oral:

(16) a. aè ʔii   'it sank'   aè ʔiîrè   'he sank (it)'
       aè pĩ́ĩ́   'he became quiet'   aè pĩ́ĩ̂nɛ̃̀ 'he quieted (s.o.)'
    b. aè gʸɔɔ   'it became wet'   aè gʸɔɔ́vɛ̀ 'he wet (it)'
       aè kã̂ã̂   'it dried'   aè kã̂ã̂mɛ̃̀ 'he dried (it)'

In (16a) the consonant is [r] or [n], as in the second person plural suffix in (14). In (16b) the consonant is [v] or [m]. This [v] is of course the realization of b intervocalically (cf. (4a)). Thus, the alternation is one between b and m.[6]

Finally, there is one grade suffix which must always be nasal:

(17) a. aè sà   'he chose'   aè sààmã̂   'he chose with (it)'
       aè bùl   'he cooked'   aè bùmã̂   'he cooked with (it)'
    b. aè gbɛ̃̀   'he ground'   aè gbɛ̃ɛ̃mã̂ 'he ground with (it)'
       aè dɛ̃̀m   'he moulded'   aè dɛ̃mã̂   'he moulded with (it)'

The instrumental suffix -mã causes a preceding single vowel to double or a preceding consonant to drop. (It has no effect on a preceding double vowel.) The result can be a surface violation of (7):

(18) a. aè bà+mã̂   →   aè bààmã̂   'he ate (meat) with (it)'
       aè bã̀+mã̂   →   aè bã̀ã̀mã̂   'he entered with (it)'
    b. aè bɛ̀l+mã̂   →   aè bɛ̀mã̂   'he ruled with (it)'
       aè bɛ̃̀m+mã̂ →   aè bɛ̃̀mã̂   'it rotted with (it)'

In (18a) there is a surface opposition between nasalized and oral (double) vowels before a nasal consonant. In (18b) there is the same opposition on a single vowel.[7] The above surface violation of (7) can of course be attributed to the fact that there is an internal morpheme boundary in the forms in (18). However, the suffixed forms in (12) - (16) also have internal morpheme boundaries, but they have agreement in nasality.

It should be evident from the foregoing that the nasal feature value spreads from the first syllable of a word rightwards until it is interrupted by the -mã suffix or a major boundary. If a suffix begins with a vowel (or certain consonants, as we have seen), a [+nasal] VB will cause this suffix (or suffixes) to become [+nasal]. The -mã suffix, on the other hand, provides the context for a change from [-nasal] to [+nasal] – a change which takes place from morpheme to morpheme, rather than from C_1 to V_1. As we shall see, there is no corresponding change from [+nasal] to [-nasal] within a ## __ # sequence.

The next question which arises concerns the nature of the "major boundary" which will interrupt nasal spreading. Clearly a full word boundary (##) is capable of interrupting nasality, e.g. mẽñ zib 'the neck of the thief', ʔú nɔ̃m 'the death of the animal', etc. However, nasality may also be checked by a single # boundary, if it is followed by a consonant:

(19) a. aè sà - n ĩ   'he chose you'   (sà # n ĩ)
     b. aè nɛ̃́- va   'he gave them (it)'   (nɛ̃́ # va)

In (19a) the verb *sa* 'choose' maintains its underlying oral vowel, even though it is followed by a nasal consonant. In (19b), the initial [v] of the object pronoun 'them' does not alternate with [m] the way we observed in (16b). As indicated, this is attributable to the # boundary which precedes all object clitic pronouns.

In summary, then, if the VB has a [+nasal] specification, so will all of its suffixes, except for the object pronoun *va* 'them'. If the VB has only a [-nasal] specification, so will all of its suffixes, except for the instrumental suffix -mã and the object pronouns nĩ 'you sg.' and m̩ 'me'.[8] Thus, the following forms, which do not involve any of these suffixes, illustrate the two nasal patterns when all of the verb slots in (11) are filled:

(20) a. oò g^y ɔɔvɛị - e 'you pl. wet him'   (g^{y}ɔɔ + vɛ + ị # e)
     b. oò kã̀ã̀ mɛ̃ĩ - ɛ̃ 'you pl. dried him'   (kã̀ã̀ + mɛ̃ + ĩ́ # ɛ̃)

4. A SEGMENTAL ANALYSIS

It is clear that much of the nasalization occurring in Gokana is redundant and therefore should be introduced by rule. The questions are: (a) how much should be predicted by rule? and (b) what conditions what? Where an alternating suffix is involved, the nasality should definitely be introduced by rule, but what about the nasality which is predictable from the constraints discussed in section 2? If we attempt to introduce some of the intramorphemic nasality by rule, where should the underlying [+nasal] specification reside? (on the V_1? on the C_1? on the C_2?).[9]

The response given in the four Ibadan studies (see note 3) is to recognize nasality on vowels and, where possible, to predict the nasality on consonants on the basis of an adjacent nasalized vowel. This works well in the case of the nasals [m̥] and [n]. Since [v] does not occur prenasally (i.e. __ Ṽ (N)), [m̥] is simply the realization of /vṼ/, e.g.

(21) /vɛ̰̃ɛ̰̃/ → [m̥ɛ̰̃ɛ̰̃] 'put'
      /vɛ̃/   → [m̥ɛ̃]   'maggot'

And since [l] does not occur in a nasal context, and [n] only occurs in a nasal context, the two are in complementary distribution and can be represented underlyingly as /l/, e.g.

(22) /lũ/ → [nũ] 'thing'
      /lɛ̃/ → [nɛ̃] 'give'

In the case of the alveolar sonorants, we have had occasion to note alternations between [r] (the intervocalic realization of /l/) and [n] in (14) and (16a). Thus, the analysis is well motivated. Pushing the analysis just a bit further we can recognize C_2 [n] as underlying /l/ too, in which case we get derivations such as the following:

(23) /vĩ́l/ → [m̥ĩ́n] 'child'
      /lɛ̃l/   → [nɛ̃n]   'person'

Thus, although nasality characterizes the whole syllable in each of the forms in (23), we can predict both C_1 [m̥] and [n] and C_2 [n] on the basis of the nasality of /ĩ/ and /ɛ̃/ in these words.

Of course the strength of the above analysis attributing underlying nasality to the V_1 will depend on its generalizability to other nasal consonants. We still must account for C_1 [m] and [ɲ] and for C_2 [m] and [ŋ].

The most straightforward of these is the velar nasal, which can only occur as C_2.[10] Although [g] occurs before nasalized vowels, as in gɔ̃ 'hide', it does not occur *after* a nasalized vowel.[11] Thus, representations such as in (24) are no problem for this analysis:

(24) /ãg/   → [ʔãŋ]   'pull out'
      /sĩg/ → [sĩŋ]   'rub off'

There will have to be two separate nasal assimilation rules such that /g/ will assimilate to become [ŋ] if preceded by a nasalized vowel, but not if followed by one.

The next entity to be addressed is [ŋ]. While Brosnahan (1964:44) treats [ɲ] as a nasalized /y/, with representations such as in (25),

(25) /yíɛ̃/ → [ɲíɛ̃]   'heart'
    /yɛ̃ɛ̃/ → [ɲɛ̃ɛ̃]   'be heavy'

this analysis is hard to maintain since there is no *oral* [y].[12] Thus, it is an ad hoc solution designed only to rid the system of [ɲ]. There is, however, an available oral segment which can be claimed to be in complementary distribution with [ɲ], namely [z], which cannot occur in a nasal context. We can propose that the words in (25) have the underlying forms /zíɛ/ 'heart' and /zɛɛ/ 'be heavy', and that when /z/ becomes nasalized, it changes to [ɲ]. This may not be as far-fetched as it seems. It is a fact that [z] derives historically from a palatal *y (e.g. *zib* 'steal, thief' is cognate with Proto-Bantu *yib, *zob* 'dance' is cognate with Proto-Grassfields Bantu *yòb, and so forth). In fact, prior to the Proto-Ogoni stage (Williamson 1979), *y becomes [z] in an oral context exactly as pre-Proto-Ogoni *w becomes [v].[13] The three segments [v, l, z] which today do not occur in a nasal context were once pronounced *[w, l, y]. Thus, while the present day rule converts voiced continuants to nasal consonants when followed by a nasalized vowel, the historical rule applied to the above class of *sonorants*. We could reanalyze /va/ 'wife' and /zɔ̃/ 'pain' as /wa/ and /yɔ̃/, but this would take us further than we need to go from the surface in order to capture the facts of synchronic Gokana.

This leaves us with only [m] to account for. In C_2 position the facts are exactly as in the case of [ŋ]: since [b] does not occur after a nasalized vowel, C_2 [m] can be represented underlyingly as /b/, just as C_2 [ŋ] was represented as /g/, e.g.

(26) /dɛ̃b/ → [dɛ̃m]   'tongue'
    /lɔ̃b/ → [nɔ̃m]   'animal'

This complementary distribution was already noted with respect to [v] (the intervocalic realization of C_2 /b/) and [m] in (16b) and (20). We were able to avoid positing an underlying /ŋ/ because phonetic [ŋ] does not occur in C_1 position. Unfortunately, [m] does occur in this position, where it contrasts with [b]:

(27) bá   'arm, hand'
    bã   'pot'
    mã   'breast'

It is commonly observed in West African languages that one nasal cannot be "gotten around". This nasal seems always to be [m] (cf. Hyman 1972: 186), as in Yoruba or Nupe. The earlier studies on Gokana follow this pattern and recognize the phoneme /m/ in *all* environments. Ekundare

(1972), as his Ibadan colleagues, has only a single nasal phoneme /m/, which he has occurring as in (28):

(28) /mɔ̃l/ → [mɔ̃n] 'voice'
      /dɛ̃m/ → [dɔ̃m] 'tongue'

However, there is redundancy in both of these underlying forms. In /mɔ̃l/, the nasality on the V_1 is predictable on the basis of the preceding nasal consonant. In /dɛ̃m/, which we would represent as /dɛ̃b/, the nasality on the C_2 consonant is predictable from the vowel. In forms such as [mã] 'breast', we shall simply have to recognize an underlying C_1 /m/. The following V_1 will receive its [+nasal] specification by rule (see below). This last decision represents the only instance in which underlying nasality is indicated on a consonant rather than a vowel.[14] It is interesting to note in this context that the syllabic nasal, which is treated in section 6, is also bilabial.

The two rules needed to specify nasality in this language are given in (29).

(29) a. [+voice] → [+nasal] / [+nasal] ___ (bounded by $\#\{{C \atop \#}\}$)

b. $\begin{bmatrix} +\text{voice} \\ +\text{cont} \end{bmatrix}$ → [+nasal] / # ___ [+nasal]
                                                                        V

Rule (29a) says that any voiced segment will become [+nasal] if preceded by any [+nasal] segment. Assuming that an underlying [+nasal] specification is indicated only on the V_1 (or on the C_1 in the one exceptional case involving /m/), (29a) will spread nasality onto a following vowel or consonant and apply to its own output until reaching a #C or # # sequence. (29a) creates all of the redundant [+nasal] specifications except those characterizing a C_1 voiced continuant. (29b) thus applies and assigns [+nasal] to C_1 /v/, /l/ and /z/ when followed by a [+nasal] V_1.

The resulting segmental analysis is, I believe, the most straightforward one possible under the assumptions inherent in this kind of phonology. The rules in (29) need only be followed by surface adjustments of the type "a [+nasal] consonant is [-cont], [-lat], etc.". This analysis will thus serve as a point of departure for discussion in the following section.

5. DISCUSSION

The simplicity of the segmental analysis is evident. All redundant specifications of [+nasal] have been removed from underlying forms whose

[+voice] segments are subject to the two rules in (29). Within this analysis the underlying nasal properties of lexical morphemes are one of the following: (a) all segments [-nasal]; (b) V_1 [+nasal], remaining segments [-nasal]; or (c) C_1 [+nasal], remaining segments [-nasal]. The [+nasal] C_1 in (c) must, of course, be /m/.

In support of our decision to restrict a [+nasal] specification to the first CV of a lexical morpheme, we note that several other distributional properties of the language depend on or refer explicitly to this initial sequence. First, it was shown in (2) that only the $C_1 V_1$ segments are obligatory in a lexical morpheme. In case there is no underlying C_1 consonant, a glottal stop is inserted, e.g. /ú/ 'death' is pronounced [ʔú]. Also, the reduplication process referred to in note 7 copies only the $C_1 V_1$ sequence of a lexical morpheme, e.g. /duùlà/ 'pull' becomes /duduùlà/ 'pulling' and /dib/ 'hit' becomes /dibib/ 'hitting', etc. Finally, properties other than nasality are controlled by the C_1 or V_1. For instance, it is only in C_1 position that consonants other than [b, l, g, m, n, ŋ] can occur. As for the V_1, it controls the distribution of tones. The above reduplicated (and corresponding non-reduplicated) forms just given are assigned a mid-low tone melody. As can be seen in forms such as [dūùrà] and [dūdùùrà], the mid tone is assigned to the V_1 and the low tone to all remaining vowels. It thus appears to be a general property of the language that the $C_1 V_1$ sequence plays an exalted role in the control and distribution of phonological features. In this respect, nasality falls right into line.

There are, however, a few unsatisfactory aspects to the solution. While all redundant [+nasal] specifications have been removed from underlying forms, the result is not redundancy-free lexical representations, but rather extensive redundant [-nasal] specifications. A more accurate reflection of the nasal properties of the language would be for all segments not marked [+nasal] to be [0 nasal], i.e. to not have *any* specification for nasality. Besides the aversion, ever since Stanley (1967), to blank feature values in underlying representations, the segmental analysis fails to explain why nasality should function in this way. The segmental model would suggest that each segment should have its own features, that there should not be blanks (except, perhaps, in cases of indeterminacy), and that there should not be feature values which have a suprasegmental domain. In Gokana we have seen that a [+nasal] feature is a characteristic of a morpheme. This fact does not receive direct expression in the above analysis, since we have disguised the different status of nasality by attributing the nasal-oral opposition to the V_1 (or C_1 /m/) in underlying forms. The only reason why this does not look totally ad hoc is because (a) almost all morphemes have a V_1 (or C_1), and (b) the rules in (29) appear to be well-motivated.

Let us look at these rules. They operate differently from one another in two senses. First, (29a) represents a perseverative assimilation, while (29b) represents an anticipatory assimilation. Second, (29a) is an iterative rule which applies to its own output, while (29b) is not. The need for *two* rules to capture the automatic spreading of nasality is unfortunate and due to our decision to "segmentalize" the suprasegmental nasal feature on the V_1.

The need to provide a segmental support for the one [+nasal] specification which can characterize a morpheme has led to difficulties in the case of [m]. Recall that the bilabial nasal consonant has two sources: in C_1 position it is the realization of /m/, while in C_2 position it is the realization of /b/. Note in this regard that the instrumental suffix -mã has to be analyzed as /-ma/, since the vowel preceding it need not be [+nasal] (cf. (17a)). While this dual representation of [m] is not necessarily damning, an analysis which would incorporate the relationship between [b] and [m], on the one hand, and the "unpredictable" occurrences of [m], on the other hand, would be preferable to one in which [m] has two unrelated sources. Such an analysis is presented in the following section.

6. AN AUTOSEGMENTAL ANALYSIS

We have seen in the preceding sections that nasality has a special status in Gokana. Rather than being an unpredictable feature on individual segments, there is at most one [+nasal] specification per morpheme. At the beginning of section 5 we spoke about three kinds of morphemes with respect to nasality. If it were possible to view [+nasal] as a feature on *morphemes*, these would now be of two types: (a) morphemes without a [+nasal] specification, and (b) morphemes with a [+nasal] specification. The former would have all oral segments, while the latter would have all "nasalizable" segments nasalized. For example, if the C_1 were /v/, /l/ or /z/, nasalization would begin on the C_1; if it were any other C_1, nasalization would begin on the V_1. In either case, the [+nasal] feature would continue to characterize all appropriate segments throughout the morpheme, and even across morpheme boundaries, as we have seen. Some special accomodation would have to be made for /m/, of course.

The essential characteristics of nasality in Gokana can most insightfully be captured within the framework of autosegmental phonology (Goldsmith 1976). In this model a feature such as [nasal] may be autosegmentalized onto a separate tier and thus formalized as separate from the remaining segmental features. Goldsmith himself applies the model to nasality in Guaraní. In Gokana I propose that morphemes either have a single [+nasal] on the nasal tier, or ∅. That is, they are either marked positive for nasality, or they have no underlying nasal specification, e.g.

(30) a. /lí/ → [lí] c. [+N]
     'root'   /l u/ → [nũ] 'thing'

   b. /bá/ → [bá]   d. [+N]
     'arm'   /bá/ → [bã́] 'pot'

In (30a, b) the morphemes 'root' and 'arm' have no specification for nasality. By convention (see below), they will thus come to the surface as [-nasal]. In (30c, d), however, the morphemes 'thing' and 'pot' have a nasal specification, which I here indicate as [+N] to indicate that we are dealing with a feature on a separate tier. The mapping of this [+N] onto the segments of each morpheme is automatic, according to the nature of the C_1 consonant. Thus, in (30c), nasality begins with the C_1 /l/, while in (30d), it begins with the V_1. The mapping rule responsible for the assignment of [+N] to the appropriate segments within a morpheme is formalized as in (31).

(31)   [+N]
                            ⋮
     #({ [-cont]   }) [+seg]$_1^n$ # { C }
        { [-voice]   }   { # }

That is, the [+N] mapping will ignore either a [-cont] or a [-voice] C_1 and assign nasality to all subsequent segments up to a #C or ## boundary. While there may be some objection to a simultaneous mapping process involving the expression [+seg]$_1^n$, it is clear that other restatements are possible. For example, we could begin with an "initial nasal association rule" akin to the initial tone association rules of Haraguchi (1977) and Clements and Ford (1979). In this case we could choose the V_1 for the first association and then let the [+N] continue associating with successive segments until hitting either a #C or ## sequence.

Or — until hitting an instrument suffix, which we represented as underlying /-ma/ in the segmental analysis. At this point we can return to the problem of [m]. First, as before, C_2 [m] can be derived from /b/, as in (32).

(32)   [+N]   [+N]
                   ∧
       /dɛb/ →   dɛb → [dɛ̃m]   'tongue'

The [+N] feature ignores the C_1 consonant /d/, since it is [-cont]. It is then associated with the V_1 and following consonant. As seen, a [+N] associated to an underlying /b/ results in phonetic [m]. In order to account for C_1 [m], however, it is necessary to assume that the [+N] is *lexically* associated with the C_1 /b/, thereby making this segment *opaque* with respect to nasality (Clements 1981 : 136). The following should be compared with (30 b, d):

(33)   [+N]   [+N]
         /   /\
       /bá/   →   bá   →   [mã́] 'breast'

As seen in the underlying representation, we can now generalize and derive *all* instances of [m] from a [+N] specification associated with the segment /b/. The mapping process in (31) is intended to continue the association of [+N] up to a #C or ## boundary whether or not the [+N] is lexically associated. The instrumental suffix will also have a lexically associated [+N], as seen in (34).

(34)   [+N]   [+N]
              /   /\
       /sìi + bà/   →   s i î + bà   →   [s i îmà] 'catch with'

Because the nasal mapping rule in (31) only associates [+N] to the right of a [-cont] C_1, we should be able to slightly modify the mapping statement so that [+N] will continue to be associated to the right of wherever an association already exists (whether lexically on a /b/, or by incorporation into the $[+seg]_1^n$ sequence in (31)). In other words, there is no provision for the [+N] to be associated onto the preceding vowels of 'catch' etc. and this is correct.

One last property of the system which falls out nicely is the treatment of syllabic nasals. Since a syllabic nasal is either bilabial (if it is a separate morpheme) or is homorganic to the following C_1 (if it is not a separate morpheme, e.g. ńnɔ̃m 'bird', ŋgà 'needle'), Brosnahan (1964) treats it as an underlying /M/. If we follow his suggestion that all homorganic nasals have the same (labial) underlying representation, we shall have to represent it as /b/ with a lexically associated [+N], e.g.

(35)   [+N] [+N]   [+N]
           | |
       / b̄   lɔb / 'bird'   / ɓ   gà / 'needle'

As seen, the form for 'bird' has two [+N] specifications, one on the syllabic nasal, which is lexically associated, the other being the free [+N] specification which is mapped by (31). By contrast, 'needle' has only the lexically associated [+N]. A problem arises, however, because the mapping rule in (31) will allow the [+N] of the initial segment in 'needle' to be associated on the following segments as well. This incorrectly produces the output *[ŋ̍ŋã]. In order to prevent this outcome, without postulating an unmotivated grammatical boundary between the syllabic nasal and the C_1, the mapping procedure in (31) is reformulated as follows:

$$(31') \qquad \begin{matrix} [+N] \\ | \\ \# \ (\ b\ ) \ (\left\{ \begin{matrix} [-\text{cont}] \\ \\ [-\text{voice}] \end{matrix} \right\}) \end{matrix} \qquad \begin{matrix} [+N] \\ \vdots \\ [+\text{seg}]_1^n \end{matrix} \qquad \# \left\{ \begin{matrix} C \\ \# \end{matrix} \right\}$$

In this way the initial homorganic nasal will be ignored in the [+nasal] mapping on subsequent segments.

Perhaps there will be some concern that I have represented a syllabic unit as an underlying /b/. As I shall show in Hyman (in preparation), the syllabicity of this nasal is predictable from the phonological context as follows: (a) after pause or a consonant or if double, [N] is syllabic, e.g. m̀ zovi mm̀ tɔ 'I dance in the house'; (b) after a vowel, single [N] is syllabic only if its tone differs from the preceding tone, e.g. aè gɔ̃ m̄ 'he hid me' vs. aè ìi ra m [ì ì ram] 'he squeezed me'.[15] A full demonstration of the syllabic properties of Gokana is beyond the scope of the present paper. However, the above facts should indicate that there is much to be gained by treating all homorganic nasals as I have done.

7. SUMMARY AND CONCLUSION

In the above sections we have examined the properties of nasality in Gokana and determined that the most adequate account is possible only if nasality is treated as a suprasegmental property. The facts of Gokana nasality are in most respects not very different from other languages in which suprasegmental nasality has been described. The autosegmental analysis adopted here recognizes only one [+nasal] specification per morpheme in underlying representations. This [+nasal] feature may be lexically associated with a morpheme-initial /b/, although in most morphemes it is not lexically associated. In either case the [+nasal] value is extended to appropriate segments until reaching a #C or ## sequence, as we saw in the mapping procedure in (31').

One question which we have not considered up to now is how segments which do not have a [+nasal] associated with them receive their [-nasal] specification. I assume that after (31') has applied, any segments still unspecified for nasality will receive a redundant [-nasal] value. The reason why this is necessary is that we have assumed that morphemes do not have

[-nasal] as a possible feature value underlyingly. This choice was made because it greatly simplified the solution, and yet it is clearly not the only way to describe these facts. One could, for instance, assume that all segments are [-nasal] but that a morpheme feature [+N] overrides the segmental [-nasal] specifications, as Morris Halle proposed for Capanahua in a recent lecture at the University of Southern California. Or, one could allow for a "boundary naseme" whereby a single [-nasal] specification is held back at an initial # boundary to be assigned to any and all following segments which have not been assigned [+nasal] lexically or by (31'). This boundary feature could affect a whole morpheme or several morphemes, or it could affect only the [-cont] or [-voice] C_1's which were exempted from (31'). While these and doubtless other analyses are possible, I believe the solution proposed above to be the most straightforward and the least arbitrary.

NOTES

1.   This paper is based on data collected during and subsequent to a Field Methods course which I gave at the University of Southern California in the Spring of 1979. I would like to thank Mr. Godwin Zoranen, the language consultant for all phases of this study, and Bernard Comrie, with whom I investigated much of the grammar of this language. In addition, I have benefitted from helpful comments from Stephen Anderson, Bernard Comrie, Osvaldo Jaeggli, Will Leben, and my Linguistics 531a class (Spring 1981), who had to solve the nasal properties of Gokana as an assignment.

2.   I wish to ignore intrinsic nasalization as well as speakers who pronounce *can't* as [kæ̃t].

3.   The Gokana language has been the subject of a number of descriptive studies. Among the published accounts are Brosnahan (1960, 1964) and Wolff (1959, 1964). In addition, I have had access to the following four "long essays" done at the University of Ibadan for which I thank Dr. Isaac George Madugu: Arekambe (1972), Asinyirimba (1972), Ekundare (1972) and Okotie (1972). Dr. Kay Williamson is also most gratefully acknowledged and thanked for sending us tapes and written stories in Gokana.

4.   In fact, I have found up to *six* identical vowels in a row, e.g.

mé é è kɔ mm̀ké̃ẽ̀ẽ́ẽ̀ẽ́ 'who₁ said I woke him₁ up?' (from ké̃ẽ̀ + ẽ́ + ẽ̀ẽ́ # ẽ̀ẽ́ # ẽ́
where 1 = 'wake up', 2 = 'transitive suffix', 3 = 'logophoric suffix', 4 = 'third sg. object pronoun', and 5 = question marker). Vowel length in Gokana is treated in Hyman (in preparation).

5.   Morphemes which are not "lexical" or stems need not begin with a consonant, e.g. *-a* 'intransitive suffix', *-i i* 'second person plural subject suffix' etc. In some cases the C_2 and/or vowel of the second syllable of lexical morphemes may be a "grade suffix", e.g. *zári* 'buy' may be analyzed as *zár+i*, although the *-i* does not have a specific meaning. The form assumed to be entered in the lexicon is *zári*, not simply the root *zár-*.

6.   The choice of [r, n] or [v, m] as the initial consonant of the transitive suffix is unpredictable. The most common shape of this suffix is without a consonant, e.g. *tá* 'finish' (intr.), *táè* 'finish' (tr.).

7. Similar violations to (7) may result from a process of reduplication which copies the first CV of a verb in order to derive a gerund, e.g. *sa* 'choose' → *sasà* 'choosing', *bùl* 'cook' → *bùbùl* 'cooking'. The problem case is created by forms such as *bɔ̃m* 'beat' which becomes *bɔ̃bɔ̃m* 'beating'. The second instance of [b] should be nasalized according to what we have said up to now. We could attempt to claim that there is a # boundary intervening between the two parts of the reduplication, although this would make it hard to explain why all such forms have a single ML tone pattern (since the mapping of tone patterns is otherwise always blocked by a #). We tentatively attribute this irregularity to the reduplication process: reduplication has to apply *after* the nasal process are in place. Thus, the [-nasal] [+nasal] specifications of the $C_1 V_1$ in 'beating' are copied along with all of the other segmental features of [b] and [ɔ̃].

8. The homorganic nasal problem is addressed in section 6. We can note here that there must be a # boundary before m̩, since nasality does not spread backwards from it, e.g. aè sà m̄ 'he chose me', where the [a] of 'chose' is not nasalized.

9. We have not even raised the question of whether the contrasting nasalization on vowels is primary. In the following section we shall see that it is not possible to posit an underlying nasal consonant from which vowel nasalization is derived.

10. In my Field Methods class some of the students noticed that [m̴] and [ŋ] are in complementary distribution: [m̴] occurs only in C_1 position while [ŋ] occurs only in C_2 position (i.e. medially and finally in words). The analysis given in this section will demonstrate the inadvisability of attributing both sounds to the same underlying phoneme.

11. This and other generalizations do not apply to words such as compounds which have an internal # boundary, e.g. *gã̂n ã̂g ĩ* 'shoulder'.

12. Asinyirimba (1972) attempts to derive [ỹ] or [ɲ] from underlying sequences of /ĩ/ plus a vowel, since many forms beginning with this sound have a vowel sequence. This will not explain other cases very readily, though. It can be noted that there is a late rule which optionally inserts a [y] or [ɲ] between a front vowel and a following vowel, e.g. *mm̀ s i í-e* or *mm̀ s i í-ye* 'I caught him'.

13. There are at least two pairs of words which may suggest an etymological relationship between [z] and [ɲ]: [zɔ́], [ɲã̂ã̂] (both meaning 'hurt') and [zɔ], [ɲɔ̃̂ɔ̃nɛ̃] (both meaning 'follow').

14. I reject any attempt to find the "missing slot" and establish an abstract set of phonological features which in conjunction with a [+nasal] specification produce phonetic [m]. The likely candidates would, however, be an implosive [ɓ'] or [β] (cf. Hyman 1972).

15. Note the final *oral* vowel in *aè ì ì ram*, since there is a # boundary between the verb and the (here, non-syllabic) object pronoun (cf. note 8).

From Cyclic Phonology to Lexical Phonology *

Paul Kiparsky
M.I.T.

The approach to word structure that I shall explore here represents a convergence of several originally independent strands of research. One is the emerging theory of morphology and the lexicon (e.g. Aronoff 1976), and more particularly the idea of a level-ordered morphology elaborated by D. Siegel (1974, 1977), M. Allen (1978) and others. Another centers around the problem of constraining lexical representations and phonological rules, beginning with various versions of the Alternation Condition (Kiparsky 1968, 1973) and continuing with the conception of Cyclic Phonology first proposed by Mascaró (1976) and subsequently pursued in a number of studies of the phonologies of particular languages (most extensively Rubach 1981). I shall also be drawing on aspects of the recent metrical theory of stress (Liberman and Prince 1977, Hayes 1981) and syllable structure. When these ideas are put together, and developed in a certain direction, they explain a series of properties of phonological rules and their relation to morphology and the lexicon that have so far appeared as unexplained generalizations, or in some cases even defied coherent formulation or escaped notice altogether.

The basic insight of level-ordered morphology is that the derivational and inflectional processes of a language can be organized in a series of levels. Each level is associated with a set of phonological rules for which it defines the domain of application. The ordering of levels moreover defines the possible ordering of morphological processes in word-formation. Following a proposal of Pesetsky (1979) let us assume that the output of each word-formation process is submitted within the lexicon itself to the phonological rules of its level. This establishes a basic division among phonological rules into those which are assigned to one or more levels in the lexicon, and those which operate after words have been combined into sentences in the syntax. The former, the rules of *lexical phonology*, are intrinsically cyclic because they reapply after each step of word-formation at their morphological level. The latter, the rules of

---

*This research was supported in part by a grant from the National Institute of Mental Health (grant Number 89283).

postlexical phonology, are intrinsically noncyclic. The lexicon is accordingly structured in the following way:

(1)

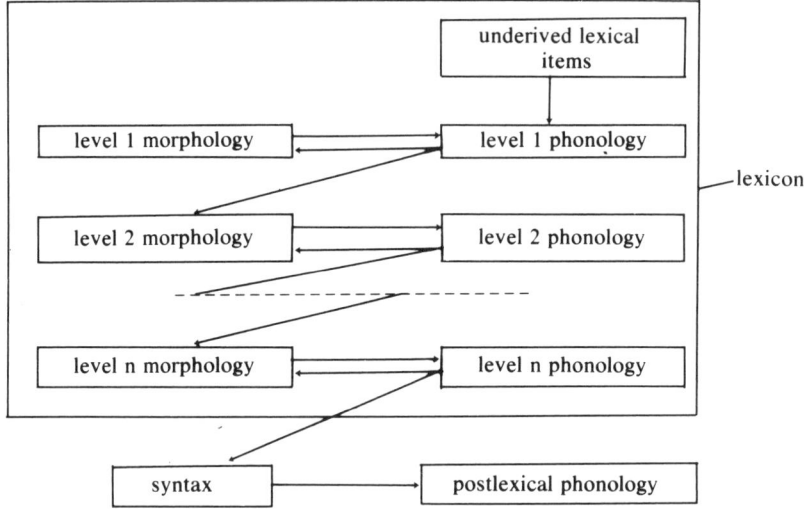

The output of the right-hand boxes collectively constitutes the set of lexical items of the language. The point that the result of every layer of derivation is itself a lexical item will have important consequences later on.

Models of this type have also been investigated by Strauss (1979a), Booij (1981), Pulleyblank (1981), and especially by Harris (1982) for Spanish and Mohanan (1981) for Malayalam, the latter also with extensive theoretical justification of the framework.

For concreteness I add a tentative sketch of how the English lexicon might be organized. It draws on previous explorations of English morphology by Siegel (1974), Allen (1978), Selkirk (MS), and Williams (1981), but differs in some respects from each. (Cf. next page).

Of the three levels in (2), the first level comprises the affixes which have usually been associated with the + boundary. They correspond to the "primary suffixes" of traditional descriptions such as that of Sanskrit by Whitney (1889). This level includes derivational suffixes such as *-al*, *-ous*, *-ity*, *-th*, and inflectional suffixes such as those in *kept, met, hidden, children, addenda, indices, foci* as well as "ablaut", "umlaut" and other stem-changing morphology as in *teethe, bleed, bathe, teeth, lice*. To the second level we assign #-boundary ("secondary") derivation

Lexical Phonology

(2)

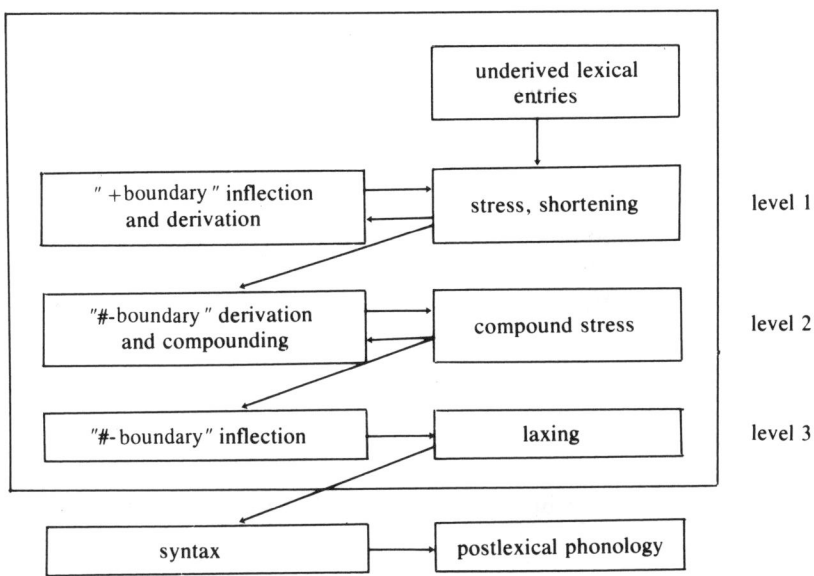

and compounding. Such derivational suffixes as *-hood, -ness, -er, -ism, -ist* belong here. The third level takes care of the remaining "regular" inflection (*leaped, pleated, books,* etc.).

Although the division between level 1 and level 2 affixes coincides entirely with the familiar distinction between the "+ boundary" and the "# boundary" affixes, we shall see that it in fact has deeper roots in the morphological system. In what follows I will first motivate (2) on morphological grounds and then proceed to develop some of its consequences on the phonological side.

First let us introduce a specific format for morphological rules in the grammar. Following Lieber (1980) I shall distinguish two basic classes of word-formation processes, compounding and affixation, and assume that all word formation is endocentric. By this I mean that the category of a derived word is always non-distinct from the category of its head, in English usually the rightmost constituent (cf. Williams 1981).[1] The categories in question include not only lexical categories but also features like Transitive, Agent, etc. In any approach to morphology it is necessary to provide certain kinds of information for any given affix: to what sorts of things the affix may be added, whether it is prefixed or suffixed, and what are the properties of the resulting form. Lieber proposes that this information is encoded in the lexical entry of the affix itself by means of a subcategorization frame and an inherent categorial specification which percolates upward from an affix to the constructions whose head it is. For our purposes it will be convenient to construe these subcategorizations and inherent feature specifications of affixes as so many contextual restrictions on the rules which insert them. Affixes will then not be lexical entries and they will have no lexical features either inherently or by percolation. Each Affix A is introduced by a rule of the form

(3) Insert A in env. $[Y\_\_Z]_X$

where Y,Z corresponds to the "subcategorization frame" of A and X corresponds to its inherent categorial specification in Lieber's format.

Consider first inflection. To illustrate, let the noun *ox* have been inserted in $[\quad]_{Noun, + Plural}$. A morphological rule at level 1 then obligatorily inserts the suffix *-en* after it:

(4) Insert /en/ in env. $[ox\_\_]_{Noun, + Plural}$

The noun *boy* is not subject to (4), but if [+ Plural] it undergoes rule (5) at level 3:

(5) Insert /z/ in env. $[X\_\_]_{Noun, + Plural}$

The morphological processes at different levels are related in certain characteristic ways which recur from language to language.

1. One phenomenon to be accounted for is the "blocking" effect, which has been discussed for derivational morphology by Paul (1896), Esau (1973), Aronoff (1976), Clark and Clark (1979), Toman (1980), and shows up still more clearly in inflection. Words which are inflected at level 1, for example, usually do not receive the general suffixes at level 3. There is no **foots, *oxes* alongside *feet, oxen,* and no **keeped, *meeted* alongside *kept, met.* We shall however have to explain not only why such is the normal case, but also how it is possible for occasional doublets to exist, e.g. *kneeled/knelt, dreamed/dreamt, crocuses/croci, indexes/indices.* In derivational morphology doublets are actually quite common, to the point that blocking there can hardly be considered more than a general tendency.

The blocking phenomenon follows from obligatoriness of morphological rules. For example, *ox,* if [+ Plural], must undergo (4) and so there is no way to derive **oxes* by the later rule (5). Failure of blocking, resulting in doublets like *crocuses/croci* and *dreamed/dreamt* — which we can take to be the marked case — is obtained by making the special rule optional for those words.

To get the blocking effect for derivational affixes, we treat them also as inserted in the context of the appropriate morphological categories. We shall suppose that lexical items are freely inserted into categorial frames [ ]$_X$, where X is a bundle of features. We illustrate with the derivation of deverbal agent nouns. A restricted set of verbs allow nouns to be made at level 1 by such suffixes as -*ant* or zero derivation (which I take to be a phonologically empty suffix). These suffixes are inserted at level 1 by such rules as (6):

(6)   Insert /∅/ in env. [V$_n$__]$_{Noun, + Agent}$

where V$_n$ = *guide, bore, gossip*...

So from [[guide]$_V$]$_{N, + Agent}$ we derive the noun [[guide]$_V$∅]$_{N, + Agent}$, which is well-formed because it is endocentric. If V is not in V$_n$, (6) cannot apply and the resulting structure is filtered out because it is not endocentric. The interesting generalization is that verbs subject to one of these level 1 rules tend not to get the otherwise productive -*er* suffix added by the corresponding rule (7) at level 2:

(7)   Insert *er* in env. [V__]$_{Noun, + Agent}$

(8)   spy$_N$: *spier
      inhabitant : *inhabiter

And when both do exist, the -*er* noun is mostly restricted to meanings not covered by the level 1 noun:

(9)   cook (person) : cooker (device)
      drill (device) : driller (person)
      divide (dividing line, ridge, etc): divider (person, device)
      stimulant, expectorant (substances): stimulator, expectorator
         (devices, persons)
      defendant (of self, in court) : defender

If we formulate the appropriate verb-particular meaning conditions on the insertion of level 1 affixes, the distribution and meaning of -*er* can be left basically unrestricted; it will simply appear whenever not pre-empted by some level 1 agent suffix.

2. An absolute constraint, on the other hand, seems to be that a blocking process can only be located at the same level or at an earlier level than the process it blocks. We do not find, for example, cases where word-

specific affixes are ordered (on phonological or independent morphological grounds) *after* the general affix for that category. An adequate theory of morphology must exclude in principle, for example, a language in which the English facts are reversed and it is the level 3 inflections which occur only with specially designated words.

Given the above format for morphology, this simply follows from the ordering of levels. It is impossible for a process to block a process that precedes it because blocking is pre-emption by prior application.

3. From this it follows in turn that among processes in a blocking relationship, those with restricted applicability have to be ordered before those with general applicability. This explains why processes at later levels are also typically more productive than functionally related processes at earlier levels.

4. Derivational processes at later levels are semantically more uniform than those at earlier levels, where various specialized uses are prone to develop. As before, the point generalizes from derivation to inflection, cf. the semantic differentiation *brothers/brethren*. The greater semantic coherence of the general word-formation processes which are ordered at later levels is a consequence of their productivity (as suggested by Aronoff 1976, 45). The fact that they do not require word-by-word specification but apply across the board to a whole category (subject to blocking as discussed above) means that there is no foothold for imposing word-specific semantic conditions on them either. In other words, imposing an additional word-particular semantic restriction adds a relatively small increment of complexity to an early (level 1) process because the words it applies to must be listed anyway, but it adds a large increment of complexity to a late process because its context can otherwise be given categorially.

5. Lexical items which are *inherent* bearers of some morphological feature do not receive the morpheme that marks that feature. E.g. inherently plural nouns like *cattle* and *people* do not receive a plural ending. Here we shall invoke the Elsewhere Condition (which will play an important role in a quite different aspect of our theory to be discussed below). The formulation in (10) modifies slightly an earlier version proposed in Kiparsky (1973), cf. Koutsoudas, Sanders & Noll (1974).[2]

(10) Rules A,B in the same component apply disjunctively to a form ϕ if and only if
    (i) The structural description of A (the special rule) properly includes the structural description of B (the general rule)

(ii) The result of applying A to ϕ is distinct from the result of applying B to ϕ

In that case, A is applied first, and if it takes effect, then B is not applied.

Consider now a *plurale tantum* like *people*. Assume its lexical entry is inherently marked [+ Plural]. We would like (10) to block such inherent plurals from being pluralized by rule (5). Suppose then we construe each lexical entry L as a rule, namely the identity rule L, whose structural description and structural change are both = L. Then the rule corresponding to the lexical entry [people]$_{+ \text{Noun, + Plural}}$ is disjunctive with (5) by virtue of (10). That is, the structural description of the lexical identity rule (namely [people]$_{+ \text{Noun, + Plural}}$) properly includes the structural description of the general plural rule (namely [X__]$_{+ \text{Noun, + Plural}}$) and their outputs are distinct (namely, *people* and *people + z*, respectively). Therefore the special rule, the lexical identity rule, sets aside the general plural rule.

6. Related to the preceding is the exclusion of stacked affixes having the same function. For example, having derived *oxen* at level 1 we cannot add another plural suffix at level 3 to get **oxens*. Nothing in (2) precludes this possibility per se. However, it now follows as in the preceding case given our assumption that the output of each stage of word-formation (with the rules of lexical phonology applied to it) is itself a lexical entry. The lexical entry [oxen]$_{+ \text{Noun, + Plural}}$ derived at level 1 is then not liable to receive a plural suffix at level 3 for precisely the same reason as the underived lexical entry [people]$_{+ \text{Noun, + Plural}}$ is not liable to receive it.

The organization of morphological rules depicted in (2) derives inflection at two levels. This predicts that irregular inflection, derived at level 1, should be available to derivational processes at level 2, while regular inflection, derived at level 3, should not. This is confirmed by the occasional appearance of level 1 plurals inside ordinary noun compounds:

(11)   a. teeth marks   b. *claws marks
         lice-infested   *rats-infested

Secondly, consider *pluralia tantum* with plural morphology, such as *alms, odds*. These nouns must be marked as inherently [+ Plural] in the lexicon. The theory consequently does not allow them to be entered as underlying /alm/, /odd/ because (10) prohibits the plural affix to be added to them by (5). Therefore the underlying form must be *alms, odds*, etc, which should also show up inside compounds, but this time *obligatorily*. This again appears to be correct:[3]

(12) almsgiving   *almgiving
      oddsmaker   *oddmaker
      painstaking   *paintaking
      Humanities Department   *Humanity Department
      clothesbrush   *clothbrush
      arms race   *arm race

The only other cases where plurals systematically appear inside compounds in English can (and in most cases must anyway for other reasons) be analyzed as involving phrases embedded in compounds. We must assume some limited recursion from phrase-level syntax back into morphology anyway. The occurrence of level 3 plurals in these cases is predicted:

(13) a. a heads-up play, a hands-off policy, a hands-down victory, hands-on training
     b. (daddy) long-legs, (Judy) blue-eyes[4]
     c. excess profits tax, the save-the-whales campaign, the Model Cities program

In the same way as (11), we predict the formation of *withstood, ı*
and similar verb compounds with level 1 inflection on their second members. Since these inflections are formed at level 1, they are available for word-formation at level 2. Moreover, the theory predicts not only that they can but that they *must* appear in past tenses of such compounds. The tensed output of level 2 is [withstand]$_{+ Verb, - Past}$ and [withstood]$_{+ Verb, + Past}$, neither of which can receive the level 3 past ending *-ed*, the former because of feature conflict, and the latter by virtue of (10) as shown above.

The prediction is particularly interesting in view of the opposite outcome in cases like *grandstanded* (**grandstood*). This too follows because of the intrinsic ordering of compounding and level 1 inflection imposed by (2). The derivation proceeds as shown in (14):

(14) level 1: stand$_V$ → stand$_N$
     level 2: grand$_A$ + stand$_N$ → grandstand$_N$
               grandstand$_N$ → grandstand$_V$
     level 3: grandstand$_V$ → grandstanded

Nouns can only be formed from untensed verbs, because tense must agree with a nominative subject (cf. Kiparsky and Kiparsky 1971, 356-7) and nouns do not have nominative subjects. Only when the verb is derived from the compound noun at level 2 can tense be assigned; at that point level 1 inflection is no longer accessible and only the regular inflectional suffixes can be assigned.

More generally, we are now in a position to explain why exocentric (*bahuvrihi*) compounds are characteristically inflected at level 3 even if their second members are by themselves inflected at level 1, whereas endocentric compounds retain the inflection that their second member has by itself. Consider e.g. *milk teeth* (endocentric) vs. *sabertooths* 'sabertooth tigers' (exocentric). As in the verb compound just discussed, endocentric noun compounds are formed at level 2 by combining words, including words derived at level 1 such as *teeth*. Exocentric compounds, however, must on our assumptions be assigned zero derivational suffixes since they otherwise would share the properties of their heads, i.e. be endocentric. But as noted in fn. 3, derivational suffixes cannot be added to derived plurals. Therefore exocentric compounds come out of level 2 with exclusively singular morphology and can receive plural endings only at level 3 where they are adjoined to the whole compound.

The model of lexical phonology directly predicts the correlation between "boundary strength" and affix order which was observed for English by Siegel (1974), and is apparently a general property of languages. The generalization is that affixes of level n are not added to stems which already contain affixes of level n+1. For example, consider the two negative prefixes *in-* and *non-*. *In-* assimilates to a follwoing consonant (Singh 1981) but *non-* does not. In standard generative phonology this is dealt with by assigning them + and # boundaries respectively and restricting assimilation to apply across + only:

(15)   in + legible   → illegible
       non # legible ↛ *nollegible

This phonological difference between *non-* and *in-* is related to the fact that *non-* can be prefixed to a word with *in-* but *in-* cannot be prefixed to a word with *non-*:

(16)   nonillegible
       *innonlegible

In the present theory both the phonology and the ordering of the two prefixes follows from putting *in-* and assimilation rule on level 1 and *non-* on level 2. No boundary is then needed to block the assimilation of *non-*. In this way, boundary symbols such as + and # can be entirely eliminated from phonological representations. The requisite information is carried by the appropriate ordering of levels and the morphological bracketing of the string, cf. Strauss (1979a), Mohanan (1981).

The cyclic application of phonological rules has generally been assumed to be subject to the convention that internal brackets are erased at the end of a cycle (Chomsky and Halle, 1968, 20). We shall assume here the weaker version (17), equivalent to the "Opacity Condition" of Mohanan (1981).

(17) Bracketing Erasure:
Internal brackets are erased at the end of a level

Hence the use of even the limited boundary information encoded in the morphological bracketing is restricted to the level at which the morphology itself is assigned. Moreover, morphological rules also do not have access to internal morphological structure of earlier levels. Pesetsky (1979) and Allen (1978) have suggested more restrictive conditions but these appear to be difficult to maintain in view of the English example in (22) below, the Malayalam cases cited in Mohanan (1981), and the extensive material discussed, from a different point of view, in Carstairs (1981).

In addition to giving a more restrictive theory of morphological junctures, lexical phonology makes it possible to deal with phenomena where boundary symbols fail. A well-known problem for cyclic assignment of word stress in English arises in zero derivation.[5] When nouns are formed from verbs they shift to the nominal stress pattern (18a), but when verbs are formed from nouns they do not shift as expected to the verbal stress pattern (18b):

(18) a. torménty → tórmènt$_N$
b. páttern$_N$ → *pattérn$_V$ (cf. *cavórt, usúrp*)

This difference in stress behavior is directly accounted for by forming nouns from verbs at level 1 and verbs from nouns at level 2, where they escape the level 1 rules of word stress. This correlates in the first instance with the productivity difference that we expect between level 1 and level 2 derivational process. N to V derivation enjoys great productivity in English (Clark and Clark 1979), while V to N derivation is comparatively restricted in scope. As a broad generalization it can be said that verbs are freely zero-derived from nouns whenever not blocked by a synonymous formation at level 1, such as *systematize* (**to system*), while nouns are zero-derived from verbs in special cases which themselves block the productive agent and action suffixes as level 2 such as *-er* (rule 7) and *-ing*.

Our proposal is borne out by a number of specific morphological facts as well.

1. It predicts that verbs zero-derived from nouns are regular in inflection. The result is that the ablaut rules at level 1 become more general. For example, it becomes a practically exceptionless rule that verbs in *-ing, -ink* are strong (*flung, stung, wrung, swung, rang, sang, shrank, sank, stank* etc.); the weakly inflected verbs (*ringed, winged, inked, linked* etc.) are derived from nouns at level 2 and hence are automatically excluded from level 1 inflection. By contrast, nouns formed from verbs at level 1 will be susceptible to level 1 phonological rules, not only stress as we have seen (*tormént$_V$ → tórmènt$_N$*) but also such rules as ablaut (*sing$_V$ → song$_N$*).

2. As for morphology, since compounds are formed at level 2 we correctly predict that noun compounds can become verbs but verb compounds cannot become nouns. This is entirely correct:[6]

(19) a. to grandstand, to wallpaper, to snowball, to quarterback
      b. *an air-condition, * a stage-manage

3. By assigning V → N and N → V zero derivation to levels 1 and 2 respectively we can also see why verbs formed with suffixes never yield zero-derived nouns:

(20)   *a publicize, *a demonstrate, *a clarify

while nouns may yield zero-derived verbs if they are formed with level 1 suffixes (21a) though not if they are formed with level 2 suffixes (21b):

(21a) to pressure, to picture, to commission, to proposition, to requisition, to trial, to engineer, to reverence, to reference

(21b) *to singer, *to beating, *to freedom, *to promptness, *to championship, *to alcoholism, *to nationalist, *to sisterhood

If we stipulate that zero suffixes cannot be added to suffixed forms

(22)   *   ] X] ∅]

these facts fall out from Bracketing Erasure (17) and the level ordering we have assumed. The verbs in (20) and the nouns in (21b) are excluded by (22) because they are zero-derived from stems which are suffixed at the same level. The verbs in (21a) do not violate (22) because the internal brackets from level 1 are erased by (17) at level 2 where N to V derivation applies.

4. Nouns zero-derived from verbs should be capable of receiving level 1 suffixes, while verbs zero-derived from nouns should not be so capable. The examples in (23) show that zero-derived nouns can indeed get level 1 suffixes:

(23)   alarmist, escapism, torturous, segmental, rebellious

And it does also seem to be true that there are no cases which would involve adding a level I deverbal suffix to a zero-derived denominal verb:

(24)   *gesturation, *figurive, *patternance, *crusadatory, *cementant

But, as predicted, level 2 deverbal suffixes can be added to zero-derived denominal verbs:

(25)   placement, commissionable, riveter, masquerading

5. A special case of this relation between level 1 and level 2 derivation is that V → N → V zero derivations are possible, while N → V → N zero derivations are not. Examples of the former type are

(26)   *protést*$_V$ → *prótèst*$_N$ → *prótèst*$_V$ 'stage a prótest' (demonstrators may *prótèst* but a child can only *protést*)
discóunt$_V$ → *díscòunt*$_N$ → *díscòunt*$_V$ 'sell at a discount'
digést$_V$ → *dígèst*$_N$ → *dígèst*$_V$ 'make a digest'
compóund$_V$ → *cómpòund*$_N$ → *cómpòund*$_V$ 'join or become joined in a compound'

Convincing N → V → N cases, such as a hypothetical triplet *pattern*$_N$ → *pattern*$_V$ → **pattern*$_N$ do not exist to my knowledge. Some cases that look like they might be of that type are probably more correctly taken as involving two distinct zero nominalizations from a verb, such as 'act' and either 'effected object' (27a), 'implement' (27b), or 'agent' (27c):

(27) a. discharge$_V$ discharge$_N$ 'act of discharging'   discharge$_N$ 'that which is discharged'
         spit$_V$ spit$_N$ spit$_N$
         shit$_V$ shit$_N$ shit$_N$
         sweat$_V$ sweat$_N$ sweat$_N$
         splice$_V$ splice$_N$ splice$_N$
      b. paddle$_V$ paddle$_N$ 'act of paddling'   paddle$_N$ 'implement for paddling'
         brush$_V$ brush$_N$ brush$_N$
      c. scrub$_V$ scrub$_N$ 'act of scrubbing'   scrub$_N$ 'one who scrubs'

The reason for taking the verbs rather than one of the nouns as basic is that various overt V → N derivations expressing each of these categories must be assumed anyway, e.g. *shavings, spittle* (effected object), *router, mixer* (implement and agent). Also, only on that assumption will level-ordering correctly predict that the verbs may undergo level 1 inflection (cf. *spat, sweat(ed)*), and that verbs which *must* be zero-derived will *not* form zero nouns but express these categories by means of other suffixes, as in (28):[7]

(28) rivet$_N$ → rivet$_V$ → riveting (act), riveter (implement, agent)
condition$_N$ → condition$_V$ → conditioning, conditioner
water$_N$ → water$_V$ → watering, waterer

Another previously problematic connection between morphology and phonology is that morphological rules may be sensitive to the output of phonological rules (Siegel 1974, Aronoff 1976). This is naturally accommodated in this theory because phonological rules operate in tandem with morphology in the lexicon. For example, the noun-forming suffix *-al* is only added to verbs which are stressed on the last syllable, e.g. *arríval, revérsal, acquíttal* vs. **depósital, *recóveral*. Therefore the derivational process that adds *-al* to verbs has to apply after the cyclic rule that assigns stress to verbs. If the grammar is organized as in (2), exactly this ordering is predicted. The claim is that only cyclic rules may be relevant to morphology, more specifically that only cyclic rules of level *n* may be relevant to morphology of level *m*, where $n \leq m$.

This organization of the lexicon, in conjunction with the proposals developed earlier, has further consequences on the phonological side. It embodies the claim that all and only lexical categories are cyclic domains. The prediction is that there should be no cyclic rule application above the word level. Up to recently this consequence would by itself have sufficed to wreck the theory in view of the fact that sentence stress was one of the castiron arguments for cyclicity. However, Rischel (1964; 1972) and Liberman and Prince (1977) have pointed out that metrical theory eliminates the need for cyclic assignment of sentence stress. In that framework the Nuclear Stress Rule, which assigns prominence to the right branch of a phrasal constituent, can apply in any order or simultaneously to all constituents in the sentence. As far as I know there are *no* rules which have to apply cyclically from the innermost phrasal constituents out and the theory of lexical phonology predicts that.

There are however cases where rules of word phonology seem to apply once at the lowest level of phrase syntax. I have argued (Kiparsky 1979) that the English Rhythm Rule applies both below and above the word level, in cases like *expéct* ~ *èxpectátion* and *abstráct* ~ *ábstràct árt* respectively. These applications take place at different stages in the derivation because the destressing of metrically weak initial syllables must crucially intervene between them. A somewhat similar situation has been found in the tonology of Ewe by Clements (1977, 119). In neither case is there evidence of cyclic iteration within the syntax itself: each rule applies once at the phrasal level and does not need to reapply cyclically on successively higher syntactic constituents.

The most straightforward assumption is that these rules belong to both the lexical and postlexical system. However, it is surely significant that they concern what may be called phrase phonology rather than full-fledged sentence phonology. Both rules are subject to a constraint which blocks their application to Verbs followed by object Noun Phrases (*màintáin órder* ≠ **máintàin órder*; for Ewe cf. Clements p. 122 ff.). Both rules have lexical exceptions (e.g. *profóund trúth* ≠ **prófòund trúth*; cf. again Clements p. 137). So one conclusion that could be drawn from this is that the lowest level of phrase structure can in some way be fed back into the lexicon. Quite apart from phonological considerations this would be suggested by the fact that phrasal combinations at this level are subject to selectional restrictions and liable to get fixed as idioms and formulas. We already noted above that they can be inputs to word-formation rules, e.g. *American history teacher, to stonewall, a hands-off policy*. A specific example of lexicalization is that *ábstràct* has for many people acquired inherently the specialized technical sense it bears in the phrase *ábstràct árt*, denoting a specific type or school of art.[8] These speakers make a difference between the sentences

(29) a. This art is ábstràct (not representational)
     b. This art is abstráct (not concrete)

In the light of such facts, the nature of phrase phonology and its relation to word phonology and sentence phonology deserves deeper investigation.

As for a lower bound on cyclicity, there is some evidence that non-lexical categories are not cyclic domains. A quite compelling case has been made by J. Harris (MS) for Spanish on the basis of a study of stress and syllable structure. One of his examples is summarized in (30).

(30) desden + es 'disdains'   (noun plural)
      desdeñ + es 'you disdain' (2. sg. subj.)

                     [desdeñ]$_N$ es]$_N$ [[desdeñ + a]$_V$ e + s]$_N$
                           \/   \/
   I Syllabification   [σ   ]   [σ   ]
      ñ → n in coda   n   (inapplicable)

   II Truncation   [———]   ∅
      Syllabification   nes   ñes
                          \|/   \|/
                           σ   σ

The point concerns the application of a cyclic rule which depalatalizes ñ to n in the coda of a syllable. The contrast between the noun plural *desden +es* and the subjunctive verb from *desdeñ+es* arises because the underlying palatalized ñ is syllable-final in the noun stem /desdeñ/ but syllable-initial in the verb stem /desdeñ+a/. These respective stems constitute the first cyclic domains and the nasal depalatalization finds its correct syllable environment there, not at the root or word level. Harris demonstrates that the cyclic domains required for both stress and syllabification in Spanish are exactly the lexical categories.

A general condition to this effect was proposed already by Brame (1974) on the basis of Arabic and English data. He noted the Palestinian Arabic contrast *fhímna* 'we understood' vs. *fihímna* 'he understood us', with the same morphemes except that *na* is an ending in the first form and a clitic in the second. As he pointed out, the data can be explained by assuming that the rule syncopating unstressed vowels is ordered cyclically after the rule assigning penult stress on the assumption that the bare verb root is not a cyclic domain:

(31)   [fihim + na]$_V$ [[fihim + ∅]$_V$ + na]$_V$

   I Stress   [fihím + na]   [fíhim   ]
      Syncope   fhím + na   —

   II Stress   —   [fíhím + na   ]$_V$
      Syncope   —   —

Brame proposed that (1) cycled substrings must occur as independent words, and (2) all and only rules mentioning brackets are cyclic. The first condition taken literally is actually too strong because stems, which must be lexically categorized as N, V or A and which do constitute cyclic domains are not necessarily capable of occurring as independent words in inflectional languages, where they may require an obligatory case ending. Moreover, in many languages word-formation must to all appearances be taken back to roots which in themselves are not necessarily members of any lexical category. If this is true, then it is necessary to stipulate that lexical rules apply only in domains delimited as lexical categories [ ]$_{N,A,V}$.

Perhaps the most significant consequences that the theory has for phonology have to do with the nature of lexical representations. Here it promises to resolve the long-standing issues that have been discussed in terms of constraints on abstractness, the Strict Cycle Condition, morpheme structure rules, and other notions. We shall summarize the problems in historical perspective and then show how they may be approached from the perspective of lexical phonology.

The theory worked out in Chomsky and Halle (1968) claims that underlying representations are chosen so as to give the simplest total grammar, where the grammar includes both lexicon and rules. The effect is to guarantee that lexical representations will be at *least* as abstract as the classical phonemic level. But they will be more abstract whenever, and to whatever extent, the simplicity of the system requires it. The simplicity of the system may require more abstract representations for several kinds of reasons. The most important kind of reason for setting up an abstract representation of a morpheme is systematically governed variation in its phonological shape. Underlying representations are set up in such a way as to permit such regular variation to be characterized by the simplest and therefore most general rules possible. Let us illustrate the point with an example from English phonology. The [s] in *dissonant* is to be derived by a degemination rule from /s+s/, on the strength of its component morphemes, which elsewhere appear as /dis/ (cf. *disreputable, discourteous*) and /sɔn + ænt/ (cf. *sonant, consonant*). Moreover, this representation directly explains why the word does not undergo the voicing rule to which single *s* is normally subject in that environment (cf. *resonant*). Similarly, the [s] in *criticize* is derived from /k/ by a "Velar Softening" rule, which applies throughout the derivational ("Romance") vocabulary of English, and accounts here for the regular relationship between *criticize, criticism* and *critic, critical*. This does *not* imply that the speaker or hearer need in any way mentally "derive" the words he says or hears by means of such rules as Velar Softening. What it *does* mean is that the alternations they govern belong to the regular phonological pattern of English, while for example a hypothetical *k*∼*s* alternation in the reverse context, such as **criti[k]ize*∼**criti[s]al*, would be irregular. The claim made is that someone who knows English implicitly knows that pattern, and will under appropriate circumstances recognize the difference between regular and irregular alternations, though he may not be able, even after reflection, to verbalize the rules that underlie it.

Lexical Phonology

The system that is set up in order to account for phonological alternations may then in turn permit further abstraction in the underlying representations of non-alternating forms as well. Often it may be positively required by the evaluation measure that selects the simplest grammar. "Abstractness" in this sense cannot be criticized on any legitimate a priori grounds; in the absence of further evidence it would indeed be demanded by sound scientific method. There is, however, evidence, which shows that at precisely this point the theory induces a characteristic type of wrong analysis. Identifying and correcting the source of error in the theory was the focus of the so-called abstractness controversy resulting in various versions of "concrete" phonology and more recently cyclic phonology.

Perhaps the most familiar English example of a rule which causes difficulties of the sort which are at issue here is Trisyllabic Shortening (or Trisyllabic Laxing). This rule shortens a vowel if followed by at least two more vowels, of which the first is unstressed:

(32) $V \rightarrow [\text{-long}] \:/\: \underline{\quad} \: C_0 \, V_i \, C_0 \, V_j$ where V_i is not metrically strong

It applies, for example, to shorten the long vowels in the initial syllables of

(33)   opacity, declarative, tabulate

(cf. *opaque, declare, table*). The rule has to be assigned to level 1 on the evidence of words like

(34)   mightily, bravery, weariness

Clearly all morphologically simple words such as

(35)   ivory, nightingale, stevedore, Goolagong, Averell, Oedipus, Oberon

must somehow be exempted from undergoing it. Standard generative phonology forces their phonological representatives to be adjusted, if possible, in such a way that the structural description of the rule is not met. For *ivory* it is possible to postulate a final /y/, which will become *i* by an independently needed rule of English phonology. For *nightingale*, Chomsky and Halle (1968, 234) rather less persuasively suggest underlying /nixtVngæl/, with $ix \rightarrow \bar{i} \rightarrow ay$ by rules they claim are required on other grounds. The reason this is ultimately unilluminating is that in the bulk of the cases – *stevedore* and so forth – the failure of Trisyllabic Shortening cannot be explained away by changing the underlying form anyway.

Along with the problem that many ordinary words have no regular derivation in the grammar, there is the complementary problem that words like

(36)   alibi, sycamore, camera, pelican, enemy, Amazon, Pamela, calendar

have *two* possible derivations, while only one is ever needed. They could be derived at face value from an underlying representation with a short vowel in the first syllable. But they could also be assigned a *long* vowel in the first syllable and taken for a "free ride" on the Trisyllabic Shortening rule.

Let us now look at some possible solutions to these problems.

A primitive attempt at solving this problem was the so-called Alternation Condition. In its strong version, it went as follows (Kiparsky 1968-1973, sec. 1):

(37)   Obligatory neutralization rules cannot apply to all occurrences of a morpheme

The general effect is to limit the "abstractness" of underlying representations to cases motivated by phonological alternations. With regard to our particular example, the Alternation Condition does two things. It resolves the indeterminacy in the underlying representation of (36) by fixing the vowels of the first syllables as short. And it prohibits the possibility of dealing with (35) by such phonological devices as postulating /x/ in *nightingale* and nonsyllabic /y/ in *ivory*. Nevertheless, the Alternation Condition as stated in (37) is unquestionably inadequate. Without attempting to do justice to the complex discussion that broke out around it,[9] let us summarize what are perhaps its most damaging flaws.

1. The Alternation Condition is not interpretable as a formal condition on grammars. In order to check whether it is satisfied in a given grammar, it would be necessary to inspect every derivation of that grammar. The only sense that can be made out of it is as a strategy of language acquisition which says that a learner analyzes a form " at face value" unless he has encountered variants of it which justify a more remote underlying representation.

2. The Alternation Condition leaves the theory with an inherent redundancy. For example, it says that words like (36) cannot be derived from underlying representations with long vowels in the first syllable. That fact ought to be of one piece with the fact that words like (35) do not undergo Trisyllabic Shortening. Yet we shall still either have to mark the latter as exceptions to the rule, or else restate its environment so that it applies only across morpheme boundaries. This is redundant because the theory already tells us, by the Alternation Condition, that these words *could not* be subject to Trisyllabic Shortening. The problem is that the constraint on underlying representations leads to a predictable restriction on the application of rules which cannot, in this formulation, be expressed systematically in the grammar.

3. The Alternation Condition is too weak in that it imposes no restrictions whatever on possible patterns of alternation. It appears that a certain type of rule, of which Trisyllabic Shortening is an example, could not apply morpheme-internally as in (35, 36) even if alternations did exist. To see what is at stake, consider the condition on Trisyllabic Shortening that the following vowel must be unstressed. It correctly blocks the rule from shortening the first vowel in such words as (38, 39):

(38) quōtátion
 flōtátion
 gȳrátion
 cītátion
 mīgrátion

(39) fīnálity
 vītálity
 glōbálity
 tōnálity
 tītánic

What does not exist, and arguably could not exist, is a pattern illustrated by the hypothetical cases in (40), where we would have to allow morpheme-internal application of Trisyllabic Shortening, on the strength of the long vowel that shows up in the derivative, where Trisyllabic Shortening is bled by stress.

(40) órigin : * ōríginal (ŏríginal)
 sýnonym : * sȳnónymous (sy̆nónymous)

The Alternation Condition is incapable of predicting that such cases do not exist.[10]

4. On the other hand, the Alternation Condition is too strong in that it excludes analyses which are well motivated on internal grounds. That is, it cannot be maintained without unacceptable loss of generalization. It is this failing which attracted the most discussion in the controversy over the Alternation Condition.

For example, while no-one will miss the putative /x/ in *nightingale*, a final /y/ is rather well motivated by the system of English word stress. Words ending in *-ory* and *-ary*, as well as words like *galaxy, industry,* systematically behave as if the final vowel was really a consonant, with respect to several of the stress rules (Chomsky and Halle 1968, 130, Liberman and Prince 1977, Hayes 1981, Ch. 5). The same final /y/ accounts for the failure of Trisyllabic Shortening in derived words like *vacancy, piracy, agency, secrecy*, where the rule would otherwise be expected to apply (Rubach 1981). Also the only exception to the generalization noted above that *-al* is added after stressed syllables is *burial*; which can be resolved by taking the final *-y* as nonsyllabic. But the required rule

(41) $y \rightarrow i / \_\_ \#$

is an obligatory neutralization rule since *i* is a phoneme of English, and so cannot apply in the proposed cases consistent with the Alternation Condition.

An alternative approach is to deny the phonological character of rules such as Trisyllabic Shortening. It is commonly said that rules of this type are to be considered as "morphological" or morphologized". This claim may actually mean a number of things, since there are several possible ways of treating morphologically conditioned rules in the phonology. But on any of the possible construals, the properties of the rule seem to be obscured rather than explained by the proposal. Let us consider three versions in turn.

The first version would be to simply add to the phonological environment of (32) a morphological environment consisting of the list of formatives before which the shortening process can take place, e.g.:

(42)
-ous	:	ōmen	~	ominous
-ate	:	pōllen	~	pollinate
-ar	:	līne	~	linear
-al	:	nātion	~	national
-ty	:	pēnal	~	penalty
-ison	:	compāre	~	comparison
-(it)ive	:	compēte	~	competitive
-(i)fy	:	vīle	~	vilify
-ent	:	refēr	~	referent

This list is, however, redundant. The suffixes which have to be included in it are simply *all* "+ -boundary" suffixes which can cause the phonological conditions of Trisyllabic Shortening to be met. The only suffixes of that class that may be omitted are those which happen never to occur in the appropriate phonological circumstances, for example deverbal -*al*, which is only added to end-stressed words (*arrival, arousal, betrayal*). The correct generalization is that all and only suffixes of the + -boundary class may trigger Trisyllabic Shortening in the environment of (32).

A second morphologized version of (32) would omit the phonological conditions entirely and state the rule simply as triggered by the suffixes of (42). It is open to the same objection as the first version and has to be rejected for that reason alone. Moreover, it misses the further generalization embodied in the *phonological* environment of the rule and therefore enormously adds to the *lexical* arbitrariness of the rule in such cases as:

(43) ŏmin + ous   vs.   heīn + ous
     pŏllin + ate   vs.   vāc + ate
     līne + ar   vs.   sōl + ar
     nătion + al   vs.   fōc + al
     compĕt + it + ive vs. invās + ive
     prepăr + at + ory vs. advīs + ory
     prĕfer + ence   vs.   cleār + ance
     rĕfer + ent   vs.   son + ant

The third version is that morphophonemic processes are integral parts of morphological operations. This is the most unfortunate treatment of all because it denies that there is a single process involved, and claims that there are as many "Trisyllabic Shortening" rules as there are suffixes that can trigger the shortening process. Since the shortening is stated separately in connection with each affixation process, there is no way in this theory to distinguish between English and a hypothetical language in which each suffix triggers its own arbitrary set of changes in the stem. It even becomes impossible to relate irregular derivations to regular ones. It seems correct to say that *obēsity* and *oblĭquity* are formed from *obēse*, *oblīque* by the same morphological process as *obscĕnity* from *obscēne* but are exceptions to Trisyllabic Shortening and Vowel Shift, respectively. But if Trisyllabic Shortening and Vowel Shift are integral parts of that morphological process, then it is necessary to say that the three derived words are formed by three *different* morphological processes.

Not only is the central regularity underlying a rule such as Trisyllabic Shortening obscured by combining it with the various suffixation processes; the very patterning of exceptions is lost sight of. For example, the morpheme /nōt/ (*note*) is an exception to Trisyllabic Shortening: cf. *denōt + ative* (vs. *compăr + ative*), *nōt + ify* (vs. *cŏd + ify*). On the proposal under consideration it would have to be considered as subject to as many exceptional, otherwise unmotivated morphological operations as happen to give rise to the conditions that ordinarily trigger Trisyllabic Shortening.[11]

The germ of truth in the morphologization idea is that instead of stating a constraint on underlying representations directly, it should be made derivative of a primary constraint on the operation of phonological rules, which limits certain rules to "derived" inputs. If we can state a principle that prohibits Trisyllabic Shortening from operating in underived cases like (35), then the desired underlying representations are at the same time automatically enforced because no others will yield the correct output in conformity with the principle.

The search for a constraint on the application of rules moreover makes more sense in the theoretical framework of generative grammar, and it is the strategy by which the most interesting discoveries of theoretical linguistics have been achieved.

We can approach the problem by introducing a notion of *derived environment*.

Def: An environment E is *derived* with respect to a rule R if E satisfies the structural description of R crucially by virtue of a combination of morphemes or the application of a rule.

We can then reformulate the Alternation Condition as restricting the corresponding class of rules as follows:

(44)   *Revised Alternation Condition (RAC)*
       Obligatory Neutralization rules apply only in derived environments.

That is, an obligatory neutralization rule can apply only if the input involves crucially a sequence which arises in morpheme combinations or through the earlier application of a phonological rule. Otherwise, that is if the environment is met already in the underlying representation of a single morpheme, the process cannot apply. Requiring that a neutralization process apply only in derived environments guarantees in particular that neutralization will always be contextual (as opposed to absolute).

The RAC, then, does double duty as a constraint on the abstractness of underlying representations and as a principle of rule application allowing us to explain a class of cases which are unstatable in the older theory.

While the Revised Alternation Condition is a substantial improvement, it still retains some of the weaknesses discussed above. In the first place, it is still not a formal condition of the desired sort because the property of being a "neutralization rule" is not determinable from inspection of the grammar. Once again it is in principle necessary to check all the derivations in order to see whether the condition is satisfied. Secondly, there remain problems of empirical adequacy. An example of a loss of generalization entailed by the Revised Alternation Condition in English phonology can be seen in the regularities governed by the Velar Softening rule. This rule, which can be formulated as

(45) $k \rightarrow s \; / \_\_ \begin{bmatrix} -\text{back} \\ -\text{low} \end{bmatrix}$

(perhaps via an intermediate c as in Chomsky and Halle 1968) is an obligatory neutralization rule, since s is phonemic in English. Because of *critic ~ criticize* and similar alternations, (45) must be in the phonology of English in any case. Prohibiting its application in non-derived cases like *conceive, proceed, recite* has several unfortunate consequences. In the first place, the explanation for the distribution of s, z and k in those stems is lost. We find one set of cases where the root initial consonant is z intervocalically and s elsewhere, and another set of cases where the root-initial consonant is s if a nonlow front vowel follows and k elsewhere:

(46)   /s/ : re[z]ist   con[s]ist
       /s/ : re[z]ort   con[s]ort

       /k/ : re[s]eive   con[s]eive
       /k/ : re[k]ord   con[k]ord

The problem is explained by assuming underlying /s/ and /k/ respectively. The independently motivated rules of Velar Softening and intervocalic voicing of s, applied in that order, account for the observed surface reflexes of /k/ and /s/. The Revised Alternation Condition loses the generalization that /z/ does not appear in roots and sets up a set of exceptions to the intervocalic voicing rule (*receive*). Furthermore, the k in the prefix of *accede, succeed, accept* (pronounced with [... ks ...]), should be attributed to the assimilation rule that operates transparently in *afford, support, account* etc., but this cannot be done if the non-alternating initial *s* has to be set up as underlying /s/ as required by the Revised Alternation Condition. Thus many of the convincing aspects of the analysis by Chomsky and Halle (1968) would have to be abandoned along with the less compelling ones.

A major step forward, which puts the whole problem into an entirely new light, was made by Joan Mascaró in his dissertation of (1976). Mascaró proposed that the class of rules which exhibits the "derived-environment-only" behavior is the class of cyclic rules, and that this behavior follows from the definition of "proper application of a cyclic rule". With some simplification, his proposal was:

(47) *Strict Cycle Condition* (SSC):
  a. Cyclic rules apply only to derived representations.
  b. Def.: A representation ϕ is *derived* w.r.t. rule R in cycle j iff ϕ meets the structural analysis of R by virtue of a combination of morphemes introduced in cycle j or the application of a phonological rule in cycle j.

The correct mode of application for Trisyllabic Shortening is thus obtained by setting it up as a cyclic rule, and the previously problematic Velar Softening rule has different properties by virtue of being a postcyclic rule.

The most important consequence of the Strict Cycle Condition is that there should be a relationship between the way a rule is *ordered* and the way it *applies*: cyclic ordering should correlate with the restriction to derived environments and postcyclic ordering should correlate with across-the-board application. Naturally, while the evidence from ordering and from application to non-derived forms should in principle coincide, we should not expect to find *both* kinds of evidence for *all* rules. There should however be no conflict between the two criteria and one would hope to find some non-trivial convergence between them. The recent study of Polish phonology by Rubach (1981) is devoted to exploring precisely this hypothesis in a rich body of material. His findings confirm it in rather striking ways.

What the theory entails for English is that Trisyllabic Shortening (and all rules that precede it) apply cyclically, and that Velar Softening (and all rules that follow it) apply post-cyclically. This is indeed compatible with what is known about English word phonology. Positive support for it may be given both directly, by evidence for the cyclic or non-cyclic application of the rules, or indirectly by transitivity, by fixing the ordering of the rules in question with respect to other rules whose cyclic or postcyclic status is established on other grounds.

Direct support for the cyclicity of Trisyllabic Shortening can be provided by a slight extension of a line of reasoning begun above. Note the contrast

(48) hy̆pócrisy   vs.   hȳpóthesis

Why is the first vowel short in *hypocrisy*? This follows if Trisyllabic Shortening is cyclic, since *hypócrisy* is derived from *hýpocrite*, where it is subject to Trisyllabic Shortening:

(49)   [[hīpo+krit]i]
      I TSS   [hipo + krit]
     II Stress   [hipókrit+i]
         Other rules   [hipókris+i]

Because Trisyllabic Shortening is blocked before a stressed vowel (cf. *hypothesis* and (39) above) it could not apply postcyclically in *hypócrisy*. Further, consider

(50)   Italy: Itálian

These words are like *Canada: Canadian* and others in (40) above. The additional twist is that the word *ītálic*, which in one listed standard pronunciation has initial [ay], indicates that the underlying vowel is /ī/. The correct forms are predicted, if Trisyllabic Shortening is cyclic, on the morphologically plausible assumption that *Italian* is derived from *Italy* but *italic* is derived from the root *ital-*:

(51)   [ītæl+i]   [[ītæl+i]æn]   [ītæl + ik]

The variant *italic* is derivable if the source is taken to be *Italy*.

The ordering of Trisyllabic Shortening can be pinpointed quite precisely thanks to the condition that it does not apply before a stressed syllable. As the data in (39) show, Trisyllabic Shortening follows the assignment of word stress (more precisely, the "English Stress Rule" of Hayes 1981). The assignment of word stress is followed by several destressing rules which basically serve to eliminate stress clashes under certain conditions. One such rule is Post-stress Destressing. This rule destresses metrically weak open syllables between a stressed and an unstressed syllable. For example, the endings *-ory, -ary* receive a stress by the English Stress Rule, which is retained after an unstressed syllable (52a) but lost directly after a stressed syllable (52b):

(52)   a. tránsit+òry   b. advís+ory
        prómiss+òry   cúrs+ory
        plánet+àry   plén+ary

Since Post-stress Destressing applies only to medial syllables and the *-y* in the above words is an underlying /y/ because of the stress considerations mentioned above, then in order to have the proper environment for Post-stress Destressing we must first syllabify the final *-y*. We already saw that the syllabification of *-y* itself follows Trisyllabic Shortening because it does not feed it in words like *vacancy, secrecy, potency*.

(53) $\begin{cases} \text{Trisyllabic Shortening} \\ y \to i \\ \text{Post-stress Destressing} \end{cases}$

By transitivity, Trisyllabic Shortening has to precede Post-stress Destressing. This predicts that vowels destressed by Post-stress Destressing will block Trisyllabic Shortening before them. The prediction is borne out by words like

(54) mīgratory, vībratory, rōtatory, phōnatory

where Trisyllabic shortening fails on account of the stress on -at- inherited from the first cycle, as shown in the derivation of mīgratory:

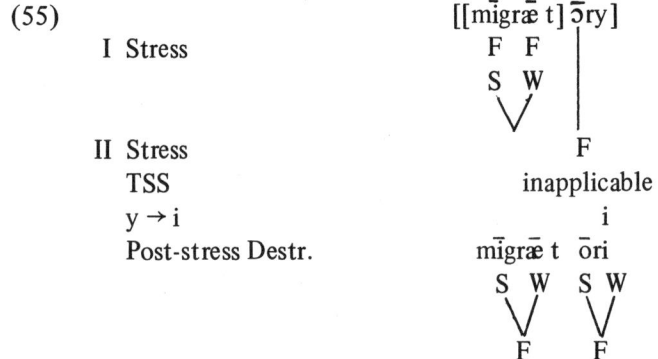

Another destressing rule eliminates metrically weak stresses medially in open syllables if another stress follows (see 56a). As (56b) shows, it is blocked in closed syllables:

(56) a. èxpla̯nátion   b. cómpènsátion
      cómbi̯nátion   indèntátion
      ínvi̯tátion   ínfèstátion
      phòneti̯cían   sýntàctícian

This rule has to precede Trisyllabic Shortening since it has to feed it in derivations of words like *proclamation, rĕstoration, rĕcitation*, where the prefix vowel is always short (cf. *prōclaim, rēstore, rēcite*, where Trisyllabic Shortening is inapplicable and the prefix consequently can be long). After application of the Rhythm Rule in the second cycle we have

Lexical Phonology

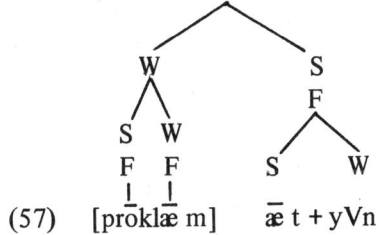
(57) [prŏklǣ m] ǣt + yVn

at which stage Pre-stress Destressing and Trisyllabic Shortening, *in that order*, apply to give

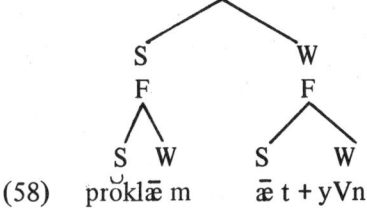
(58) prŏklǣ m ǣt + yVn

from which the phonetic form is directly derivable.

Because Pre-Stress Destressing precedes the cyclic rule of Trisyllabic Shortening, it must itself by cyclic, and so in turn must every rule that has to be ordered before it. As far as I can see, this is entirely compatible with the theory of English word stress that has been worked out so far.

For comparison, consider the rule which lengthens the vowel in such cases as *Newton ~ Newtōnian, Canada ~ Canādian, Athens ~ Athēnian*:

$$(59) \quad \begin{bmatrix} V \\ -high \end{bmatrix} \rightarrow \bar{V} / \_\_ C \begin{bmatrix} i \\ -stress \end{bmatrix} \begin{bmatrix} V \\ -stress \end{bmatrix}$$

This rule is ordered after Trisyllabic Shortening (Chomsky and Halle 1968, 181) and in fact it seems to be postcyclic on the basis of examples like *mániac ~ maníacal* (not **māníacal*). Hence the rule is free to apply in nonderived environments and an underlying V: $\bar{V}$ contrast is possible in the environment of (59), cf. *ammōnia : ammōnify, ammōniátion* with /ɔ̄/.

The theory of cyclic phonology we have considered so far raises a number of questions. Some are more or less conceptual: Why should there be two types of phonological rules, cyclic and postcyclic? Why should the definition of proper cyclic application have the particular and very complex form it has? What is the *inherent* connection between cyclicity, a property of rule ordering, and the restriction to derived environments? These questions become particularly troublesome if Freidin (1978) is right that the (strict) cyclic application of transformational rules in syntax does not have to be stipulated as an autonomous principle in the theory of grammar, because its effects can be derived from the "Opacity" (Tensed S and Nominative Island) conditions. If cyclicity is indeed derivative in syntax then surely it will not be primitive in phonology. For these reasons one is tempted to look for a reformulation which succeeds in reducing the theory of strict cyclicity in phonology to independently given principles of grammar.

There are also some empirical problems with the theory. For one thing, cyclic rules are known which do not show the expected "strict cyclic" properties, in that they must apply to non-derived environments on the first cycle. We have encountered one such example in the Spanish syllabification rule (see 30). A notorious case is stress in English. Although a metrical treatment eliminates the need for cyclic assignment of sentence stress, it remains true that lexical stress must be assigned cyclically (Kiparsky 1979, Hayes 1981). And it is evidently assigned by exactly the same rules to non-derived stems as to derived stems. That is, the antepenult stress in *Menómini* is an instance of the same regularity as the antepenult stress in *synónym+y*. The formulation of (47) incorrectly entails that this cannot be the case.

A second question that the Strict Cycle Condition leaves unanswered harks back to the original "abstractness" issue. One of the basic observations that the Alternation Condition set out to explain was the tendency for non-derived outputs of obligatory neutralization rules to get lexicalized. Mascaró suggested that this class of rules is necessarily cyclic, but this is evidently untenable for the reasons already discussed in connection with the Revised Alternation Condition. The weaker formulation that obligatory neutralization rules are cyclic in the so-called "unmarked case" is at the very least ad hoc. And finally, if nothing at all is said beyond (47), the theory is simply left with two classes of rules, cyclic and noncyclic, and does not have the leverage required to account for the observed drift into the lexicon. The problem, then, is to develop a theory capable of explaining why, in case after case, obligatory absolute neutralization rules bequeathed to a language by sound changes that merge segments are reanalyzed out of it, and non-derived outputs of obligatory contextual neutralization rules are lexicalized, so that the actual phonologies of languages are practically always more concrete than history would make one expect.

A third question concerns the relation between the morpheme structure of a language and its cyclic rules. Typically, the output of the cyclic rules (again excluding metrical rules) has the same form as do underlying representations, both as regards the segment inventory and the possible combinations of segments. In other words, cyclic phonology is structure-preserving. The theory as it now stands does not explain why it should be

Lexical Phonology 159

so. Moreover, it saddles grammar with a characteristic redundancy, where phonological rules recapitulate the unmarked structure of morphemes. For example, the theory cannot relate the existence of the (cyclic) Trisyllabic Shortening rule (32) to the fact that non-derived words that violate it, such as (35), are nevertheless much rarer than non-derived words that conform to it, such as (36). In the theory of Chomsky and Halle (1968) the former are outright exceptions, in cyclic phonology they are entirely on a par with the latter and fully as regular; the truth would rather seem to be that morpheme-internal $\bar{V}CVCV$ sequences are "marked" relative to $\breve{V}CVCV$ within English phonology.

In sum, the class of cyclic rules seems to be distinguished from the class of postcyclic rules by a syndrome of properties which define a special mode of rule application, and which have no apparent intrinsic connection either with each other or with rule ordering. Why are cyclic rules structure-preserving? Why do cyclic rules characterize unmarked morpheme structure? Why do obligatory neutralization rules tend to become cyclic? Why do *metrical* cyclic rules seem to work differently? And more generally, why do these properties go together and what do they have to do with cyclicity?

The answers to these questions are actually already at hand. The Strict Cycle Condition does not have to be stipulated in the theory. A version of it is deducible from the Elsewhere Condition. The version so deduced, unlike the original version, directly predicts the apparently deviant behavior of cyclic metrical rules as well as the relationship we noted between cyclic phonology and the lexicon.

The basic point is that the blocking of cyclic rules in nonderived environments effected by the Strict Cycle Conditions follows from the Elsewhere Condition under the assumption, already justified on morphological grounds above, that every lexical entry constitutes an identity rule whose structural description is the same as its structural change. For example, we shall then have the two rules

(60)   a. /nītVngǣl/
       b. Trisyllabic Shortening (32)

The structural description of (60a) properly includes (60b), i.e. (60a) defines a subset of the contexts of (60b). The outputs of (60a) and (60b) are distinct, with (60a) specifying a long vowel in a position where (60b) specifies a short vowel. So the Elsewhere Condition is applicable and says that only rule (60a) is applied to the string /nītVngǣl/, which gives us the desired result that the word is not subject to the Trisyllabic Shortening rule. The rule is, however, free to apply to derived inputs such as [[sǣn]$_A$-iti]$_N$, because they do not constitute lexical entries.

160 *Paul Kiparsky*

(61)   [[sǣn]$_A$iti]$_N$ [nĭtVngǣl]$_N$
   I   [—]   (blocked by E.C.)
   II   [[sæ̬n]$_A$iti]$_N$
        sanity   *nightingale*

We not only derive the special case of blocking on the first cycle, but the full effect of the Strict Cycle Condition, which blocks rules on any cycle *n* from applying to inputs which are not derived (in the sense of (47b) on cycle *n*. This is by virtue of the principle, which we also saw to be necessary on independent morphological grounds above, that the output of every layer of derivation, such as [sæ̆niti], is itself a lexical entry, and thereby an identity rule which enters into a disjunctive relation with other lexical rules such as Trisyllabic Shortening by the Elsewhere Condition in exactly the same way as underived lexical entries do.

Finally, the reason postlexical rules such as Prevocalic Lengthening are free to apply to nonderived inputs is that being in a different component they cannot be linked disjunctively to a rule in the lexicon by the Elsewhere Condition.

The version of strict cyclicity that we arrive at in this way however differs crucially from (47) in that it blocks conjunctive application only when the outputs are *distinct*. That has been the case in the examples considered so far, but it is not the case in a large class of other cases, most obviously in rules that assign metrical structure to strings not already bearing metrical structure. Consider the lexical entry *parent* and the rule of English word stress that assigns it the stress pattern ∧̅SW̅. We have two rules whose respective outputs when applied to the string *parent* are

$$\overset{F}{\underset{S\ W}{\wedge}}$$

parent itself (the identity rule) and *parent* (the stress rule). These outputs are not distinct in that they do not have contradictory feature specifications or contradictory metrical structure. Rather, one has a specified metrical structure where the other is unspecified as to metrical structure. The outputs not being distinct, clause (ii) of the Elsewhere Condition is not met, and both rules accordingly apply, which means that stress is free to apply on the first cycle. In the same way, syllable structure in Spanish is assigned on the first cycle by rules with the effect of (62b) (among others) because condition (ii) of (10) is not met and (62a,b) therefore apply conjunctively.

(62)   a. desdeñ
       b. VC → V̂C

Lexical Phonology

We also correctly predict that cyclically derived phonological properties can trigger subsequent rules on the same cycle. Thereby even feature-changing rules can apply on the first cycle if they are fed by cyclic rules. This is illustrated in the Spanish example we cited from Harris, where the cyclically assigned syllable-final status of *n* causes depalatalization:

(63) a. desdeñ
     b. Vñ → Vn

Here (10) is not met and the rules therefore apply conjunctively. Hence we have the correct derivation *desdeñ* (62a = 63a) → *désdeñ* (62b) → *désdéñ* (63b), all in the first cycle.

A further corollary is that rules which assign metrical structure *will* be blocked on the first cycle to the extent that the input is metrically structured already in the lexicon. In Spanish, cases like *huir* (two syllables), *oiremos* (four) can be simply marked so in the lexicon (as suggested by Harris) and the syllabification rules will not apply.

These assumptions afford a series of major simplifications in Hayes' theory of English word stress. Hayes introduces two basic rules of stress assignment (foot formation): the English Stress Rule (ESR) and Strong Retraction Rule (SRR). The ESR applies at the right edge of the word, assigning maximally binary feet labeled S W, where W may not be a heavy syllable (not counting "extrametrical" material). The SRR applies iteratively from right to left, also assigning maximally binary feet labeled S W, but without restrictions as to syllable weight. As proposed by Selkirk (1980), stress is not a feature but the property of being the strong or only syllable of a foot, Thus, we have such derivations as (64), where parentheses denote extrametricality:

(64)

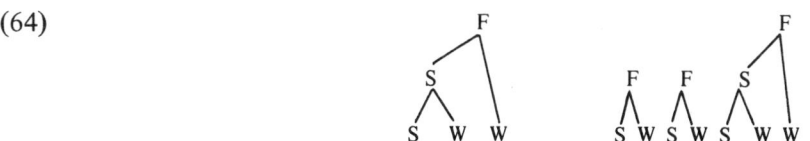

a. hamamelidanthemum → (ESR) hamamelidanthe (mum) → (SRR) hamamelidanthemum

b. Tīconderōga → Tīconderō (ga) → Tīconderōga

The resulting feet are then joined into a word tree, whose right branches are labeled strong unless they consist of single syllables.

Two special sets of assumptions are required in order for the analysis to work out right. The first is that the stress rules, though necessarily cyclic, do *not* observe the principle of strict cyclicity. This is forced by the need to apply stress rules on the first cycle, i.e. in non-derived environments. The second is that the grammar may specify in what manner stress rules apply, specifically whether they may override existing foot structure in the string, or whether they only assign metrical structure to syllables which are not yet organized into feet. The two English rules differ on this score. The ESR belongs to the first type in that it applies regardless of whether the string is already provided with a metrical organization or not. The SRR, on the other hand, strictly respects existing metrical structure. The contrast can be seen in the following examples. Parentheses show extrametricality.

(65) a. parent → (ESR) par(ent) → parent + al → (ESR) parent(+al)

b. illustrāte → (ESR) illustrāte → (SRR) illustrāte (↛*illustrāte)

c. standard → (ESR) stan(dard) → standard +īze → (ESR, word tree)

standard +īze (↛ (SRR) * staṅdardīze) → standardīze + ation

→ (ESR, word tree) standardīze + ātion (↛ (SRR) * standardīze + ātion)

Example (65a) shows how the ESR wipes out the metrical structure assigned by itself on a previous cycle. Example (65b) shows how the SRR respects the metrical structure assigned by the ESR previously on the same cycle. If the SRR were allowed to wipe out the metrical structure assigned by the ESR, we would derive the wrong form *illústràte, and more generally, all evidence that the ESR even existed in the grammar would disappear. Example (65c) shows how, in addition, the SRR respects the metrical structure assigned by the ESR and by itself on a previous cycle. This is why we do not derive the wrong final form as indicated there (*standàrdizátion).[12]

In the present theory, nothing at all need be stipulated in the grammar of English about the mode of application of any of the stress rules. It follows outright from the Elsewhere Condition. In the first place, the ESR and the SRR must be disjunctively ordered. Secondly, being cyclic (i.e. lexical) rules they are blocked from applying in a structure-changing function in non-derived environments. This jointly defines the correct conditions for their operation and interaction. The details are as follows.

The SRR is applicable to any string of syllables and the ESR is applicable to right edges of constituents, i.e. to domains bounded by]. Thus the structural description of the ESR properly contains the structural description of the SRR. By virtue of the Elsewhere Condition, the rules must apply disjunctively, with ESR, as the special rule, taking precedence over the SRR where they conflict. This explains their interaction in (65b). On the rightmost domain, ESR assigns a unary foot, taking precedence over the SRR which would assign a binary foot over the last two syllables to give penult stress. Proceeding leftwards, we come to the string *illu-*. The ESR is not applicable since the string is not at the right edge of a constituent, and so the SRR puts a binary foot on it, stressing the initial syllable. The usual word tree rule labels the left foot strong to complete the derivation.

As for the application of the ESR and the SRR to strings with pre-existing foot structure, the theory requires that *both* rules should be subject to the principles that govern the application of cyclic rules. Cyclic rules are subject to "strict cyclicity", which by our earlier argument again reduces to the Elsewhere Condition. Its effect is to block cyclic rules from applying in a structure-changing function in non-derived environments. We shall now take up the various possible cases for both rules in turn and show that everything works as predicted.

There are three kinds of cases to consider:

1. Non-structure-changing applications. As predicted, both rules apply: see e.g. (65b).

2. Structure-changing applications in non-derived environments. Both rules should be blocked.

164 *Paul Kiparsky*

As far as the SRR is concerned, it is just this blocking which lies behind its failure to erase metrical structure assigned (in whatever way) on earlier cycles. In the derivation of *standardization* (see 65c), the application of the ESR to *-ation* on the third cycle yields the structure (66):

(66)   [[standardīze]_V ātion]_N

By virtue of our assumption that the output of every cycle is entered

into the lexicon, the string to the left of *-ation*, [standardīze]_V, constitutes a (derived) lexical entry which is fully organized into feet. The Elsewhere Condition prohibits the SRR from overriding the foot structure of this lexical entry.

Now we are committed to the prediction that the ESR too behaves in exactly the same way. Where does the ESR encounter pre-existing foot structure? The case occurs in words like *Attila, Kentucky, Mississippi*, which have a stress on a syllable where it cannot be assigned by the standard stress rules. They are very reasonably treated as being represented prior to the application of the stress rules with a foot on that syllable:

(67)   Attila   Mississippi

What prevents the ESR from applying to such nouns, eliminating the stress on the second syllable to give the incorrect forms (68)?

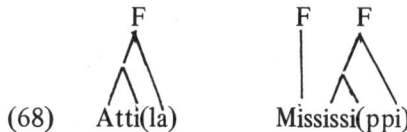
(68)   Atti(la)   Mississi(ppi)

Strict cyclicity, i.e. the Elsewhere Condition. So we must assume that structure-changing applications in non-derived environments are prohibited for the ESR as well as for the SRR. It is thus not true, even in terms of Hayes' own analysis, that the ESR is simply free to erase whatever metrical structure lies in its way. Like the SRR it submits rigorously to the conditions that govern the application of cyclic (lexical) rules.

Lexical Phonology

3. Structure-changing applications in derived environments. Both rules should apply. First consider the ESR. In examples like *parental* (65a) the ESR overrides existing metrical structure because it can apply in a derived environment. That is, the string under consideration in the second cycle (marked off in (69)) is not a substring of a lexical entry which bears a contradictory foot structure:

(69) [[parent]$_N$ (al)]$_A$
            └─────────┘
                 ESR

(with foot structure S W over *parent*)

The Elsewhere Condition is inapplicable, and the ESR is free to form a foot at the right edge of the word, giving *paréntal*.

Again we expect to find corresponding cases with the SRR. The reason they were not obvious before is that in most cases, the interior of a word will have been metrically organized in full at any cycle but the first. So observationally the generalization that the SRR never reorganizes existing foot structure approximates the truth fairly closely. But it is only by accident that it seems so nearly true. It breaks down in the crucial cases where more material than can be accomodated by the ESR is introduced on a given cycle. There the SRR completes the foot assignment on the extra syllables to the left and may combine it with material contained in existing foot structure. Consider *falsify, solidify* derived from *false, solid*. Coming out of the first cycle we have (70):

(70) [[fals]$_N$ ifȳ]$_V$ [[solid]$_A$ ifȳ]$_V$

The ESR now assigns a foot to -*fȳ*. If the SRR were now to form a foot solely on that part of the string which does not already belong to a foot, namely the -*i*- which precedes -*fȳ*, the final outcome would be the wrong forms **fàlsífy, *sòlidífy*. Rather, the SR must form a foot on *falsi-, -lidi-*, eventually yielding *fálsify, solídify*. This shows that the SRR too is free to apply to material already contained within feet, provided it does so in a derived environment.

In sum, there is no essential difference in functioning between the ESR and the SRR. Being cyclic, both are restricted by strict cyclicity, and being in an inclusion relationship they apply disjunctively. Both properties are guaranteed by the Elsewhere Condition and nothing need be stipulated about their mode of application in the grammar of English. In addition, two sets of cases which escape even the fine-meshed net of Hayes' analysis are now hauled in along with the rest: the failure of the ESR to apply in non-derived environments, as in *Attíla* (see 67) and the applicability of the SRR in derived environments, as in *solídify* (see 70).

As a result, a further substantial simplification of the stress rules becomes possible. We are free to collapse the ESR and SRR into a single rule in which the ESR appears as a mere condition on the constituent-final environment:

(71) Assign maximally binary S W feet from right to left, where W may not branch in env. ___].

Finally, under our theory the decision to enter idiosyncratic metrical structure in the lexicon assumes rather more significance than before. At least the following empirical consequences are at stake. First, it predicts, surely correctly, that arbitrary exceptions to stress rules add relatively less complexity to the grammar in basic stems than in derived stems. Furthermore, it follows that such lexical exceptions should be typical of languages with *cyclic* stress assignment, such as English. Postcyclic stress rules, such as the initial stress rule of Finnish, cannot be contravened simply by inherent lexical specification of stress; exceptions to them are costlier in that the lexical items in addition must be marked as not undergoing the stress rules. In languages where word stress is assigned postcyclically it should therefore be characteristically more regular. And this is obviously the case.

This issue arose in an interesting way in the original discussion of the SSC by Mascaró (1976). Mascaró was forced by his version of cyclic phonology to set up phonemic stress in Catalan stems. Yet it is clear that there is an unmarked stress pattern much as in Spanish. This can now be done justice to by assigning it by a cyclic stress rule, with underlying stress restricted to exceptional antepenult or final stress (e.g. *défisit* 'deficit', *papá* 'father'). Support for this alternative is provided by a cyclic segmental rule that depends upon stress. In the environment $\acute{V}$___ l, there is devoicing of *b* (and sporadically of other stops also), e.g. *diáplə* 'devil' (cf. *diabólik* 'devilish'). The devoicing rule must apply even if the vowel subsequently loses its stress to a following suffix, e.g. *diaplǝria*. Hence it is cyclic. But the environment ... $\acute{V}$bl ... is always contained within the *first* cycle. Now if stress is underlying, the environment of devoicing will be non-derived and the rule should not be able to apply (even on our theory, since it is feature-changing). But if stress applies on the first cycle, then it can feed devoicing on the first cycle and there is no difficulty with these derivations.

Lexical Phonology

A further important point is that *vacuous* application creates derived environments in Mascaró's theory but not in ours. Mascaró indeed found an interesting case in his Catalan material which seemed to work crucially as his version predicts, but it yields entirely to the reanalysis just indicated.

Moving now to the problems involving lexical representations, we can resolve them in essentially the same way. We shall simply take the "morpheme structure rules" of a language to be so many rules of its lexical phonology. Then lexical rules, rather than being simply inapplicable on the first cycle, will apply on the first cycle as redundancy rules to fill in lexically unspecified feature specifications, in addition, of course, to applying as before in derived environments in a feature-changing function. For example, the distinction between *nightingale* and *sycamore* is that the first vowel is specified as long in the former – blocking Trisyllabic Shortening as shown above – and *unspecified* for length rather than specified as [-long], in the latter. Then the Elsewhere Condition will not block Trisyllabic Shortening from applying to *sycamore* as its clause (ii) is not met, so that the rule will specify the vowel as [-long], as desired.

A priori the elimination of a special category of "morpheme structure rules" is welcome because the status of these putative rules has almost from the beginning of generative phonology been beset with problems. Kenstowicz and Kisseberth (1977) identify four of them:

1. Condition or rule: are MSRs to be construed as rules that fill in predictable feature specifications left blank in the matrices entered in the lexicon, or are they to be construed as static well-formedness conditions that check the acceptability of fully specified lexical entries?

2. The duplication problem: why are regularities expressed by morpheme structure rules often recapitulated by phonological rules proper, applying to derived forms?

3. The domain problem: on what sorts of entities are lexical constraints defined – morphemes, stems, or finished words?

4. The level problem: to what stage of derivation are lexical constraints applicable – underlying representations, the phonetic output, or some intermediate level?

In the approach proposed here, the answers to these questions must run as follows:

1. Predictable feature specifications are left unspecified in lexical entries and are filled in by the system of universal and language-particular rules of lexical phonology.

2. There is no duplication problem because the rules that apply to non-derived forms in a blank-filling function, governing the structure of primitive lexical entries, are the same lexical rules that apply after the first cycle in a feature-changing function, governing the structure of derived lexical forms.

3. The domains on which lexical constraints are defined are *lexical categories*, i.e. the cyclic constituents N, A, V. Lexical constraints are therefore only indirectly pertinent to morphemes (roots, affixes etc.).

4. Lexical constraints are applicable in lexical (cyclic) phonology as determined by the ordering of the relevant rules. Thus they are not necessarily true either of underlying representations or of the phonetic output. In particular, the application of postlexical rules may totally obscure the canonical structure of lexical items.

From our point of view, "duplication" between morpheme structure rules and rules of lexical phonology, far from being a problem, is actually the predicted normal case. We do not allow rules whose domain is defined as the morpheme; minimally they must belong to level 1 and apply also to such derived forms as meet their structural description. This does not mean that all rules will actually exhibit duplication. It can very well happen that the environment of a level 1 rule occurs only in underived lexical items or only in forms derived at level 1; what is predicted is that *if* it occurs in both then the rule will indeed apply to both.

It is of course still necessary to make some distinction between those lexical rules which govern the structure of underived lexical items merely in the unmarked case and those which govern it absolutely. That is, when are lexical rules contradicted by inherent feature specifications in lexical items and when are they not? Even in its present skeletal form our theory makes an interesting prediction on this score. Namely, lexical rules which apply in non-derived environments should all be potentially "cancelable" on the first cycle, while lexical rules which apply in derived environments on the first cycle should not be cancelable. The only way a lexical rule can come to be applicable on the first cycle in a derived environment is for it to be fed there by a previously applying lexical rule (which by what we have said must either have applied in a non-feature-changing way or itself have been fed by an earlier rule). The obvious examples are segmental rules that apply within metrical domains such as stress feet or syllables themselves assigned by earlier lexical rules. We had such a case in the Spanish depalatalization rule (63b), which applies within a syllable structure created earlier on the same cycle. So it follows that we cannot keep a syllable-final ñ in Spanish simply by marking it as /ñ/ in the lexicon. And in fact, it appears that this is never necessary.

If we are to allow unspecified feature values in the lexicon, then it becomes incumbent upon us to answer the well-known objections of Stanley (1967) against that procedure. We shall do this by stipulating that no feature can appear marked both + and - in the same environment in the lexicon.

For our starting point we revert to the natural assumption of early generative phonology that phonological features are unspecified in under-

Lexical Phonology

lying representations if their value can be assigned by a rule. The theory of grammar will provide a set of universal redundancy rules functionally analogous to the markedness principles of Chomsky and Halle (1968), but formally identical to ordinary phonological rules. In particular, assume that for every feature F there is minimally a rule

(72)   [   ] → [α F]

where α (+ or -) is the "unmarked" value. In addition other rules may be applicable in specific syntagmatic or paradigmatic contexts. For example, for voicing we may have the rules

(73)   a. [   ] → [+ voiced]
       b. [+obstr] → [- voiced]

putting the unmarked value as [- voiced] for obstruents and [+ voiced] elsewhere. We now say that voiceless obstruents and voiced sonorants are represented as [0 voiced], that is, unspecified for voicing, and that their respective specifications for voicing are filled in by the application of rule (73). This much is quite in the spirit of traditional markedness theory.

Suppose further that the lexical phonological rules of a language apply to lexical entries together with universal rules such as (73), as part of the system of lexical redundancy rules. For example, the English lexical rule of regressive voicing assimilation applies on the first cycle as a lexical redundancy rule that assigns [α voiced] as the normal value to obstruents in the context   [α voiced]. This again means that obstruents in that context are [0 voiced] in lexical entries of English.

We thus obtain a hierarchy of successively more specific rules, all but the first rule (73a) applying in domains included in more general rules and superseding them in the shared domain. The portion of the hierarchy that we have seen so far is shown together in (74):

(74)   (a) [   ] → [+ voiced]
       (b) [+ obstr] → [- voiced]
       (c) $\begin{bmatrix} + \text{obstr} \\ \alpha \text{ voiced} \end{bmatrix}$ → [α voiced] /___ $\begin{bmatrix} + \text{obstr} \\ \alpha \text{ voiced} \end{bmatrix}$

The disjunctive ordering among such sets of rules comes by the Elsewhere Condition.

Clearly, lexical redundancy rules must not be allowed to change lexically specified features. For example, rule (74b) only "fills blanks", and does not apply to segments inherently specified as [+ voiced], such as /z/.

This does not have to be specially stipulated in the theory, but falls out directly from (10) if we construe each lexical item L as a rule as proposed above. Suppose we have the English words *sip* and *zip*. We then have the rules (75 a-c), where (a) and (b) are disjunctive by (10) but (a) and (c) are not disjunctive because their outputs are not distinct (condition (ii) of (10) is not met).

(75) a. $[+\text{obstr}] \rightarrow [-\text{voiced}]$

b. $\begin{bmatrix} +\text{obstr} \\ +\text{cor} \\ \text{etc.} \\ +\text{voiced} \end{bmatrix}$ *ip* (disjunctive with (a))

c. $\begin{bmatrix} +\text{obstr} \\ +\text{cor} \\ \text{etc.} \\ 0\text{ voiced} \end{bmatrix}$ *ip* (conjunctive with (a))

In exactly the same way, the /b/ of *absent*, lexically specified as [- voiced], does not undergo the voicing assimilation (74c), while the unspecified /b/ of *abdomen* does. Thus the lexical entries themselves are the end points of the above-mentioned hierarchies of successively more specific rules:

(76)
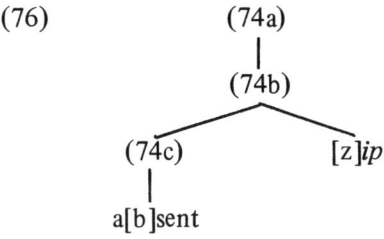

It follows that in every context C, only two lexical specifications will be possible for any feature F, viz. [0F] and [αF], where [αF] is the unpredictable value. Therefore we escape Stanley's (1967) objection that allowing unspecified features in the lexicon amounts in introducing a three-valued feature system.

Not every context allows both possible feature specifications. If only one specification of F occurs in some context C', i.e. if some branch of the hierarchy for F does not terminate in any lexical items but in the rule for C' itself, then we shall say that F is *non-distinctive* in C'. Its lexical specification in C' is then necessarily [0F].

We still have an IOU to pay off to the abstractness issue. Although we have been able to derive the "cyclic syndrome", including the properties associated with the Strict Cycle Condition, from independently motivated principles governing the lexicon, we have as yet no explanation for why rules should become lexical in the first place. After all, sound changes enter a language as postlexical rules and there is no a priori reason why they should in time tend to graduate to lexical status, with concomitant reanalysis of their synchronically nonderived outputs. More particularly, as was made explicit in several formulations of the Alternation Condition and the Strict Cycle Condition, obligatory neutralization rules have a special affinity for the cycle/lexicon which still needs to be accounted for.

To begin with this last question, the answer is evidently that obligatory neutralization rules are precisely those rules whose outputs are potentially subject to lexicalization without complicating the grammar. Why neutralization rules? They are rules which merge one set of representations with another:

(77)

where possibly C = A or B. So in this case C derived from A has by definition another possible source in the lexicon, namely B or whatever is the source of B. The lexicalization of the output of a non-neutralization rule (say, aspiration in English) requires adding some redundant category to underlying representations, which other things being equal will be rejected on grounds of simplicity. And why just *obligatory* neutralization rules? If the output of an *optional* rule is lexicalized then its relationship to the other variant cannot be accounted for by the rule. This will again be rejected on grounds of simplicity. Imagine, for example, that the Trisyllabic Shortening rule in English was postlexical and optional. Then obviously the shortened variant of *nightingale* would not be lexicalized because it could not then be related to the variant with a long vowel. So if a postlexical rule is non-neutralizing or optional, simplicity considerations will generally require that it continue to apply to non-derived forms, and the Elsewhere Condition then entails that it remain in the postlexical component.

This does *not* mean that there could not be non-neutralizing rules or optional rules in the cyclic phonology. Such cases have certainly been documented in the literature. All that is predicted is that postlexical rules can shift into the lexicon without either overt changes in their non-derived inputs or loss of generality only if they are obligatory non-neutralization rules.

Assuming this account of why it is obligatory non-neutralization rules that may become lexical, we now come to the question why the rules that may become lexical so readily do so. To postulate a principle that the "unmarked" status of a rule is lexical is no more than a restatement of the observation that we wish to explain. Assume instead that the language learner is guided by a principle that selects the simplest available derivation, the criterion of derivational simplicity being length. By "available" I mean "allowed by the evaluation measure." This means that derivational simplicity is strictly subordinated to grammatical simplicity, and only comes into play when the evaluation measure is indeterminate as between alternative grammars. The principle that the shortest derivations are preferred is related to Zwicky's (1970) "No Free Ride" Principle and more distantly to Postal's Naturalness Condition, which is formulated as a condition of adequacy on phonological theories, rather than as a principle for selecting between alternative descriptions within a theory. The idea was actually implicit in some generative treatments of analogical leveling, e.g. the discussion of the loss of final devoicing in Swiss dialects in Kiparsky (1968). We shall call it the Derivational Simplicity Criterion (DSC) and formulate it as follows:

(78) *Derivational Simplicity Criterion* (DSC)
Among alternative maximally simple grammars select that which has the shortest derivations.

The favored status of lexical phonological rules is derivable from the DSC because putting a rule into the lexical phonology always enables non-derived forms to be derived from the shallowest source, in satisfaction of (78). As a schematic example, consider how Trisyllabic Shortening might have become a lexical rule. Suppose that at a certain period there arose surface exceptions to it such as *nightingale*, from degenerate compounds, vowel lengthening, and other sources. Faced with data such as *nightingale* two analyses are available to the learner. The first possibility is to take the word "at face value" set up /nītVngæ l/, with an underlying long vowel. The second, assuming for the sake of the example that an /x/ deleted with compensatory lengthening can still be motivated for this stage of English, is the more abstract /nixtVngæ l/. These two alternatives commit the learner to different assumptions about the phonological rules as well. Underlying /nītVngæ l/ entails that Trisyllabic Shortening is lexical. Underlying /nixtVngæ l/ entails that the rule deleting /x/ is postlexical. But the DSC fixes the underlying form as /nītVngæ l/, in turn forcing Trisyllabic Shortening into the lexical phonology. Such restructuring erodes the support for the /x/-deletion rule and eventually brings about its demise.

Lexical Phonology

To summarize, we have arrived at the conclusion that what is right about the Strict Cycle Condition is derivable from the Elsewhere Condition on the assumption that word phonology is integrated with the morphology in the lexicon. The resulting theory can be considered an advance from both the conceptual and the empirical point of view. Conceptually, it achieves a greater explanatory depth in that various principles that had to be stipulated previously are now derived from the interaction of more elementary principles. Empirically, it marks a step towards overcoming the tension between two goals, each legitimate in themselves but so far curiously difficult to reconcile with each other in generative phonology: maximal generality and elegance of descriptions on the one hand, and maximal realism, naturalness etc. on the other. It no longer seems necessary to make compromises in one in order to achieve the other.

The notable feature of this theory when compared to earlier approaches to the same problems in generative phonology, as well as to current trends in syntax, is that the main explanatory burden is carried by simplicity and the structure of the grammar itself, as opposed to conditions on rules or representations. The only condition we required was the essentially trivial Elsewhere Condition, which may very well be reducible to a more general cognitive principle.

NOTES

1.   Marchand (1969, p. 228) accurately points out that "... a prefix is the determinant of a syntagma whereas a suffix is the determinatum." "A prefixal derivative joins the category the unprefixed word belongs to. In a suffixal derivative, however, the suffix is the grammatically and semantically dominant element. In combinations such as *father-hood, father-ly*, the word *father* merely determines what is essentially a '-hood' or '-ly' respectively." He further observes that the order of determinant and determinatum (modifier and head) is reversed in "combinations based on the underlying theme of appreciation": diminutives and hypocoristics (*booklet, daddy*), approximatives (*yellowish*), frequentatives (*crackle*).

2.   The formulation of (10) is generalized from that of Kiparsky (1973) in that it need specify only that the structural changes effected by the rules be incompatible (condition ii). The earlier version had to apply also to cases where the structural changes are identical. But, as pointed out by Howard (1975), the case where the changes are identical was only necessary for stress rules. For example, the two rules collapsed in the schema

$$V \rightarrow \acute{V} \quad / \quad \underline{\quad} \; C_0(V\,C_0)\,\#$$

must apply disjunctively so that a stress is assigned to the final syllable only if there is no penult (i.e. in monosyllables). However, if we adopt metrical phonology, the stress patterns ($\ldots \overset{F}{\overset{\frown}{S\ \ W}}\#$ and $\ldots \overset{F}{|}\#$) are distinct if we construe distinctness for metrical structure in the obvious way as incompatibility of labeling or bracketing. And in any case, the metrical version of the rule simply assigns a maximally binary foot to the right edge of a word, and so does not properly constitute a schema abbreviating two rules. We therefore need only specify distinctness of outputs as in (ii) of (10).

3. The model predicts that level 1 plurals should not only be inputs to compounding, but also to level 2 affixation. This possibility is to my knowledge not realized. We therefore require an ad hoc constraint that blocks it. Interestingly, this constraint does *not* apply to *inherent* plurals, cf. *to people, to dice, dicey, sudsy, woodsy*.

Another point is that nouns which denote things that are classified as coming in pairs, e.g. (*a pair of*) *trousers*, systematically deviate from the pattern of (12) in that they do not require plural endings in compounds:

trouser pockets	(trousers)
scissor tail	(scissors)
spectacle case	(spectacles)
pincer movement	(pincers)

They must therefore be considered as morphologically derived plurals, however this is to be done. This is independently required because the stems *trouser* etc. that we are forced to set up in the lexicon are indeed *not* bound to the plural morpheme, for they show up also in derivatives like *trousered, bespectacled, to scissor*.

4. These examples were called to my attention by Nigel Fabb.

5. For discussion of zero derivation see Marchand (1969), Rardin (1975), Allen (1978, 271 ff), Clark and Clark (1979), as well as the criticism by Lieber (1980, Ch. 3) and Carlson and Roeper (1981).

6. *Breakin, showoff* etc. are not zero-derived from verbs but compounds formed at level 2, as we shall see below.

7. Actual words which appear to be N → V → N zero derivatives are *feed*$_N$ 'food for feeding livestock; (← *feed*$_V$ ← *food*$_N$) and perhaps *breed*$_N$ 'genetic type produced by breeding' (← *breed*$_V$ ← *brood*$_N$, if the latter is really the synchronic base). The first step of the derivation, N → V, would have to be at level 1 in order to feed V → N, which itself is at level 1. But this conclusion is forced independently on phonological grounds. One reason the verb has to be derived at level 1 is in order to undergo the vowel change (umlaut), which must be confined to level 1 because it is never triggered by any level 2 or level 3 affixes. Second, the verb has to be derived at level 1 because its past tense and participle forms have level 1 morphology (*fed, bred*, derived by the level 1 rule of shortening from /fēd + t/, /brēd + t/). Therefore these words do not refute the theory but on the contrary confirm it.

8. I owe this observation to Richard Oehrle.

9. See e.g. Kenstowicz and Kisseberth (1977, Ch. 1) for a review of the issue.

10. The pronunciations cited here and below follow the norm given by Webster's Dictionary (Third Edition). It should be noted that many speakers show some variation in quantity in initial open syllables, apparently involving both shortening of long vowels (*tonálity* → *tŏnálity*) and lengthening of short vowels (*prŏ́gress* → *prṓgress, pŏlíce* → *pōlíce, rĕsídual* → *rēsídual*).

11. Taken literally, this is what Linell (1979) must be advocating when he says that "phonotactic rules" and "morphophonological rules proper" are not "separate rules" but "aspects of certain morphological operations" (p. 131, 142). For example (p. 133) Trisyllabic Shortening and Vowel Shift are both considered by him as a part of the morphological operation by which the suffix -*ity* is added to adjectives

Lexical Phonology

(and, presumably, of the many other morphological operations that can cause the relevant alternations to come into play). Similarly, epenthesis of [I] between sibilants and devoicing of z after voiceless obstruents are considered by him part of plural suffixation (and, presumably, duplicates of these rules are part of genitive and 3. sg. suffixation as well as applying somehow to the reduced forms of *is* and *has*.

12. Apparent exceptions like *demócratize, oríginate* (vs. the regular *álphabetize, cápitalize, sýcophantize, rélativize, óxygenate, mýelinate* etc.) should be taken as instances of derivation not from nouns but from roots. The first cycle is then [democrat +ize]$_V$, [origin +ate]$_V$. Since there is no internal cycle, the ESR and SR apply to give the correct stress pattern.

Metrical or Autosegmental

William Leben
Stanford University

1. INTRODUCTION

In recent years a great deal of work has gone into the description of prosodic processes in language, and two advances that have come out of this work are the frameworks of autosegmental phonology and metrical phonology. These two frameworks provide ways of escaping the assumption, which used to be quite ordinary in phonological theory, that speech and phonological representation could both be represented linguistically as unilinear sequences of discrete symbols. This development seems particularly fortunate, since the approaches in question appear to express some of the prosodic properties of speech much more adequately and elegantly than previous ones. However, for a given prosodic phenomenon in language, it is not always easy to determine which sort of analysis — metrical or autosegmental — will be the most appropriate. Halle (1980) is the first attempt to deal with this problem, though almost totally in the area of vowel harmony. The present paper will attempt to deal with this question in a somewhat more general way.

Anderson (1980), surveying a wide variety of different vowel harmony systems, shows that there are real problems with the autosegmental treatment of vowel harmony in some languages. For example, he shows that sometimes the autosegmental system is ambiguous as to whether a particular harmonic element should move from the left or from the right. Anderson avoids such difficulties elegantly with an iterative segmental rule. Halle (1980) responds to this challenge in a different way. He proposes that vowel harmony systems occur basically in two types: dominant (or bidirectional) harmony and directional (or unidirectional) harmony. Halle suggests that bidirectional harmony, in which harmony can theoretically spread both to the right and to the left from a particular ("dominant") morpheme or segment should be analyzed autosegmentally, since it shares the property of bidirectional spreading with tone languages for which the autosegmental formalism has been shown to be extremely well motivated (Goldsmith 1976b). In this vein, Halle gives Akan advanced tongue root (ATR) harmony, which he adapts slightly from Clements (1976) as an example:

(1)   ɔ + fItI + I   ɔ + fItI + I   (which is interpreted as [o
              | \|/   + fiti + i] 'he/she pierced
           [+ATR]   [+ATR]   it')

(2)   ɔ + bIsa + I   ɔ + bIsa + I   (which is interpreted as [o
           \   \/ \/   + bisa + i] 'he/she asked
        [+ATR] [−ATR]   [+ATR] [−ATR]   him/her')

However, for cases where this bidirectional spreading is not evidenced, which as Anderson notes cause the autosegmental formalism to more or less get in the way rather than helping matters out, and for which Anderson adopts a segmental solution with iterative rules, Halle instead proposes that such vowel harmony systems are to be analyzed metrically rather than autosegmentally. A good example is Khalkha Mongolian, where rounding harmony is roughly described by Halle as follows:

(3)   /a/ is replaced by a rounded vowel if the preceding non-neutral vowel is a mid rounded vowel. /i/ is neutral.

For Halle, the domain of rounding harmony is the metrical foot, and we can define the metrical foot in the following way, using a two-step process that Halle attributes to J. R. Vergnaud.

(4)   a. Assign a left-dominant metrical foot from left to right such that no recessive node is a high rounded vowel.
       b. Delete branches whose terminal elements are high vowels.

By left-dominant we intend that the rounding value of the left-hand node determines the rounding value for all vowels in the same foot. Rule 4a produces 5a, which provides input to rule 4b. The result of applying 4b is 5b.

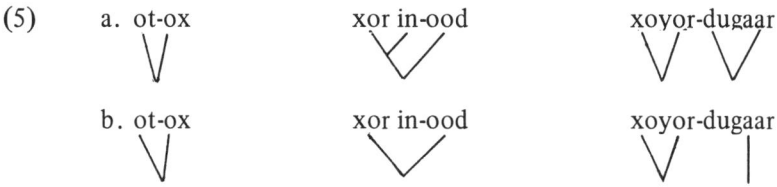

Thus, there is a metrical alternative to Anderson's iterative segmental formulations. Although the choice between these alternatives deserves more detailed treatment than it is receiving here, I believe that the metrical alternative is preferable, if only because the constraints it posits are needed independently, for the description of stress systems (cf. Liberman and Prince 1977, McCarthy 1979, Hayes 1981).

2. SIMILARITIES BETWEEN METRICAL AND AUTOSEGMENTAL STRUCTURES

One particularly attractive aspect of Halle's proposal is that it helps to solve the problem of excessive power resulting from the incorporation of two very powerful frameworks, autosegmental phonology and metrical phonology, into generative phonological theory. The way Halle curbs the power is, in effect, to place these two frameworks in complementary distribution, at least as far as vowel harmony is concerned. Harmonic systems that are bidirectional are to be described autosegmentally, while those that are unidirectional are to be described metrically.

Of course, there is another general approach we could take to the problem of excessive power posed by the fact that there are two competing frameworks, metrical and autosegmental, for dealing with the prosodic properties of speech. This is to show that these two frameworks are really not distinct but are instead one and the same. This is the argument that I will attempt to make in this section. First I will attempt to show that autosegmental and metrical structures have much in common. Then I will attempt to show that many of the differences that appear to distinguish the two frameworks are in fact based on questionable assumptions.

One of the most obvious similarities between metrical and autosegmental analyses is that they are constructed on the same sorts of projections of phonological units. In metrical analyses, we are accustomed to seeing metrical structures whose terminal elements are restricted so that rather than including every segment in a linear sequence, they are restricted to projections such as syllable rhymes, vowels, or consonants. For example, in the Khalkha Mongolian example above, the feet for vowel harmony were constructed on vowels, with high vowels later exempted. In some of the stress systems mentioned by McCarthy (1979) and by Hayes (1981), metrical structures are built on syllable rhymes. Though in autosegmental analyses the term "projection" is not frequently used, it is indeed assumed that autosegmental association lines are assigned only to certain units in the linear sequence of segments. For example, Clements and Ford (1979) treat the syllable as the "tone-bearing unit" in their autosegmental account, and Clements (1976) treats the vowel as the recipient of an autosegmental harmony feature.

Any difference between the specific *sorts* of projections that metrical and autosegmental analyses apply to can be attributed to the type of process involved rather than to the fact that it is specifically metrical or specifically autosegmental. That is, for example, tones attach naturally to syllable projections (or to syllable rhyme projections in languages in which the consonantal onset is irrelevant to tone) but not to consonant projections.

A second similarity between metrical and autosegmental structures is that they obey identical well-formedness constraints. Let us take as a model the standard convention for associating autosegmental tones:

(6)   Well-formedness condition (Goldsmith 1976).
   (1) All vowels are associated with at least one tone; all tones are associated with at least one vowel.
   (2) Association lines do not cross.

Parallel to condition (1) is the fact that metrical structures cannot skip over projections[1] or be assigned to non-projections. Violations result in ill-formed structures (7a,b). And, by the same token that autosegmental association lines may not cross, metrical structures may not overlap, in the sense illustrated by (7c).

(7)   a. *XXX   b. *XX X   c. *XXXX
         \|/   \|/   \|/
          V   V   V.

Another way in which metrical and autosegmental analyses resemble one another is that they contrast prominent vs. non-prominent elements. Metrical analyses may oppose strong to weak, while autosegmental analyses may oppose starred to non-starred elements. The starred element of a string might just as well be interpreted as the element which is in the metrically strongest position in that string. Note, too, that the strong/weak distinction is used similarly to the starred/unstarred distinction in that in certain structures they may have no role at all to play. This is true of Halle's (1980) metrical proposal for Russian obstruent voicing assimilation and of the analysis of Mende in Leben (1978), for example.

A fourth similarity is that operations on prosodic structures do not automatically affect the projections on which they are constructed. In autosegmental phonology, this is the stability phenomenon illustrated in Goldsmith (1976). For example, when we delete a syllable (say by a historical change), we do not automatically lose that syllable's tone. There are certain proposals, e.g. by Ingria (1980) and Stemberger (1980), that make the same argument for metrical structures involving length.

Another resemblance is the following. Although many metrical and autosegmental structures are produced by rules (e.g. the creation of metrical feet by a rule beginning at the right hand side of a word and creating a left-branching structure whose dominant node is a branching rhyme, as well as the mapping of autosegmental tones onto syllables from left to right on a one-to-one basis), sometimes these structures must instead be represented lexically for special words whose phonological (or whatever) characteristics are insufficient to receive the appropriate structures by the regular rule, even though these words behave as if the structures in question are present. A metrical example is in Hayes' (1981) account of Aklan, where certain phonetically non-heavy syllables count as feet even though the only single syllables that regularly count as feet in this language are heavy. A corresponding autosegmental example is Leben's (1978) analysis of Mende, where certain syllables are lexically assigned a High tone even though the majority of syllables in the language are underlyingly toneless and receive their tone by regular rules.

A final parallel between the two systems rests on an observation made by John Goldsmith at the Lake Arrowhead, Calif., Conference on the Formal Treatment of Nonsegmental Properties in Phonology. In autosegmental phonology, there are two types of spreading. One is maximal and proceeds by a general convention, the well-formedness condition, and the other is confined to a limited domain, e.g. only one or two syllables, and this is achieved by language-specific rule. The first is the sort of process that might automatically associate the tone of a given syllable with all of the toneless syllables to its right. The second is the sort that might move the point of transition from High to Low in a word from its first syllable to its second syllable. In metrical phonology, analogously, there are essentially two types of tree: unbounded and binary, whether we follow McCarthy's (1979) system or Hayes' (1981) system. The unbounded spreading of an autosegmental feature may just be another way of capturing the notion of maximality inherent to unbounded metrical trees.[2]

3. APPARENT DIFFERENCES BETWEEN THE TWO SYSTEMS

Metrical and autosegmental structures do appear somewhat different in certain respects, at least superficially, and at first this makes it difficult to imagine how they could be regarded as the same. Yet where metrical and autosegmental structures differ most, their properties are the least well motivated. Consider the most obvious difference, that autosegmental structures are much flatter, from a geometrical point of view, than the binary branching hierarchical trees of metrical phonology:

(8)   a. autosegmental tree   b. metrical tree

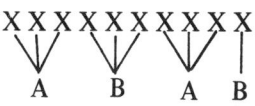

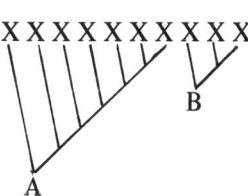

Of course, we could reconcile this difference trivially by imposing binary branching structure on autosegmental tree (8a), converting it into (9):

(9)

But I know of no evidence to suggest that this extra structure would be justified. A better tack to take, I believe, is to question the extra structure in metrical trees such as (8b). By and large, the binary branching nested structures of metrical phonology, and particularly of those structures internal to the metrical foot, have been assumed with no explicit justification. This is the case, for example, in Hayes (1981). Hayes presents a remarkably successful typology of stress systems, but it is interesting to observe that the assumption of foot-internal binary branching appears to play no role whatever.[3] For example, in (10) I give a schematic version of a stress rule employing a variety of devices that Hayes adopts, and the structure generated by this rule appears in (11a). Now suppose instead that we wished to generate the flatter structure in (11b).

(10) Assign maximal unbounded right-dominant feet right to left such that no recessive node contains [+A].

(11) a. binary branching tree   b. n–ary branching tree

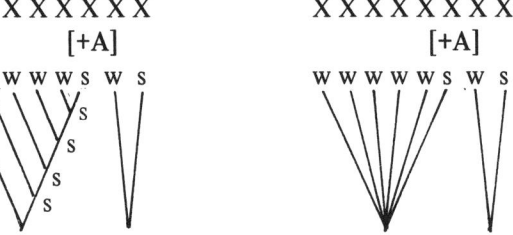

This would be accomplished by the very same rule, (10).[4] As far as the stress system schematized in this example is concerned, the more intricate structure in (11a) gives the same amount of information as the humbler structure (11b) — necessarily, since we can convert one into the other by the appropriate adjustment of Hayes' definitions. In particular, we do not need foot-internal structure in order to signal relationships between primary and secondary stresses, since on current assumptions the foot is defined as containing one and only one stressed syllable. For hierarchical

Metrical or Autosegmental

relationships among stresses, it does appear useful to assume binary branching hierarchical groupings of feet. The point here is that below the level of the foot, these groupings are unnecessary. Note, incidentally, that Hayes' system also tacitly distinguishes foot-internal structures from other metrical trees. This can be gathered from examining the following passage (Hayes 1981:47):

> We will say that any pair of sister nodes contains one dominant node and one recessive one. All metrical rules must specify whether in the structures they create it is right nodes or left nodes that are dominant. The single node of a non-branching tree is counted as dominant, ... Using this terminology, we can now state the principal constraint on rules of tree construction:
> (1) Recessive nodes may not branch.

Now if we attempted to apply these definitions to metrical structure above the foot, say to the expression *community center finance committee*, which has the metrical structure

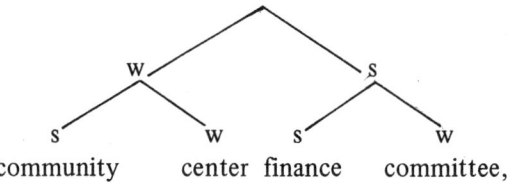

the node that would be called recessive by Hayes' definition —the *w* node dominating *community center*— in fact branches. I conclude from this that in Hayes' system, as in any other I can imagine, foot-internal constraints are different from foot-external ones.

Perhaps the most interesting and most explicit arguments in favor of the more intricate foot-internal structures are given by McCarthy (1981a). In dealing with the question of where the infix "fuckin" can be inserted into English words, McCarthy observes that in a word like *Tatamagouchee*, the infix can be inserted either after the second syllable, giving *Tata-fuckin-magouchee*, or after the third, giving *Tatama-fuckin-gouchee*. The latter possibility can be accounted for by claiming that "fuckin" can always go between two metrical feet. But in accounting for *Tata-fuckin-magouchee*, McCarthy suggests that this fact demonstrates that there is a "more intimate connection between the two most deeply embedded syllables of a foot than either has with the third syllable." In other words, the foot "tatama" has the structure in (12), and infixation can break off the least deeply embedded syllable but nothing else.

(12) tatama
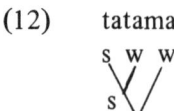

However, Meg Withgott (personal communication) has suggested that this phenomenon instead provides evidence of two different foot structures. The first is the one assumed for *Tatama-fuckin-gouchee*, with the first foot as it appears in (11). The second divides *Tatamagouchee* in a different way, namely, *Tata-magouchee*. Evidence for this division comes from English feet that are entire words and whose form matches *magouchee*, e.g. words like *aroma, proposal*, etc., which contain only one stressed syllable and hence only one foot. Furthermore, the fact that *tat-fuckin-amagouchee* is impossible would follow from the fact that *amagouchee* is not a possible foot. Indeed, English has no words that begin with two unstressed syllables, and this would follow from a constraint on foot division ruling out an initial sequence of unstressed syllables. Since this constraint must figure in any grammar of English, and since it does not apparently require internal branching within the foot, McCarthy's first argument is answered.

A second argument from McCarthy comes from data in (13), where [D] stands for the alveolar flap. (McCarthy also refers the reader to Stampe's 1972 dissertation for similar facts.)

(13) a. repe[t^h]i[t^h]ive
      b. repe[D]i[t^h]ive
      c. repe[D]i[D]ive
      d. *repe[t^h]i[D]ive

His explanation for these facts is again based on binary branching foot structure, where the foot in question takes the form:

(14) pe ti tive

McCarthy claims that "flapping may occur at the juncture of nonterminal and terminal nodes of a foot only if it applies also at the juncture of terminal nodes." In other words, flapping does not occur on a segment within a less deeply embedded portion of the foot if it hasn't also applied within a more deeply embedded portion of the same foot where it could have applied. But there is an adequate restatement of this observation that makes no reference to hierarchical organization within feet but that rather makes reference to the left-right order of segments and syllables within the foot. Namely, flapping does not apply farther away from its trigger (the stressed syllable) unless it has also applied closer to its trigger where it could have applied. This obviates the need for hierarchical organization, but there may be a preferable statement of the phenomenon illustrated in (13), one that is more general. Flapping appears more likely to take place the closer it is to a stressed syllable on the left. This seems true even in cases where only one segment is subject to flapping:

(15) a. $\left\{\begin{array}{l}\text{flee}\\\text{scurry}\end{array}\right\}$ to a hiding place

  b. They look $\left\{\begin{array}{l}\text{free}\\\text{angry}\\\text{ornery}\end{array}\right\}$ to me

Pronouncing *to* with an aspirated [t^h] rather than with a flap strikes me as overly formal after monosyllabic *flee* and *free*, but more natural after disyllables *scurry* and *angry* and even more so after trisyllabic, initial-stressed *ornery*. Obviously, a full-fledged study is needed to back up this intuition. But note that even if this intuition proves misguided, there is still the linear formulation given earlier that avoids the need for hierarchical foot-internal structure. Of course, it is not surprising that there is an adequate linear restatement of McCarthy's hierarchical formulation. Given the way that hierarchical foot structure is created (for example, see the quote from Hayes 1981 above), it seems by and large to merely encode the linear order of syllables within the foot.

Another apparent difference between autosegmental and metrical processes, following Halle (1980), is that autosegmental structures lend themselves well to nondirectional (or bidirectional) processes. Metrical structures, because they are created in a fashion that moves either from left to right or from right to left but not in both ways at once, lend themselves more readily to directional processes. But this does not argue that the two formalisms are or should be different. In fact, I believe that there is an argument here that the two formalisms must be viewed as one and the same. The reason is that certain prosodic phenomena exhibiting bidirectional tendencies — tone is the obvious example — still often possess directional characteristics as well. Clements and Ford (1979) discuss this point explicitly. They note (p. 207):

> that tones which are "set afloat" due to the deletion of vowels (or, as in the case of glide formation rules, to the loss of their syllabicity) reas-

sociate to the tone-bearing unit that *conditioned* the deletion (or loss of syllabicity). This observation shows that the reassociation of floating tones cannot be predicted without reference to the specific rules conditioning the deletion of the vowels to which they were previously associated in the derivation, ...

Moreover, Hyman (1978) observes that in Standard Igbo, [éwú] 'goat' and [àtó̩] 'three' combine to form [éwú ꜜ átó̩] 'three goats'. In effect, the low-toned initial syllable of the second word has gravitated to the left, causing this phonologically low-toned syllable to receive the high tone of the syllable to its right and causing these high-toned syllables to be downstepped. On the other hand, in Aboh Igbo, [éwú] 'goat' and [ètó̩] 'three' form [éwú é ꜜtó̩] 'three goats'. Here the low tone of the initial syllable of the second word has gravitated to the right, downstepping the second syllable of the second word and causing a high tone to move from the left onto the syllable [e] of [eto̩]. Here there is no apparent conditioning for the direction of tone movement. Instead, the directionality must be written into the tone rules.

Likewise, metrical processes, which as noted are typically directional, sometimes require separate statements because they fan out in opposite directions. An example is Hayes'(1981) analysis of Garawa, which has main stress on the initial syllable, secondary stress on the penult, and tertiary stress on alternate syllables preceding the penult. Schematically, the facts are as they appear in (16), where ˆ indicates a tertiary stress:

(16)   a. X́ X   b. X́ X X̀ X   c. X́ X X̂ X X̀ X

Hayes' analysis is this:

(17)   a. Assign a binary, quantity insensitive, left dominant foot at the left edge of a word.
   b. Group the remaining syllables of the word into similar feet, going from right to left.
   c. Form a left dominant word tree. Remove non-branching feet in weak position.

Hayes does not specify that the operation in (17a) must be left-to-right, but his system does seem to require this. For one thing, other rules (such as (17b) along with many others that Hayes posits) do require that their direction of operation be specified. Presumably, then, this is posited as a property which may vary from rule to rule and which must thus be specified individually for each rule. Now if the direction of (17a) were specified as right-to-left, then for this rule to operate correctly, we would

Metrical or Autosegmental

have to scan every string twice, the first time to find where the leftmost syllable is (and in the process passing over the second syllable), and the second time to make the second syllable the recessive node. The easiest way to avoid this procedure would be to specify that rule (17a) operates from left to right, a possibility which Hayes' system freely allows in other instances. Thus we have a metrical account of stress assignment that goes in two directions, left-to-right and right-to-left.

Thus the facts of tone and stress appear to demand a single formalism that is versatile enough to express both directional and non-directional processes. Now consider the following illustration, which schematizes a case that arises frequently with tone, nasal prosodies, and vowel harmony. A root with a given lexically specified prosodic pattern for tone, nasality, or vowel harmony is combined with a prefix and a suffix, both of them inherently unspecified for the prosodic feature in question. The affixes receive the relevant feature of tone, nasality, or vowel harmony by copying the closest relevant feature of the root, as illustrated schematically in (18a,b):

(18)

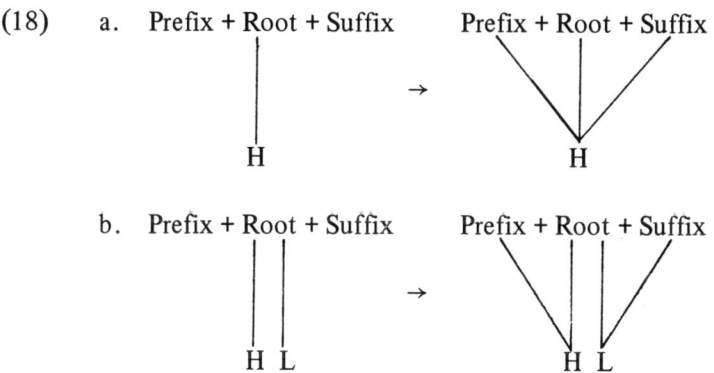

How can this rightward and leftward spreading process be expressed metrically? What we must do is create two trees in each case. The tree that expresses the prefix tone will make the right node dominant, and the tree that expresses the suffix tone will make the left node dominant. The rules might be expressed as:

(19) a. Prefix rule. Construct a right-dominant tree such that no recessive node contains a tone.
b. Suffix rule. Construct a left-dominant tree such that no recessive node contains a tone.

These generate structures similar to those in (18). A clearer picture of the output is in (20a,b). The reason for the condition on recessive nodes is to prevent the wrong tone from being taken as dominant when the root has more than two tones. For example, in (20c), the middle tone is wrongly taken as dominant, giving the suffix a High tone.

(20) a. Prefix + Root + Suffix   b. Prefix + Root + Suffix

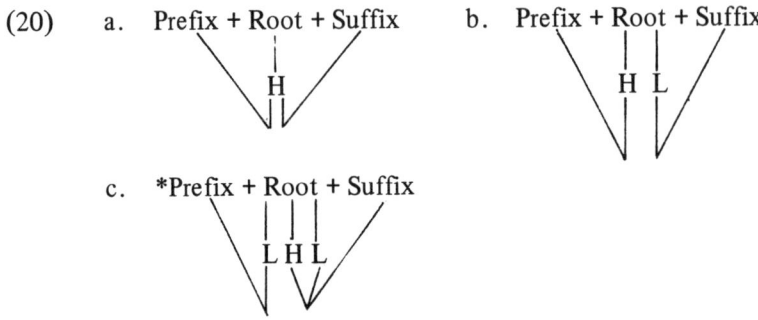

c. *Prefix + Root + Suffix
       L H L

This assumes that the feature of the dominant node percolates up the tree and thereby comes to be articulated on all of the projection material within the tree. (This same assumption was made in the Khalkha Mongolian example above.) The wrong output in (20c) is avoided by the condition that no recessive node contains a tone.

One may wonder about the ability of two metrical trees to terminate on one and the same node, such as the node H in (20a). But in fact there are precedents for this in metrical phonology. For example, in proposals that posit ambisyllabic consonants, such as Kahn (1976) and Leben (1980), the trees for two separate syllables share a common terminal node, the ambisyllabic consonant:

(21)   C V C V C
       w s w s w
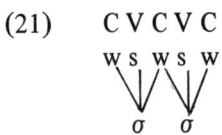
       σ   σ

Another potential case, suggested by David Gil on the basis of Hayes' (1981) treatment of Winnebago, is the following. Hayes uses the basic facts of stress placement in Winnebago as an argument in favor of extrametrical nodes. Stress placement goes as follows: Stress is final in disyllables, but on the third syllable in longer words. Secondary stress is placed on every other syllable to the right of main stress. By assuming the first syllable to be extrametrical, Hayes manages to give an elegant account of stress placement in Winnebago. He posits binary branching, right dominant feet, so that words of three and five syllables receive the foot structure in (22).

(22)   a. X X X   b. X X X X X
              w s   w s w s
               V   V   V

But, Gil has privately suggested, if we wished to disallow extrametrical syllables, and if we permit ternary feet, then we could generate the correct stress placements by instead assuming right-dominant ternary feet, but with the added provision that feet overlap with one another as much as possible. This last provision ensures that the last syllable of the first foot will simultaneously become the first syllable of the second foot in (23b):

(23)

The fact that the third syllable in (23b) is simultaneously a strong member of the first foot and a weak member of the second might seem problematic or self-contradictory, if we took the convention used by Prince (1980:522) (citing the work of Selkirk 1977, 1980) literally. According to the convention, within a foot the metrically strongest syllable is interpreted as stressed and all the weaker ones are stressless. This yields a contradictory reading for the third syllable in (23b). To avoid this, we may rephrase this convention to say that the stressed syllable of a foot is its strong member. All other uninterpreted syllables of a foot are interpreted as weak. By this convention, the third syllable of (23b) is interpreted as stressed.

The considerations just outlined make it possible to reinterpret autosegmental phonology as a special case of metrical phonology. Where Halle (1980) has proposed to solve the problem of excessive power of the two frameworks by limiting them in ways that guarantee total non-intersection, I have argued for solving the problem in just the opposite way, by making them intersect totally. From a theoretical point of view, either of these approaches would limit the range of choices equally well. What would be useful now is a comparison of the different analyses that these two theories permit.

NOTES

1.   It might be thought that Halle's (1980) proposal which involves first assigning a metrical structure and then deleting parts of it, as illustrated by (5) in the text, violates this condition, but it does not. This condition applies to projections and states that projections may not be skipped over by metrical structures. Halle's proposal involves, in effect, a two-step process in the definition of projections. The output of the second step, that is, what is left after erasure of certain lines, is the projection, and it is these projections that cannot be skipped over.

2.   For example, McCarthy (1979:86) stipulates that "the n-ary branching foot has the additional property of being maximal; it is as large as possible consistent with any conditions on its terminal nodes with respect to the form to which it applies."

Binary feet require an additional comment. Later I will propose that some metrical feet of finite length have more than two branches. This need not destroy the parallel with autosegmental spreading, however, since in some languages tones spread a finite number of syllables, but more than one, from their source. Hyman and Schuh (1974) mention Sukuma and Kanakuru as possible examples, under the name "displacement".

3. Special thanks to David Gil for first impressing this point on me.

4. In this case we would of course also have to adjust Hayes' definitions appropriately. For example, the stipulation that the recessive nodes of a metrical foot may not branch would be changed to specify that neither dominant nor recessive nodes branch within a foot.

Prosodic Templates, Morphemic Templates, and Morphemic Tiers *

John J. McCarthy
University of Texas at Austin

1. INTRODUCTION

In recent work (McCarthy 1979, 1981; Halle and Vergnaud 1980; Harris 1980; Marantz, to appear; Yip, to appear) a new model of morphology has been emerging, one in which nonlinear phonological representations play a central role. This model, which I will refer to as *prosodic*, was originally developed in an analysis of the complex system of nonconcatenative morphology found in Semitic languages, Classical Arabic in particular. It has since been extended to other, typologically and genetically quite different sorts of phenomena. In this paper, we will see still further empirical consequences of the adoption of this theory.

The fundamental characteristics of the prosodic model of morphology can be described quite briefly. The notational apparatus — association lines and tiers or simultaneous levels of representation — are taken from autosegmental phonology (Goldsmith 1976). But this formalism is given a quite different interpretation. The central notion is that information about the canonical pattern of segments in a form is represented on a different tier from information about the kinds of segments occurring in a form. The canonical pattern tier is called the prosodic template, and a particular type of prosodic template, composed of the units C and V, can be referred to as a CV-skeleton. Other sorts of prosodic templates may consist of higher-level, prosodic units, like syllables σ, metrical feet Φ, subunits of these, and perhaps combinations of units from different levels. The tiers with segmental material are then mapped onto the prosodic templates by the operation of autosegmental rules of association.

Morphemes play a central role in this model. In nonconcatenative morphological systems, morphemes may be segmentally discontinuous. Most importantly, the identity of morphemes or morpheme classes defines

---

* In examples cited in this article I have occasionally changed transcription symbols in accordance with more familiar usage. Any special features of the transcription are described in the footnotes.

I am indebted to Morris Halle, Alan Prince, and Mark Feinstein for adding to my understanding of the issues discussed here.

the different autosegmental tiers — that is, different morpheme classes are represented on different tiers. The prosodic template is itself in some cases a morpheme or string of morphemes, and the other various tiers will each contain the segmental properties of a particular morphological class. Each such level can be characterized as a morphemic tier. Furthermore, the recognition of morphemes as distinct formal units permits a further abstraction: the number and distribution (in effect, the canonical pattern) of morphemes in a form can be stipulated independently of morpheme identity. Thus, languages may also indicate *morphemic* templates composed of morpheme positions μ, with association of morphemes to these templates also accomplished by autosegmental principles.

These concepts can be illustrated by some examples from the Classical Arabic verb system, discussed more fully in McCarthy (1981). Consider the second derivational class of the verb, which has a transitivizing or ditransitivizing meaning. A representative member of this class, the stem *kattab* 'caused to write', is given in (1):

(1)   Vocalic melody tier

       Prosodic template tier   [CVCCVC]

       Root tier   ktb

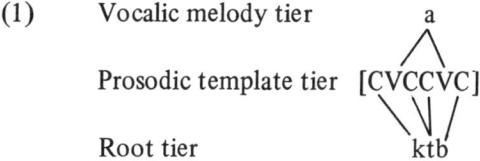

All three of the tiers in (1) constitute separate morphemic levels. The vocalic melody tier contains the inflectional specification of perfective aspect/active voice. This melody can be varied independently to yield, for example, the perfective passive *kuttib*. The root tier is characterized as containing the fundamental lexical morphemes — [ktb] appears in forms referring to writing. And the template is the morphemic mark of the second derivational class. So changing the template to, say, [CVVCVC] yields the third class reciprocal *kaatab* 'corresponded', with the segmental elements assuming a different canonical pattern.

The prosodic template, then, allows us to extract from each derivational class the characteristic pattern assumed by roots and vowel melodies — in fact, the basic generalization underlying Semitic morphological systems. Placing the vowel melody and the root on separate tiers permits these two levels to associate with the prosodic template essentially independently of one another. The levels further allow any one property to be varied apart from the others.

Another effect of morphemic tiers appears in the eighth derivational class *ktatab* 'was registered'. The first *t* of this form is an infixed morpheme with detransitivizing or reflexive force, appearing also as a prefix in the sixth form *takaatab* 'wrote to each other' (and the nonoccurring fifth form *takattab*). *ktatab* is represented formally in (2):

(2) Vocalic melody tier

t-morpheme tier

Prosodic template tier

Root tier

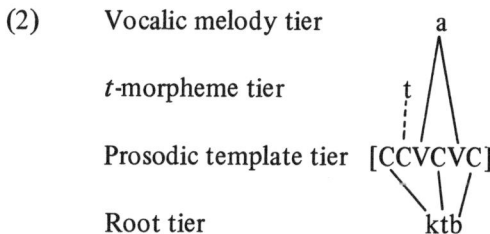

The broken lines connecting the element *t* with the template indicate that it is on a separate morphemic tier from either the vowel melody or the root, although this situation cannot be conveniently represented in a two-dimensional image. Thus, association of *t* with the template is independent of the root or vocalism — the fact that it is infixed is indicated by its association with the second C-slot of the skeleton, and not by insertion into a linear string. This apparent infixation is accomplished by a simple rule of reassociation, accounting for the systematic alternation of *t* between a prefix in the fifth and sixth derivational classes, and an infix in the eighth.

Morphemic templates arise in another set of cases. There is a sense in which such templates have played a role in much earlier morphological models. Structuralist descriptions often contain templates specifying the order of morphemes, the relative positions of different morpheme types with respect to one another and the root. But a considerably more interesting application of morphemic templates develops when they express multiple occurrences of a single morpheme in a form. The particular example of root reduplication, which is met with in many languages, is germane to this point.

Classical Arabic has a root reduplication process applicable to biconsonantal roots, doubling them and associating them with the prosodic template [CVCCVC]. So, the root [zl] appears as *zalzal* 'shook' in the perfective active, represented in (3):

(3) Vocalic melody tier

Prosodic template tier

Morphemic template

Root tier

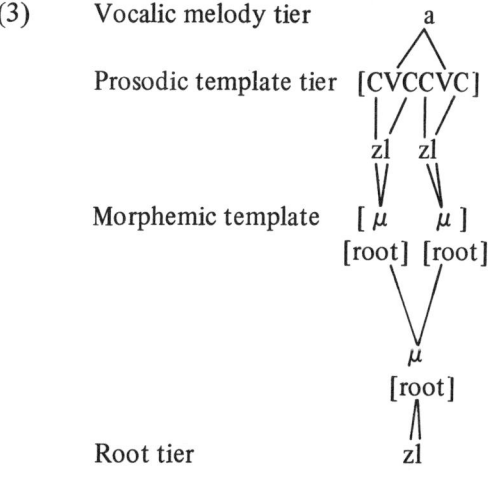

This pattern of verbal derivation, then, stipulates a morpheme template [μ   μ], indicating that the root is to be mapped onto two [root] [root] morpheme positions. The product of this mapping is itself then associated with the positions on the CV-skeleton.

In the discussion below we will find considerable empirical justification for this formal system. Section 2 begins with a consideration of a language game in an Arabic dialect in which the root tier, distinct from other representational layers, plays an essential role. A language game in the Philippine language Hanunóo provides further support for the root/template dichotomy, while several other language games involve basic operations on the template, with the recognition of an affix tier like that in (2). Section 3 treats two morphological systems that share many formal properties with Semitic. In the first case, from the South Munda language Gtaʔ, a tier with vocalic melodies is necessary to account for complex patterns of what is called echo-word formation. In the second, the Malayan language Temiar displays an elaborate system of verbal derivation that requires the full use of all aspects of the theory. A concluding section suggests some further consequences, particularly in the realm of higher-level organization of prosodic templates.

But first we will deal briefly with those aspects of the prosodic model that have not yet been adumbrated but that are essential to the analyses. Association between autosegmental tiers is governed by the theory of tonal association of Clements and Ford (1979). Clements and Ford present three universal conventions for association of tonal elements (t) with tone-bearing elements (T). These are summarized in (4):

(4)   Universal Association Conventions

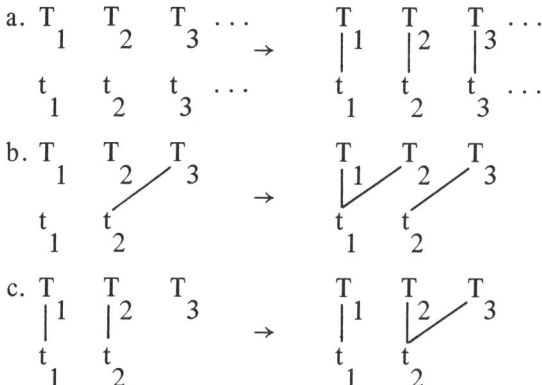

Convention (4a) provides for a left-to-right one-to-one mapping of several melodic elements to several unassociated melody-bearing elements. (4b) gives precedence in spreading to an unassociated tone over one that already bears an association — for instance, by the prior application of a language-particular rule. (4c) ensures that all tone-bearing elements will have at least one association (though not the converse), garnered if necessary from the tonal element on the left.

Under the prosodic model of morphology, these association conventions, together with the prohibition against lines crossing of Goldsmith's (1976) Well-formedness Condition, will apply to the units on morphemic tiers, mapping them onto slots on templates. Language-particular association rules, which are met with in many tonal systems, occasionally arise and take precedence over these universal conventions. We will assume that the tier to template association is subject to two further conditions, neither of which has a direct counterpart in the autosegmental theory of tone.

First, following a suggestion made by Halle and Vergnaud (1980), we will say that there must be a matching in major-class membership between any melodic element and the template position with which it is associated. Specifically, I will assume, in view of the essential elimination of the feature [syllabic] in recent nonlinear studies of syllabification, that the feature [vocalic] is the basis of this matching. Thus, only [+vocalic] elements may be associated with V-slots in the skeleton, and only [-vocalic] elements with C-slots. Similarly, the association of morphemes with morphemic templates will be sensitive to the matching of morphological features like [root]. Explicit stipulation in a grammar can override this matching requirement, as when a glide spreads into a V-position.

A second important addition to the tonal autosegmental theory is a prohibition against many-to-one associations. This excludes the mapping of several melodic units onto a single position of the template, and thus has the natural consequence of ruling out in the unmarked case individual segments with multiple specifications for point and manner of articulation. Since such complex segments do arise, as with the short diphthongs discussed in section 3.1, we will permit the stipulation of dispensations from this requirement.

These three conventions — the association rules in (4), the matching rule, and the prohibition of many-to-one associations — constitute the unmarked basis for mapping in this model. Language-particular rules have the freedom to contravene any of these conventions, but only at cost. And, as we will see in section 3.2, language-particular rules can sometimes function as parameters, providing an elegant account of otherwise puzzling interlinguistic variation.

2. NONLINEAR LANGUAGE GAMES

Many previous studies have dealt with language games or secret languages, systematic distortions of speech. Earlier treatments of a phonological sort have been largely concerned with only a single theoretical consequence of such games: their significance for determining the so-called psychological reality of abstract phonological representations. Here we will approach the separate question of the form of phonological representations, which has not usually figured in such discussions.[1]

In particular, the facts of language games provide strong support for the conception of phonological representation outlined above. A Semitic example, taken from the modern Arabic dialect of Hijazi Bedouins, involves a free transposition of elements only on the consonantal root tier, apart from all other levels. Another transposition game, occurring in Hanunóo, also effects only the root tier, leaving the prosodic template unaltered. Further, a very common type of infixing game, illustrated by several languages, inserts material into the CV-skeleton, with associated consonants, while leaving the root tier unchanged.

As with any linguistic phenomenon, data from language games cannot be applied incautiously to theoretical problems. Games which are highly limited in use or which require extensive training to master may invoke nonspecific intellectual capacities rather than purely linguistic ones. We would expect such games sometimes to contravene otherwise reliable notions of phonological representation, as in the case of games that make use of information from another language or the orthography. Clearly no formal linguistic theory should offer a direct account of them.

2.1. Bedouin Hijazi Arabic Transposition Game

The Modern Arabic dialect spoken by Saudi Arabian Bedouins is extremely conservative, retaining many features of Classical Arabic, including such properties as the characteristic passive vocalic melody. In view of this, we can assume that the morphological analysis of Classical Arabic presented above and in McCarthy (1981) carries over with few changes to Bedouin Hijazi Arabic (BHA). BHA segmental phonology has been described in great detail by Al-Mozainy (1981).[2]

BHA has the language game that is illustrated in (5). Forms in the game can be produced and understood unhesitatingly, and to my knowledge it is not explicitly taught.

Prosodic Templates

(5)

Derivational Class	I	II	III	IV	V	VII	VIII	X
Base Form	difa9	kattab	kaatab	ʔarsal	tikattab	nkisar	jtima9	staslam
Game Forms	da9af	battak	baatak	ʔaslar	tibattak	nrakas	mta9aj	stalmas
	fida9	takkab	taakab	ʔasral	titakkab	nrasak	mtija9	stamlas
	9adaf	tabbak	taabak	ʔalsar	titabbak	nsarak	jta9am	stasmal
	fa9ad	bakkat	baakat	ʔarlas	tibakkat	nsikar	9timaj	stalsam
	9afad	kabbat	kaabat	ʔalras	tikabbat	nkaras	9tijam	stamsal
	'pushed'			'sent'		'broke'	'met'	'surrendered'

I have listed these stems from the verbal system according to the traditional Western system of numbering. The list contains the base word at the head of each column and an exhaustive accounting of the game forms possible with that base. Initial epenthetic vowels have been suppressed.

It is apparent that this game involves scrambling the order of consonants in a form. Some examples, like *da9af* or *nrakas*, also show a change from the vocalism of the base. Al-Mozainy (1981) has convincingly demonstrated that this game is prephonological, and that any change in the vowels can be attributed to the operation of rules sensitive to the quality of the neighboring consonants. Thus, we can completely define the transformation wrought by this game solely in terms of consonantism.

What makes this game inherently interesting is that many possible transpositions of consonants are judged as ill-formed, considered as outputs of the game. While all 3! permutations of the three consonants in I *difa9* or III *kaatab* are well-formed, only those listed in (5) are possible for II *kattab*. We would expect a total of 4! outputs in this case, but the rest, like *taktab* or *baktat*, are ill-formed.

This observation follows directly from the representational apparatus inherent in the prosodic model. The BHA language game involves free permutation of consonants on the root tier. This scrambling process must necessarily precede the operation of rules of association, since otherwise association lines would cross in violation of the Well-formedness Condition of Goldsmith (1976), as shown in (6a). A sample grammatical output, scrambled before association, is given in (6b).

(6) a. *[CVCCVC]   b. [CVCCVC]

Under this account, prohibited outputs like *taktab* or *baktat* could not possibly be generated without crossing association lines or violating the rules of association applied in this derivational class.

In V *tikattab* and VIII *jtima9* we have to reckon with the affixal element *t*. Again, not all possible results of scrambling all the consonants in the stem are grammatical. Some, like V **tikabtat* or **tibaktat*, are ruled out for exactly the reasons adduced above. Others that are ill-formed include V **kibattat* or VIII **m9ataj*, **mjata9*, **jmata9*, and **9jatam*, in all of which the prefix/infix *t* is scrambled along with the root consonants.

This property also follows from considering the language game to be limited to permutations on the root tier. Affixes like *t*, although composed of consonantal material and even when infixed, are not part of the root proper and therefore do not appear on that morphemic tier, as shown above in (2). Precisely the same mechanism limits the possible game derivatives of classes IV, VII, and X to those listed. Affixal *?*, *n* and *st* all lie on separate tiers from the root. Similar considerations hold too for inflectional morphemes, which are prefixed or suffixed to the stems in (5). Thus, from *difa9na* 'we pushed', it is possible to derive *fida9na*, *9afadna*, and so on, but not **na9adfa* or **fina9da*. Furthermore, nouns, which are also subject to the game, cannot have affixes scrambled with the root. Thus, the noun *miftaah* 'key', which has a deverbal prefix *m* with the root [fth], can yield *mifhaat*, *mitfaah*, or *mihfaat*, but not **tihmaaf* or **tihfaam*.

Further data from roots with other than three consonants also confirm this approach. As expected, a quadriliteral verb like *taržam* 'translated' can be transformed to *tarmaž*, *martaž*, *žamrat*, *žartam*, and so on for 4! possibilities. Biliteral roots, discussed in detail in McCarthy (1981), form only a single output in the game. The class I verb *hall* 'solved' and the class II verb *sammam* 'poison' can become *lahh* and *massas*, respectively, but not **lalh*, **lahl*, **masmam*, or any others. This result follows from the independently-motivated representation of these forms given in (7):

(7) a.   a   a   b.   a   a
         | | /\   /\
       [CVCC] ~ [CVCC]   [CVCCVC] ~ [CVCCVC]
        \V/   \V/   \V/   \V/
        hl   lh   sm   ms

Scrambling on the root tier before association could yield only the indicated game derivative of each of these forms.

A final point of interest in the BHA language game concerns the treatment of forms with reduplicated biconsonantal roots, like *zalzal* in (3). Scrambling on the root tier, before association, gives the well-formed output *lazlaz*, with all other conceivable possibilities judged ungrammatical: **lazzaz*, **zallal*, **lazzal*.

Prosodic Templates

These data, then, provide very strong confirmation for the conception of Arabic morphology in McCarthy (1981). The basic process in this game is quite simple: permute on the root tier. Nothing else need be said, since other results – ordering of scrambling before association and the exclusion of ill-formed outputs – follow from either the representational system or independently necessary properties of the analysis. It is difficult to imagine how else this complex set of facts could be explained.

2.2. Hanunóo Transposition Game

Several games of the Philippine language Hanunóo have been described by Conklin (1959). Here we will be concerned with one that, like the game in BHA, involves scrambling of root material. This game is apparently used productively by young people and learned in early adolescence.

The Hanunóo game exchanges the first and last consonant-vowel sequences in the stem with one another, as shown in (8):

(8) | Base Form | Game Form | |
|---|---|---|
| rignuk | nugrik | 'tame' |
| bi:ŋaw | ŋa:biw | 'nick' |
| ʔusah | saʔuh | 'one' |
| balaynun | nulayban | 'domesticated' |
| ba:raŋ may bu:ŋa | ra:baŋ may ŋa:bu | (phrase of greeting) |
| ʔa:san sa kanta | sa:ʔan sa tanka | |
| katagbuʔ | kabugtaʔ | |

Two observations Conklin makes about this language game suggest its relevance for a theory of phonological representations. First, vowel length remains unchanged despite the transposition of vowels. So, for example, the long vowel-short vowel pattern of *bi:ŋaw* persists in the game form *ŋa:biw* even though *i* and *a* have been exchanged. Second, only the segments of the root participate in the transposition. Because of this, the prefix *ka+* in *katagbuʔ* is unaltered in the game form *kabugtaʔ*. Both of these phenomena – the invariance of canonical pattern and the limitation of scrambling to root material – are obviously reminiscent of the situation in BHA. The formal interpretation is essentially the same.

We can recognize in Hanunóo two basic levels of representation in a morphologically simplex form. The prosodic template will describe the canonical pattern of the word. Clearly, however, the Semitic consonantal root/vowel melody dichotomy does not carry over to a language of this type. The root tier, then, will contain both consonantal and vocalic elements, mapped according to the matching convention described in section 1. Some sample representations appear in (9):

(9)   a.   b.   c.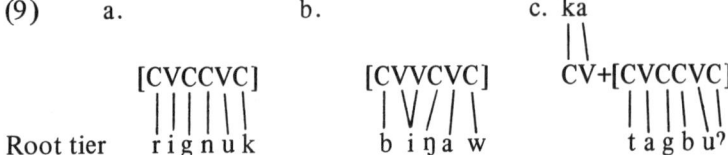

In this model, then, the Hanunóo game can be seen as a transposition of the first and last consonant-vowel sequences in the root tier. Material in the prosodic template is unaffected, and thus vowel length remains unchanged (9b). Elements on other morphemic tiers — like the prefix *ka+* in (9c) — are similarly unaffected by the root tier operation.

This preservation of the prosodic and morphological patterns of a word, despite massive segmental disruptions produced by a language game, is met with in the related language Tagalog as well (Conklin (1956)). As in BHA, the segregation of information about canonical form and about other morphemes on different formal levels allows essentially independent manipulation of any one of these factors. The transposition games depend crucially on this formal isolation.

2.3. Infixation Games

An extremely common type of language game involves the insertion of some sequence into every syllable or every word of the base. In some cases, the inserted material is fully specified, as in the English Alfalfa and Ob games (Donegan and Stampe 1979). Games of this sort are compatible with the model presented here, but do nothing to distinguish it from others. Many games, however, involve the insertion of only partly specified strings, and, as we will see, provide strong support for the prosodic theory.

Two Cuna play languages described by Sherzer (1976) illustrate this claim. The first, known as *ottukkuar sunmakke* 'concealed talking', is exemplified in (10a); the second, which is unnamed, appears in (10b).

(10) a. Base Form   Game Form
         merki   mepperkippi   'North American'
         pia   pippiappa   'where'
         ua   uppuappa   'fish'
         perk^{w}aple   pepperk^w appapleppe   'all'
      b. merki   mererkiri
         pe   pere   'you'
         pia   piriara
         tanikki   taranirikkiri   'he's coming'

Clearly, the basic observation underlying these facts is that both games involve inserting after the nucleus of every syllable the consonant(s) *pp* or *r* followed by a copy of the preceding vowel. The prosodic interpretation of this is quite straightforward. The infix is of the form CCV (or CV) with both C-slots preassociated to the melody *p* (or *r*), but with the V-slot unspecified. Then, automatic spreading in conformity with clause (4c) of the Association Conventions will yield apparent copying of the preceding vowel. This derivation is illustrated in (11):

(11)

$$
\begin{array}{c}
 p p p p \\
[CVCCV] \rightarrow [CVCCVCCVCCV] \rightarrow [CVCCVCCVCCV] \\
 merki merki merki
\end{array}
$$

Only one aspect of (11) requires special mention. The melodic elements *p*, which specify the consonants of the infix, are represented on a separate autosegmental tier from the root or any other part of the form. This reflects a plausible conception of these elements as quasi-morphemes, distinct from other morphological units. The result of this representation is that automatic spreading alone is sufficient to yield the observed vowel copying.

It appears that language games with copying infixes are extremely common, and thus it is a distinct advantage of this theory that it is able to provide an elegant account of them. Sherzer (1976) describes two games of Javanese with *fV* and *pV* infixes. Price and Price (1976) describe games collectively known as *akoopína* in Saramaccan creole, some of which involve infixation of an *IVIV* sequence. This circumstance, in which more than one infixed vowel is unspecified, is clearly documented in some of the Tagalog language games called *baliktád* (Conklin 1956). In one version, a V*g*VV*d* sequence is infixed after every syllable-initial consonant. This is exemplified in (12a) and represented formally in (12b):[3]

(12)   a. Base Form   Game Form
           hindí?   higí:dindigí:di?   'no, not'
           taŋhá:li?   tagá:daŋ hagá:daligí:di?   'noon'

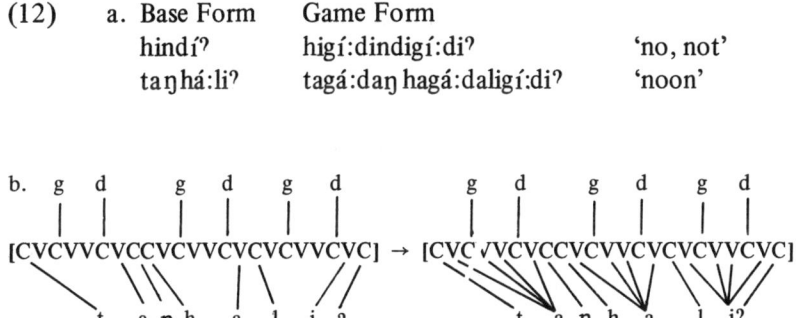

As in the simpler cases, the melodic specification of the infixed C-positions appears on a separate tier, allowing free (and automatic) association to specify the infixed V's. Other infixes appear in *baliktád* games, including the striking VV*p*V*nd*VV*p*, and these are often combined with one another or with transposition games in a single form.[4]

Although I have been unable to document the existence of such a process, this model predicts that there should be games of some language with CV or VC (or longer) infixes where the consonants are unspecified and the vowels are fully specified. What is much more difficult for this theory to express, and therefore ought to be highly marked if not nonoccurring, is a situation in which both elements of the inserted VC or CV are unspecified and copy adjacent material. This hypothetical case must, of course, be distinguished from syllable copying or the like, which is not uncommon, but apart from this the prediction of the prosodic model is clear.

3. TWO NONCONCATENATIVE SYSTEMS

3.1. Gta?

A remarkable example from outside the Semitic family in which the vocalic tier figures prominently is presented by Gta?, a South Munda language. Although the phenomenon we will discuss here is apparently an areal feature of South Indian languages, it is most elaborated in Gta? and has been carefully described there by Mahapatra (1976).

Gta? has a productive process of echo-word formation, a term originally due to Emeneau (1967). These derivatives form a kind of paradigm for each word, as illustrated in (13):

(13) Base Form   Echo Forms

    a. kitoŋ 'god'   kataŋ 'being with powers equal to *kitoŋ* (e.g., a benevolent ghost)'
                              kitiŋ 'being smaller, weaker than *kitoŋ* (e.g., a minor deity)'
                                kitaŋ 'being inferior in status to *kitoŋ* (e.g., a bad ghost)'
                        or katoŋ
                              kutaŋ 'being other than *kitoŋ* (e.g., spirits, ghosts, etc.)'
    b. kesu 'wrapper worn against cold'   kasa 'cloth equivalent to *kesu* in size and texture'
                                kisi   'small or thin piece of cloth'
                                kesa   'large piece of thick cloth, torn

	or kasu	or worn out, serving as a *kesu'*
	kesi	'like *kesa/kasu*, but small, thin piece'
	kusa	'any other material usable against cold'
c. bole 'rice'	bala	'food stuff usable as main dish (e.g., millet gruel)'
	bili	'snacks and the like, not constituting staple food'
	bale	'food not made of grain (e.g., tubers or mango stones)'

As is clear from (13), echo-words involve some systematic modifications in the vocalism of the base with a concomitant change of meaning. According to Mahapatra, changing all base vocalism to *i* yields a diminutive or hypochoristic sense, while changing all vocalism to *a* has the opposite, augmentative effect. Changing fewer than all vowels to *i* or *a*, respectively, has the same result, but with an added sense of inferiority. Another vowel pattern, *u-a*, indicates a type "different from" the meaning of the base. Zide (1976) confirms the substantial semantic regularities in echo-word formation.

We will first see a formal analysis of these alternations, and then consider some further details that lend added support to this analysis.

As in the voice and aspect inflection of the Classical Arabic verb system, we can isolate a set of morphemes whose sole realization is as vocalic melodies on a morphemic tier. One subset of these melodic morphemes is purely formal: the vocalic melodies associated with the base words. The other subset, which appears in (14), consists of the echo-word melodies which have the meanings indicated above.

(14)　　Gtaʔ Echo Word Melodies
　　　　[i]
　　　　[a]
　　　　[u a]

Presence of one of these melodic morphemes on the vocalic tier marks a form as an echo-word.

The formation of echo-words will proceed as follows. In one type, represented in (15b, c, d), one of the echo-word melodies appears alone on the morphemic tier. That is, the base-word melody in (15a) is lost:

(15)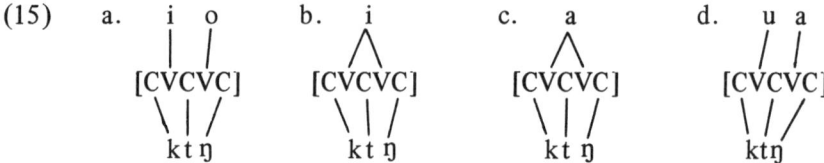

In the other type, those forms with the added meaning of inferiority, the base melody and echo melody appear together on the same tier, in either order:

(16) a. e u a   b. a   e u   c. e u   i
          \\ / /   \\   \\ /   \\ \\ /
          [CVCV]   [CVCV]   [CVCV]
          | / | / | /
          k s   k s   k s

Here, the prohibition of many-to-one associations between the melody and a position on the prosodic template ensures a one-to-one mapping, with the echo-word melody partly displacing the base melody. The unassociated melodic elements in (16) receive no phonetic interpretation.

A number of further facts suggest slight extensions of this analysis. First, the "differential" melody [u a] is nonoccurring with monosyllabic forms, although the other melodies are possible. This is shown in (17):

(17)   Base Form   Echo Forms
      a.   gnaʔ 'basket'   gniʔ
      b.   mni 'name'   mna
      c.   gsuʔ 'dog'   gsaʔ
                                gsiʔ
      d.   gbug 'pig'   gbag
                                gbig
      e.   sle 'work'   sla
                                sli
      f.   tboʔ 'earth'   tbaʔ
                                tbiʔ
      g.   gsɛŋ 'chicken'   gsiŋ
                                gsaŋ

The absence of monosyllables with the melody [u a] follows from the prohibition against many-to-one association. This melody cannot be realized on a single element without such a configuration arising. We may presume that association of part of the echo melody, which would be formally permissible, is ruled out by essentially functional considerations of morphological opacity or recoverability. That is, the full melodic morpheme must appear as a mark of the echo-word class. Similar factors exclude the partial association (as in (16)) of the [u a] melody with disyllables. We shall have occasion to come back to this notion of opacity in greater detail in connection with root association in Temiar, in section 3.2.

This argument is vitiated somewhat by the absence of [u a] echo words among trisyllabic stems, suggesting that perhaps this melody must in any case be limited to disyllables. It may be, however, that the lack of [u a] echoes of trisyllables is an accident due to the relative scarcity of such stems in Gtaʔ. And interestingly, the facts of echo-words in the Desia dialect of Oriya, an Indo-Aryan language also described by Mahapatra (1976), support the explanation offered for (17). In Desia the [u a] melody occurs with disyllabic nouns as in Gtaʔ (18a). It can also occur with monosyllabic nouns, but the template is extended by the addition of a final V position (18b). No information is provided for trisyllables.

(18)   Base Form   Echo Form
    a.   sili   'wheel'   sula
           celi   'goat'   cula
           poti   'book'   puta
           pani   'water'   puna
    b.   git   'song'   guta
           dud   'milk'   duda
           tel   'oil'   tula
           dol   'drum'   dula
           jɔr   'fever'   jura
           mac   'fish'   muca

The augmentation in (18b) does not occur with monosyllabic verbs, which echo with the simplex melody [a] or [u] (the latter when the base is [a]): *por* 'to burn' becomes *par*; *baj* 'to fry' becomes *buj*. These observations make sense only under a theory in which the [u a] melody must be fully associated with the template, consistent with the prohibition of many-to-one associations.

Another interesting set of facts is presented by base-forms containing diphthongs, as in (19):

(19)   Base Form   Echo Forms
    a.   bcueʔ   'tamarind'   bciʔ
                                bcaʔ
    b.   luen   'road'   lin
                                lan
    c.   nsua   'spade'   nsi

The base diphthongs obviously echo as single, short vowels. The diphthongs do not behave like disyllabic words; they fail to accept the [u a] melody or partial replacement of the base melody by [i] or [a]: *bcuaʔ, *bcieʔ, *bcuiʔ.

Zide (1976) suggests a compelling explanation for this pattern. If the diphthongs are short – that is, monomoraic – then they would be expected to echo as short vowels, as shown in (20):[5]

(20) a. Base Form   b. Echo Forms

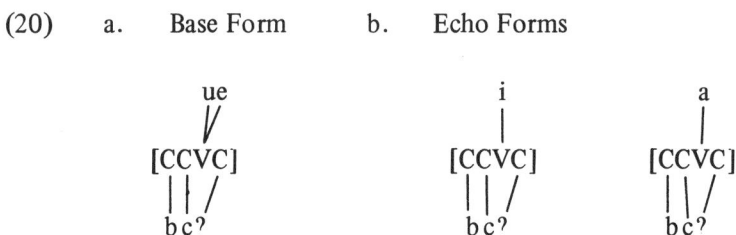

This account obviously presupposes that the prohibition on many-to-one associations is applying in (20b) and the like, to rule out the [u a] melody or partial replacement of the diphthongal melody. The obvious question is why this prohibition does not exclude all representations of monomoraic diphthongs, as in (20a). It would seem that the lexical melody – the base vocalism – is associated with the template in the lexicon, and thus can constitute an explicit exception to the prohibition. Derived melodies in the echo words are nevertheless subject to it. This makes the apparently correct claim that echo-words never contain diphthongs.

The form (19c) brings in a further point of analysis. Zide (1976) points out that the general participation of vowels in the formation of echo words is systematically violated by syllabic nasals: thus ṇsua echoes as ṇsi, not as *isi or *ĩsĩ. This demonstrates that echo formation is not simply an operation on syllable nuclei, but specifically a matter of adding a vocalic melody on a morphemic tier. The representation of ṇsua and its echo appears in (21):

(21) a.   ua   b.   i

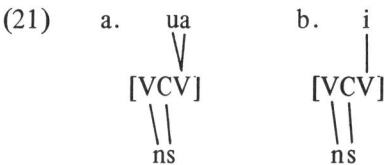

That is, the lexical representations of Gtaʔ explicitly permit the association of [-vocalic] n with a [+vocalic] V-position of the template, and therefore this consonant can constitute a syllable nucleus even though it does not appear on the vocalic tier. Further discussion of syllabic

Prosodic Templates 207

nasals in a representational model of this sort can be found in Yip (to appear).

A final point of Gta? echo formation provides quite strong support for the analysis presented here. The melodies [a] and [i] occur quite freely with trisyllabic words, as shown in (22):

(22) Base Form Echo Forms
a. aṛatra 'up' iṛitri
 iṛitra
 iṛatra
b. picoṛi 'a bat' pacaṛa
 piciṛi
 pacaṛi
 picaṛa
 pacoṛi
 picaṛi
c. sewari 'free drink' sawara
 siwiri
 sawari
 sewara
 sewiri

As the analysis predicts, the echo melody can fully replace the base melody (*iṛitri, pacaṛa, sawara, siwiri*). The echo melody can also occur in any position on the vocalic tier with the base melody: before it (*iṛitra, iṛatra*), after it (*picaṛa, sewara*), or in the middle of it (*picaṛi*). What Mahapatra (1976) explicitly rules out, however, is the possibility of the echo-word vocalism affecting vowels in nonadjacent syllables, so hypothetical **iṛatri* or **pacoṛa* are excluded. This follows directly from the formalism; a single melodic element cannot be mapped onto two nonadjacent vowels without violating the Well-formedness Condition, as illustrated in (23):

(23)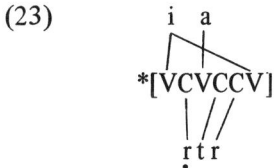

Under any account of this phenomenon that did not incorporate vocalic melody levels, this observation would necessarily be stipulated in the analysis, whereas here it is a property of the representational system.[6]

There are some remaining puzzles of Gta? echo-word formation. Chief among them is the nonoccurrence of some expected echo-word derivatives of various stems. Mahapatra presents a number of complex principles to exclude certain arrangements of base-word and echo-word vocalism, and it is possible, though unrevealing, to translate these principles into the melodic notation adopted here. Another puzzle is the apparent acceptance of the echo-word melody by prefix vowels: *aʔ+coŋ* 'feed' echoes as *iʔ+ciŋ*; *ma+coŋ* 'eat (pl. obj.)' echoes as *mi+ciŋ*. Since the vocalic melodies associated with the prefix morphemes must appear on different morphemic tiers from the root melodies, they ought to be able to echo or fail to echo independently. This is precisely the behavior in the echo words derived from compounds — the two morphemes constitute separate domains of echo formation. As the analysis currently stands, an ad hoc rule spreading the echo melody to the prefixal template is necessary to explain *mi+ciŋ* and the like, with the spread association displacing the basic melody of the prefix.

3.2 Temiar Morphology

The verbal system of Temiar, a language spoken on the Malay Peninsula, is striking in its heavy reliance on both prosodic (CV) and morphemic (μ) templates. The system has close structural parallels with Classical Arabic and is fully compatible with the theory offered here. The data are drawn from a fairly lengthy description by Benjamin (1976).

Verb roots can be divided into three classes according to canonical pattern: biconsonantal roots CVC (*kɔ̃w* 'to call'); triconsonantal roots CCVC (*slɔg* 'to lie down, marry'); and longer roots CV(C)CVC (*halab* 'to go down-river', *sindul* 'to float').[7] These longer, disyllabic roots are largely uninflected and consequently fail to participate in the morphological alternations discussed here, a fact that we will return to at the end of this section. Inflection of the shorter verbs for aspect and voice is largely a function of modifications of this canonical form, sometimes with root reduplication and various affixation phenomena. Representative paradigms, including bracketed forms formed by rule but not actually given for these particular roots, are presented in (24):

(24)		Biconsonantal Root	Triconsonantal Root	
Active Voice				
	Perfective	kɔ̃w	slɔg	
	nominal	[knɔ̃w]	[snlɔg]	
	Simulfactive	kakɔ̃w	salɔg	
	Nominal	[kanɔ̃w]	[snalɔg]	
	Continuative	kwkɔ̃w	sglɔg	
	Nominal	[kwnɔ̃w]	[snglɔg]	(Kelantan dialect)
		[nwkɔ̃w]	[ngslɔg]	(Perak dialect)

Prosodic Templates   209

Causative Voice
    Perfective   trkɔ̃w   srlɔg
    Simulfactive   [trakɔ̃w]   [sralɔg]
    Continuative   trwkɔ̃w   srglɔg
    Nominal   [trnkɔ̃w]   srnlɔg

The verb forms, except for the simulfactive causative, are apparently productive; the other forms somewhat less so. Nevertheless, these data are faithful to the formal possibilities in Temiar morphology. They are also not as limited in function as (24) indicates. Most deverbal nouns (other than the nominalizations in (24)) are formed according to one of these schemata, and noun plurals follow the active continuative pattern.

Let us first consider the active voice verb forms and then extend the analysis to the causative and the various nominalizations. It is apparent that the perfective active is the formally unmarked category, retaining the unchanged form of the stem. The two perfective types in (24) can be represented as in (25), with root and prosodic template constituting different levels:

(25)   a. Template   [CVC]   b.   [CCVC]

           Root   kɔ̃w   slɔg

The templates in (25) are the characteristic morphology of the perfective active, since different templates appear in other categories. Thus, the two levels in (25) constitute separate morphemic tiers.

The simulfactive has two stem syllables (with *a* in the first one) and, in the case of the biconsonantal root, reduplication of the initial consonant. Unlike the perfective, in the simulfactive one template suffices for both root types. It appears as in (26), with *a* preassociated to the first V-slot:

(26)   Simulfactive Active Template

        a
        |
    [CVCVC]

The element [a], part of the characteristic simulfactive morphology, appears on a separate tier from the root. Association will proceed as in (27):

210   John J. McCarthy

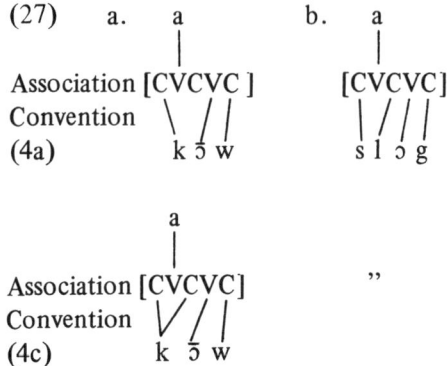

In particular, the reduplication of initial *k* in the biconsonantal root follows directly from universal principles. Left-to-right association is governed by the prohibition on many-to-one mappings, which blocks association of ɔ̃ with the first V-slot of the skeleton. *k*, then, must spread to fill the unspecified second C-position. Just as in Arabic, shorter roots are expanded by spreading (with the apparent effect of reduplication) to fill templates that are exhaustively occupied by longer roots.

The continuative form shows a different sort of reduplication – partial copying of the root in both the biconsonantal and triconsonantal types. This is analyzed as full root reduplication – the mapping of the root onto a morphemic template of two μ-categories, just as in the Arabic form in (3) – with association of portions of the copied root to the prosodic template. Formally, for the continuative we will stipulate the prosodic template (28a) and the morphemic template (28b):

(28)   Continuative Active Templates

   a.   [CCCVC]

   b.   [$\begin{matrix}\mu\\ \text{[root]}\end{matrix}$ $\begin{matrix}\mu\\ \text{[root]}\end{matrix}$]

The full representation of the continuative active form appears in (29) (see next page).

The roots are copied fully by the morphemic template (28b), but the prosodic template of the continuative (28a) provides positions for only four consonants and one vowel, and so only portions of the copied root are mapped onto template positions – just the opposite of the situation in the simulfactive of biconsonantal roots. Remaining, unassociated segments do not receive a phonetic realization. Since the association of the root morpheme with the two positions of the morphemic template is a

Prosodic Templates

(29) a.   b.

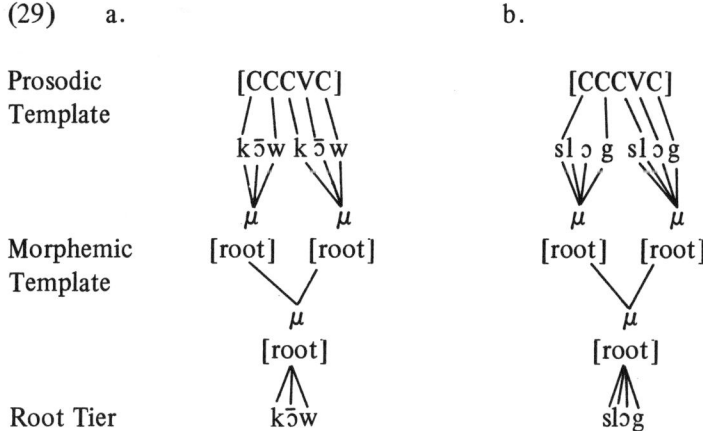

trivial case of spreading, the real problem presented by (29) is that of accounting for the mode of association between the copied roots and the prosodic template.

It is clear that the universal principles — left-to-right association (4a) in particular — will not yield the relationships in (29) without further modifications. I suggest, then, the language-particular association rule (30), which associates the last element (α) in the first copy of the root with the second C-position of the prosodic template (this will be modified later):

(30)   Continuative Association

[CCCVC]
  |
[[x α]   [y]]

For a biconsonantal root like $k\bar{\jmath}w$, left-to-right association applied to the output of (30) yields the correct result, as the derivation in (31) shows (only the relevant parts are shown here and in (32)):

(31)
Association   [CCCVC]
Rule (30) |
              kɔ̄w kɔ̄w

Association   [CCCVC]
Convention   /|\\\
(4a)   kɔ̄w kɔ̄w

But the mapping of the triconsonantal root *slɔg* requires the invocation of the functional exclusion of morphological opacity, alluded to earlier. The output of (30) is transformed, by the Association Conventions alone, into the ill-formed structure in (32):

(32)

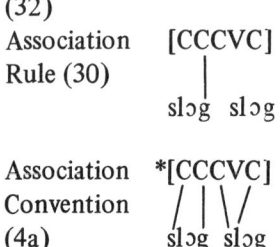

Association Rule (30)   [CCCVC]
                          |
                        slɔg slɔg

Association Convention (4a)   *[CCCVC]
                              / | \ /
                              slɔg slɔg

In (32), neither copy of the root element ɔ is associated with a template position, and consequently this element receives no phonetic realization. If, as seems reasonable, this sort of situation, where a portion of the root is lost, is ruled out in principle, then we can derive the correct result. Left-to-right association proceeds normally, subject to the condition that all elements of the root must appear at least once in the output.[8] The actual continuative active structure (29b) is the only result that meets this requirement.

This addition to the formal morphological theory is strongly supported by some data from Levantic Arabic which is strikingly similar to the Temiar continuative, differing only in a parameter set by the language-particular association rule (30).

Many Levantine Arabic dialects have a process of intensive/pejorative verb formation that is applicable to both biconsonantal (33a) and triconsonantal (33b) roots:[9]

(33)		Root	Derived form	
a.		lf	laflaf	'wrapped (intensive)'
		ḥl	ḥalḥal	'untied, undid'
b.		frḥ	farfaḥ	'rejoiced'
		bḥš	baḥbaš	'sought'
		mrṭ	marmaṭ	'cut unevenly'
		brd	barbad	'shaved unevenly'
		dḥl	daḥdal	'rolled gradually'
		šrḥ	šaršaḥ	'criticized severely'
		ḥlṭ	ḥalḥaṭ	'sheared unevenly'
		qrṭ	qarqaṭ	'crunched'
		šḥṭ	šaḥšaṭ	'dragged roughly'

Prosodic Templates

All of these derived forms are regularly associated with verbs in the first derivational class, to which they bear a fairly consistent semantic relationship.

These verbs are formed on the [CVCCVC] template, the unmarked category for stems with four consonants, including quadriliteral roots. They also clearly have root reduplication by virtue of a morphemic template [$[\text{root}]^\mu$ $[\text{root}]^\mu$], like the Classical Arabic form in (3). But unlike this Classical Arabic pattern, Levantine Arabic reduplicates both biliteral and triliteral roots, to yield the output structures in (34):

(34) a.

Prosodic Template: [CVCCVC] — lf   lf

Morphemic Template: [$[\text{root}]^\mu$ $[\text{root}]^\mu$]

Root Tier: lf

b.

Prosodic Template: [CVCCVC] — frh frh

Morphemic Template: [$[\text{root}]^\mu$ $[\text{root}]^\mu$]

Root Tier: frh

There is nothing particularly notable about (34a); simple left-to-right association produces this pattern without other considerations arising. But (34b) is clearly a more complex case. For a triliterial root C_1 C_2 C_3 in Arabic, the surface schema of reduplication is C_1 C_2 C_1 C_3, whereas the schema is C_1 C_3 C_2 VC_3 in Temiar. This interlinguistic difference in two such similar modes of reduplication can be attributed to the setting of a simple parameter: Temiar has the language-particular association rule (30), while Levantine Arabic has that in (35):

(35) Intensive/Pejorative Association
      [CVCÇVC]

      [[x]   [αy]]

This rule, then, associates the initial element of the second copy of the root with the third C-slot of the prosodic template.

The Association Conventions alone, applied to the output of Intensive/Pejorative Association (35), yield the ill-formed structure in (36), in which neither copy of the root-final consonant ḥ is associated with the prosodic template:

(36)

```
              a
             /\
        *[CVCCVC]
         |/ |/
         frh frh
         \\: \\:
      [ [roöt]μ [roöt]μ ]
            \\/
           [roöt]μ
            /|\
            frh
```

Here again we must invoke considerations of morphological opacity, requiring that all root elements be mapped onto template positions, to generate the correct pattern of association. The difference between Arabic and Temiar in the realization of reduplicated roots where insufficient template positions are available can be referred solely to a difference in simple language-particular rules of association, providing we have this principle.

The causative voice verb forms of Temiar are related in a systematic way to the corresponding active voice ones. We can recognize essentially three formal differences between the active and causative. First, the causative is formed on a prosodic template taken from the set in (37):

(37) Causative Prosodic Templates
    a. Perfective   [CCCVC]

                            a
                            |
    b. Simulfactive   [C+CVCVC]
    c. Continuative   [C+CCCVC]

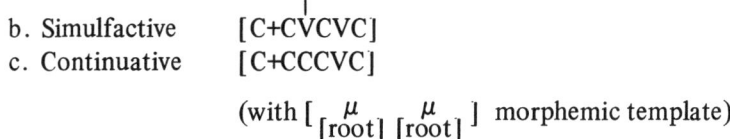
(with [[root]μ [root]μ] morphemic template)

As I have indicated by the internal boundary in (37b and c), the causative templates of the simulfactive and continuative are identical in all respects to the corresponding active ones, except that they have C prefixed to the template — that is, a template morpheme. No such decomposition is possible with the perfective, however: the perfective active form is different for the two root types ([CVC] and [CCVC]) but the perfective causative is the same for both.

A second difference between active and causative forms is that the latter have the melodic morpheme [r] associated with the second C-slot

Prosodic Templates

of the template. This is accomplished by rule (38), applied before and taking precedence over the mapping of the root onto the template.[10]

(38)   *r*-association

[CC x| [causative]
 |
 r

The morpheme *r* will appear on a separate morphemic tier from the root, and thus (38) in some cases has the apparent effect of infixation. This is formally similar to the Arabic representation in (2).

Finally, all causative forms based on a biconsonantal root like *kɔ̄w* have another melodic morpheme, *t*, in prefixal position, associated with the initial C-slot of the template. Like (38), this association will also take precedence over the mapping of root material.

Full representations of the causative verb forms appear in (39):

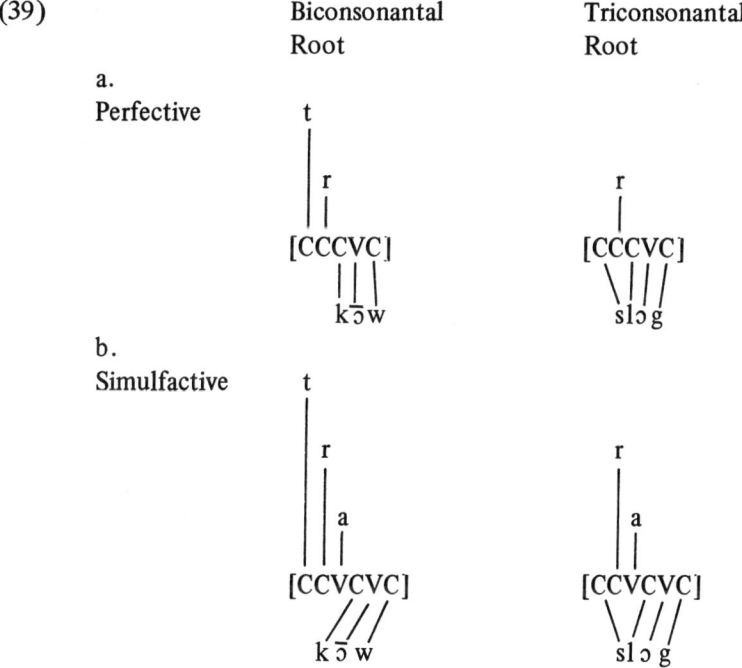

216 *John J. McCarthy*

c.
Continuative

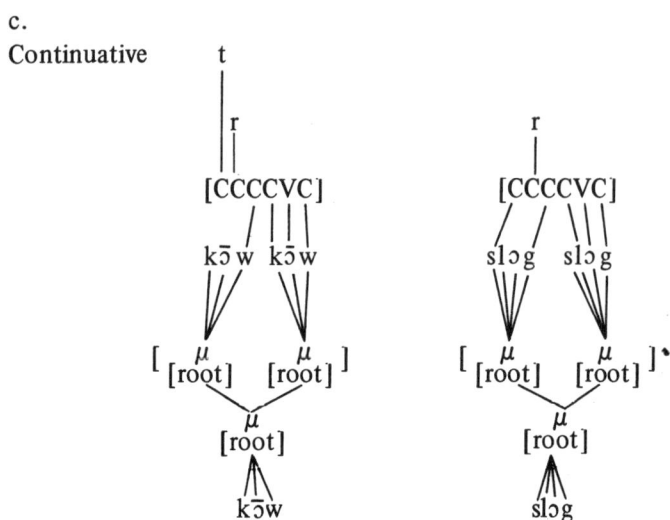

The derivation of the perfective forms is unremarkable. After the affixation processes attaching [t] and [r], there remain an equal number of unfilled skeleton slots and unassociated root elements, so left-to-right association (4a) applies normally. In the simulfactive, the prior association of melodies [t] and [r] with the first two C-slots blocks the spreading of k found in the biconsonantal active simulfactive form *kakɔ̄w* (27a). That is, Association Convention (4c) is inapplicable here, because of the prohibition of many-to-one associations, and the entire result follows from left-to-right association. The model, then, accounts directly for this difference in the surface form taken by the simulfactive morphology in the two voices. Because spreading is impossible in the causative, only the active form shows reduplication.

The continuative aspect of the causative voice involves one additional complication over the corresponding active. By the application of the Continuative Association Rule (30) the active continuative shows copying of the root-final consonant in the second C-position of the template: *kwkɔ̄w*, *sglɔg*. But the causatives have this same root consonant associated with the third C-slot of the skeleton. This calls for a small revision in the Continuative Association Rule, along the lines in (40):

(40)   Continuative Association (Revised)
       [(C)CCCVC]
         /
       [[xα] [y]]

This new version of the association rule distinguishes the two voices ac-

Prosodic Templates

cording to their templates: active [CCCVC] has mapping onto the second C-slot, while causative [CCCCVC] has association with the third C-position.

With this question aside, we can consider the full derivations of the causative continuative forms. These appear in (41) (again, irrelevant structure has been suppressed):

(41)   Biconsonantal Root   Triconsonantal Root

Affix association:

Biconsonantal:
$$\begin{matrix} t \\ | \\ r \\ | \\ [\text{CCCCVC}] \end{matrix}$$

Triconsonantal:
$$\begin{matrix} r \\ | \\ [\text{CCCCVC}] \end{matrix}$$

Continuative Association (40):

Biconsonantal:
$$\begin{matrix} t \\ | \\ r \\ | \\ [\text{CCCCVC}] \\ / \\ k\bar{ɔ}w \; k\bar{ɔ}w \end{matrix}$$

Triconsonantal:
$$\begin{matrix} r \\ | \\ [\text{CCCCVC}] \\ / \\ slɔg \quad slɔg \end{matrix}$$

Association Convention (4a):

Biconsonantal:
$$\begin{matrix} t \\ | \\ r \\ | \\ [\text{CCCCVC}] \\ /||| \\ k\bar{ɔ}w \quad k\bar{ɔ}w \end{matrix}$$

Triconsonantal:
$$\begin{matrix} r \\ | \\ [\text{CCCCVC}] \\ /|\backslash \\ slɔg \quad s\,l\,ɔg \end{matrix}$$

Morphological Opacity:

Biconsonantal: "

Triconsonantal:
$$\begin{matrix} r \\ | \\ [\text{CCCCVC}] \\ /|\backslash|| \\ slɔg \; slɔg \end{matrix}$$

The causative has full morpheme reduplication, by virtue of the morphemic template (28b), like the corresponding active. The causative also clearly presents the same problem of too few slots for the available root material. After the application of Continuative Association (40), left-to-right mapping (4a) can proceed, associating the triconsonantal root's *s* with the first template slot. But this association by convention is blocked in the biconsonantal root by the prior association of affixes [t] and [r]. The effect of this is that the biconsonantal root appears to have a preposed copy of its final consonant, a surprising situation that arises quite automatically under the analysis developed here. Notable also is that prior association of these affixes accounts for the difference in reduplication between the active and causative continuative of the biconsonantal root, parallel to the result presented above for the simulfactive. Finally, we see in (41) that morphological opacity blocks left-to-right association for its failure to associate ɔ, and so the correct output provides a realization for all root elements.

The nominalizations constitute an interesting and complex variation on the verb analysis. Part of the complexity is no doubt due to their lesser productivity and the indicated dialect variation. Nominal forms are not given for the active and simulfactive causative; they are given, however, for disyllabic roots, which participate in no other aspect of the morphology that we have discussed. Related to the disyllabic roots *golap* 'to carry on shoulder' and *sindul* 'to float' are the nominalizations *gnolap* and *snindul*.

We will first look in (42) at the prosodic structures of the nominalizations of the biconsonantal and triconsonantal roots, and then turn to the rules creating these structures and the special problem of the disyllabic roots.

(42) Biconsonantal Triconsonantal
      Root   Root

a.
Perfective   n   n
Active | |
              [CCVC]   [CCCVC]
               kɔw   slɔg

b.
Simulfactive   a   a
Active | |
                 n   n
                 | |
              [CVCVC]   [CCVCVC]
               kɔw   slɔg

Prosodic Templates

	Biconsonantal Root	Triconsonantal Root

c.
Continuative
Active

Kelantan
dialect

Perak dialect
(abbreviated
structure)

d.
Continuative
Causative
(abbreviated
structure)

As indicated in (42), I have suppressed the morphemic template and associated root-reduplication structure where it is merely repetitious.

It is clear that the nominalizations are formally derived from the corresponding verb forms, to which they bear many similarities. The rules of derivation, however, are of considerably less generality than those described above for the verb system, and so our analysis must tolerate a good deal of unexplained government of rules by morphological category or root type.

Prefixation of a C-slot to the template of the corresponding verb takes place in the nominalizations of the perfective of all root types and the nominalizations of the active simulfactive and continuative of the triconsonantal root. I have discovered no systematic character to this distribution, so it must be assumed that the prefixation rule (43) is controlled by category and root type:

(43)   Nominal Prefixation
        $\emptyset \rightarrow C \ / \ [\_\_x]$

Another process, applied after (43), maps the characteristic nominal melody [n] onto some C-position of the template. In most cases, this can be attributed to the rule (44), which associates [n] with the second C-slot from the left:

(44) n-association
        $[C(V) \underset{|}{C} x]$
        n

Rule (44) accounts directly for the perfective and simulfactive nominalized forms.

On the basis of these two nominalization rules, we can consider the treatment of disyllabic roots like *golap* and *sindul*. The structures of their nominalizations are given in (45):

(45)   a.   b.

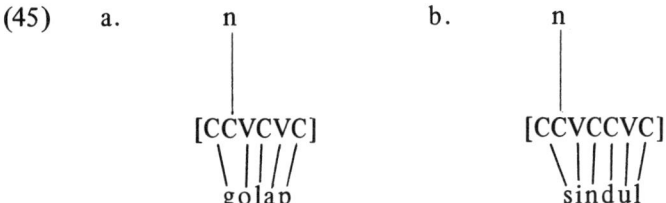

These nominalizations can be derived from the corresponding stem forms by Prefixation (43) applied to the template, with subsequent n-association (44). These forms are clearly consistent with this much of the analysis, but there is a deeper moral here as well.

Recall that the disyllabic roots do not undergo any of the verbal morphology described here — they remain uninflected or are subject to some simple affixation processes. It is obviously of some interest to account for the fact that these roots eschew all other nonconcatenative morphology but do undergo nominalization. The disyllabic roots are blocked from appearing in the other morphological categories because the templates stipulated for those categories all contain only one free V-slot. That is, these templates have the property of providing insufficient V-positions, so a portion of the disyllabic root would remain unassociated, in contravention of the functional avoidance of morphological opacity. The nominalization, which is derived from the basic disyllabic root template by prefixing C, does provide two V-slots in the skeleton, and so is permissible.

The distribution of the [n] melody in the biconsonantal and triconsonantal continuative forms is essentially inexplicable in terms of (44). The failure of [n] to associate with the second C-slot of the causative continuative forms is conceivably due to the prior association of the distinctive causative melody [r] with that position. The [n] might thus shift association to the right, where an unfilled slot is located. But the position of [n] in the active continuative forms must apparently be stipulated for each dialect.

The association of the root with the prosodic template is unremarkable in all nominal forms but the continuatives. The causative continuatives show the expected blocking of Continuative Association (40) by the prohibition of many-to-one associations. The third C-slot in each template is already filled by [n], and therefore Continuative Association cannot apply. The effect of this is that only a single copy of the biconsonantal root appears on the surface, and only the first consonant of the first copy of the triconsonantal root. The active continuative forms show the anticipated pattern of association in the Kelantan dialect, but we would expect Continuative Association to yield *$nsgl\mathfrak{o}g$ as the active continuative nominalization in the Perak dialect. In the absence of other information about these dialectal differences, we can only stipulate a special association rule in the latter.

This completes the analysis of the extremely complex morphological system of Temiar. A few other formations described by Benjamin (1976) are clearly compatible with this treatment. For example, expressives — ideophone-like derivatives — involve further cases of root reduplication: *bguy* 'waft (smoke)' becomes *bybguy;* *rwēg* 'stand conspicuously upright' becomes *rgrwēg*. On the whole, then, Temiar morphology largely confirms the need for all the theoretical devices proposed here.

4. CONCLUSION

There are three major areas for further research in this theoretical model. First, morphemic templates promise an even more general account of reduplication than the one here or in McCarthy (1981). Recent work by Marantz (to appear), done in a slightly different formal framework, shows the need for some sort of root copying operation to account for reduplication of initial CV (or final VC) and the like, which occurs in a wide variety of languages. Second, much richer and more complex systems of morphemic tiers appear in some morphologies or subparts of morphologies. For example, it appears that the system of ideophones in Korean is largely dependent on the recognition of distinct, meaningful morphemic tiers for vowel quality, consonant quality, and the laryngeal state in obstruents. Equally elaborate is the system of levels underlying the inflectional morphology of Western Nilotic languages. Third, the possibilities of forming prosodic templates are undoubtedly richer than just linear strings of C's and V's. In McCarthy (to appear) I discuss cases of prosodic templates demonstrably made up of syllables and of metrical stress feet. These are but a few of the issues that considerations of this sort can lead us to.

NOTES

1 Yip (to appear) is a notable exception.

2 I am grateful to Hamza Al-Mozainy for providing me with information about his language and for his perceptive grasp of the issues. The Arabic transcription has the following special features. A subscripted dot in t, d, and s indicates emphatic (pharyngealized) articulation. 9 and h are the voiced and voiceless pharyngeal glides, respectively. Other symbols have their familiar values.

3 In the transcription of the game form for *hindi?* I have corrected an obvious typographical error; in the original it reads with final η. Note that we would expect infixation alone to yield . . *ha:gá:da* . . . for the second game form, rather than the observed . . . *hagá:da*. As Conklin (1956) points out, this and the other trisyllabic sequences are each treated as single prosodic words, with stressed penults. Long vowels do not occur to the left of the penult in Tagalog (Carrier 1979), so shortening is to be expected in this and similar cases.

4 Conklin (1956) stipulates that transposition precedes infixation in forms that combine these two game processes. This ordering has the effect of ensuring that the infixed vowels copy adjacent vocalism, rather than copy some vowel that is subsequently transposed to the other end of the word. This result follows without ordering from the nature of the representational system in the prosodic model, since such nonlocal vowel copying would necessarily require crossing association lines.

5 Zide (1976) indicates that this conception of Gta? diphthongs as short is supported elsewhere in the phonology, but he gives no details. Both sources sometimes write diphthongs with onglides, but I have ignored this subtlety here.

6 Of course, it would be possible to affect two nonadjacent vowels by adding the vocalic melody twice, say at each end of the basic melody. But this is entirely excluded by the nature of all morphemes, including melodic ones: morphemes do not double or reduplicate except by explicit stipulation. No such stipulation is made in this case since no evidence supports it.

7 Two points are of significance in the phonemicization of Temiar followed here. First, I assume that vowels with a macron are distinguished from vowels without one by the feature values [±tense]. This accords well with the detailed phonetic description by Benjamin (1976) and the lack of evidence from syllable structure and phonological rules for a moraic length distinction. Second, the phonemicization abstracts away from entirely regular processes of epenthesis described by Benjamin (1976) and Diffloth (1976), which serve to break up many of the initial clusters in the cited forms.

Prosodic Templates

8   Apparently somewhat marginal categories, like the Arabic quinqueliteral roots described in McCarthy (1981), can lose root material in templates that simply contain too few positions.

9   The significance of these data for nonconcatenative morphological theory was first noted by Munther Younes. I am indebted to him for bringing them to my attention and for providing me with a wealth of examples.

10   *r* could as well be preassociated with the templates in (37). This alternative would not affect the overall analysis.

Prosodic Domains of External Sandhi Rules

Marina Nespor and Irene Vogel
University of Amsterdam and University of Nijmegen

1. INTRODUCTION

The organization of the phonological component of a generative grammar has changed considerably since the proposal made in *The Sound Pattern of English* (SPE) (Chomsky and Halle, 1968). According to SPE, phonological rules apply to the linear surface structure of a sentence, that is, to the output of the syntactic rules. The phonological and syntactic components of the grammar were thus seen as independent from each other; the phonological rules were blind to syntactic structure. At most, phonological rules could make reference to boundaries in their input strings (cf. also Selkirk, 1972; 1974).

Napoli and Nespor (1979)[1] have shown, however, on the basis of an external sandhi rule in Italian, raddoppiamento sintattico (RS), that there is a much closer relationship between syntax and phonology. Specifically, the facts of RS cannot be accounted for merely in terms of boundaries, but rather seem to reflect syntactic information to a larger extent. That is, phonological rules must be able to distinguish between right and left branches in a syntactic tree. Similarly, Clements (1978) has argued that tone sandhi rules in Ewe cannot be handled by making reference only to boundaries between terminal elements, but rather depend crucially on such notions as left branch, right branch and nonpreterminal node. In these works, while the relation between the syntax and the phonology is viewed in a new light, the traditional view of the hierarchical organization of syntax as opposed to the non-hierarchical representation of the phonology is maintained.

The theory put forth by Liberman (1975) and Liberman and Prince (1977) introduced another significant modification in the organization of phonology. According to their metrical theory, certain (prosodic) aspects of phonology, such as English word and phrase stress, "are not to be referred primarily to the properties of individual segments (or syllables), but rather reflect a hierarchical rhythmic structuring that organizes the syllables, words, and syntactic phrases of a sentence" (p. 249). This hierarchical structure consists of binary branching trees, and it is to the constituents of such trees that relative prominence is assigned by projection rules. Linguistic rhythm is then seen "in terms of the alignment of linguistic material with a 'metrical grid' " (p. 249). Vergnaud and Halle (1978) extend Liberman and Prince's proposal, which was based exclusively on English, to an analysis of the stress systems of several languages. They claim that the languages of the world "may differ in choosing between the two types of directional trees and the two labelling conventions made available by universal grammar", though they explicitly state that each level of metrical structure consists of uniformly right or left branching trees. What this amounts to is that there are two independent parameters in the stress component, one that establishes the geometry of the tree (right or left branching) and one that establishes the relative prominence of the nodes, that is, their labelling. In a discussion of this proposal, Wheeler (1981) points out that such a system predicts the existence of stress patterns that do not exist in natural languages. To restrict the proposal so that it will not systematically produce patterns that do not exist, Wheeler provides a constraint called the Branching and Prominence Constraint that establishes a correlation between the geometry of the trees and the labelling of their nodes. According to this constraint, right branching trees are labelled w s (weak / strong) and left branching trees s w, independently of whether or not their nodes branch.

While the proposals of Liberman and Prince and of Vergnaud and Halle differ from previous ones in that they introduce a hierarchical structure in the phonology, the relationship between the branching structure of the phonology above the word level and that of the syntax is not clear. Selkirk (1978, 1980a), on the other hand, in addition to accepting the proposal that not only syntactic, but also phonological representations are hierarchical in nature, actually formulates explicit rules for building the phonological categories above the word level. She demonstrates, furthermore, that certain phonological rules make crucial use of these categories. Thus, while some phonological rules may make reference to labelled bracketings, other make reference to a distinct prosodic structure which includes the following categories: syllable, foot, prosodic word, phonological phrase and utterance. Selkirk points out that, while prosodic and syntactic constituents are not isomorphic, a mapping between the syntactic and prosodic structures "can and must be defined . . . for the prosodic structure reflects syntactic structure in certain ways." The fact that the hierarchical prosodic structure makes use of syntactic information but is not necessarily isomorphic to syntactic structure, is not surprising in that it parallels the situation below the word level, where the phonological and morphosyntactic structures do not necessarily coincide. The mapping conventions Selkirk provides, however, are based solely on English. In this paper, we will investigate further the relation between syntax and prosodic phonology by examining a number of phonological phenomena in Italian and other languages. We propose a series of mapping conventions for Italian which we will then argue are sufficiently general to be able to account for any X-bar type language once the values of certain syntactic parameters have been assigned. Thus we find an illustration of the interpretive role of the phonological component in the sense that the phonology makes use of certain syntactic parameters. That is, at least some aspects of the prosodic structures found in the languages of the world can be seen as dependent variables whose value is automatically assigned once the values of certain independent variables (parameters) of the syntax are known.

2. PROSODIC STRUCTURE OF ITALIAN.

In this section, we will present our analysis of the prosodic structure of Italian based on two suprasegmental phenomena, raddoppiamento sintattico (RS) and intonation contours, and show how this structure allows us to account for additional prosodic phenomena of the language, specifically stress retraction (SR) and the Gorgia Toscana (GT). Since we are particularly interested in the relationship between phonology and syntax, we will limit ourselves to the discussion of prosodic units larger than the word, and thus to those rules that apply above the word level, external sandhi rules, even though we recognize that there is also hierarchical prosodic structure below the word level.

2.1. The phonological phrase: raddoppiamento sintattico.

We will begin by considering what is probably the best known external sandhi rule of Italian: raddoppiamento sintattico, the rule which accounts for the lengthening of the initial consonant of word$_2$ in a sequence word$_1$ word$_2$, under certain phonological and syntactic conditions (e.g. *parló [b]ene → parló[b:]ene*, 'he spoke well'). While RS is found in all varieties of Central and Southern Italian, the environments for its application vary from region to region. We will restrict our attention here to the Tuscan variety of Italian as spoken in Florence. The phonological conditions for RS in this type of Italian are that word$_1$ must end in a stressed vowel and word$_2$ must begin with a consonant, optionally followed by a liquid or glide, and by a vowel (cf. Vogel, 1978).

While it is clear that RS does not apply between just any two words, predicting exactly where it can occur is a problem which has puzzled scholars of Italian linguistics for years (cf. Camilli, 1941; Fiorelli, 1958; Pratelli, 1971, among others). The problem is, in fact, quite complicated since it is not sufficient to know which two words are involved, but it is necessary to know what relationship exists between them. For example, RS occurs between the words *perché* 'why' and *Carlo* in sentence (1a) but not in (1b).

(1) a. Perché [k:] arlo non é ancora arrivato?
'Why has Carlo not arrived yet?'
b. Che c'é un perché [k] arlo lo sa.
'That there is a reason is known to Carlo.'

As we mentioned above, Napoli and Nespor (1979) have, in fact, shown that without reference to syntax, specifically constituent structure, it is not possible to specify the environments for RS. For example, in a sentence such as

(2) Devi comprare delle mappe di cittá vecchie.
a. 'You must buy some old maps of cities.'
b. 'You must buy some maps of old cities.'

which can have two meanings corresponding to two different syntactic structures, RS can occur to lengthen the initial consonant of *vecchie* only in the second meaning, that is, only when *vecchie* is a complement of *cittá*; it cannot occur when *vecchie* is a complement of *mappe*. While Napoli and Nespor's analysis defines those contexts in which RS is allowed, it is incapable of expressing precisely where RS actually occurs. In addition to the syntactic structure, it seemed that the length of the constituents involved, might somehow influence the occurrence of RS, although there was then[2] no part of the grammar that could distinguish between constituents of different lengths. The most recent developments in phonological theory mentioned above, however, suggest that these differences might not be merely a question of length but rather of how constituents of different lengths are organized into prosodic structures.

Data we have gathered on RS[3] have led us to establish the first prosodic category above the word level, the phonological phrase (ϕ). That is, ϕ delimits the domain for the obligatory application of RS; outside of ϕ RS is prohibited. While ϕ's do not necessarily correspond to syntactic constituents, syntactic information is needed for their construction. In (3) the rules are given for mapping syntactic structure onto the prosodic constituent ϕ.

(3) a. *ϕ construction.*
Join into a ϕ any lexical head (X) with all items on its non recursive side[4] within the maximal projection and with any other non lexical items on the same side (e.g. prepositions,

complementizers, conjunctions, copulas...).
b. φ *constituency*.
   φ branches in the same direction as the syntactic trees.

Since Italian is right branching, φ's are also right branching. Furthermore, assuming Wheeler's proposal that the direction of branching determines the labels of the nodes, each pair of sister nodes is labelled w s.

It should be noted that the only items that are considered lexical heads in φ construction are N, V and A. Why P does not belong to this group is not entirely clear, since, in some syntactic analyses P is, in fact, considered a lexical category (cf. van Riemsdijk, 1978). It is worth noting, however, that in SPE only N, V and A are considered lexical categories for the purpose of stress assignment. Thus, independently of syntactic reasons for considering P a lexical category, it seems that there are phonological reasons for distinguishing P from other lexical categories.

The application of the rule in (3) is illustrated in the examples in (4). It should be noted that although φ is necessary for the specification of the environments for the application of RS, it is not sufficient. In addition, the phonological environment mentioned above must be present in order for RS to apply. Those contexts in which RS actually applies are marked in the examples below by '‿'.

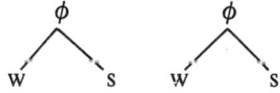

(4) a. Ho‿mangiato da‿Carla.
       'I ate at Carla's,'

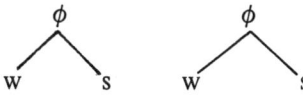

b. Ho‿creduto che‿venisse.
   'I believed that he would come.'

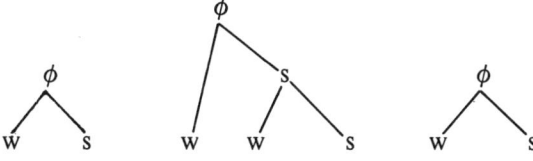

c. 'E‿passato con tre‿cani molto belli.
   'He passed by with three very beautiful dogs.'

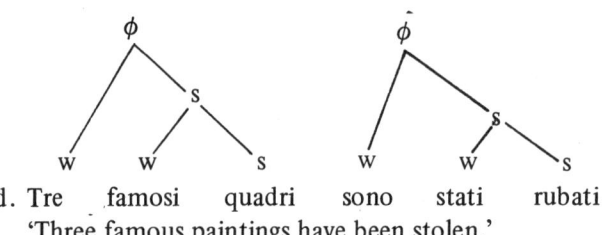

d. Tre famosi quadri sono stati rubati.
'Three famous paintings have been stolen.'

In (4d), we have an example of a Noun Phrase with a prenominal adjective as its complement. Note, though, that in Italian, the position of complements is usually to the right, i.e. recursive, side of the head (cf. 3.1. below). This means that for adjectives the right side is the unmarked position. There are, nevertheless, some cases, as in (4d), in which an adjective can be found to the left, i.e. non-recursive, side of the head; this is the marked case. When they are in the marked position, adjectives do not count as heads of syntactic phrases for the construction of ϕ, but rather are subsumed under a ϕ with the following noun. This particular case may, in fact, be part of a more general principle according to which major categories count as heads for prosody only when they are in the unmarked position. Independent evidence for this characteristic of syntactic phrases has been given by Emonds (1980). To explain the possibility of some extraction transformations and the impossibility of others, Emonds gives the 'Generalized Left Branch Condition', according to which "no syntactic phrase C to the left of the lexical head (N,A, V) of a larger phrase is analyzable as C". He also makes explicit that "on the non recursive side" should replace "to the left".

The rule given in (3) to construct ϕ's, can produce non-branching ϕ's. To eliminate such ϕ's, a restructuring rule may apply, which creates a new node ϕ' under certain syntactic conditions. These conditions are given below in (5).

(5) *Optional ϕ restructuring.*
A non branching ϕ which is the first complement of X on its recursive sides loses its label and is joined to the ϕ containing x under a new node labelled ϕ'.

Note that ϕ' is constructed in such a way that it branches only once. It is therefore impossible to determine its direction of branching. We assume, however, in accordance with Vergnaud and Halle that trees within a stratum, in this case the phonological phrase, are uniformly branching. Thus the relative prominence of the terminal nodes of ϕ' is w s. Illustrations of restructuring are given in (6)-(8), where the forms in *a* are the result of the application of (3) and the forms in *b* are the result of the application of (5).

(6) a. Le cittá vecchie sono belle.
  'Old cities are beautiful.'

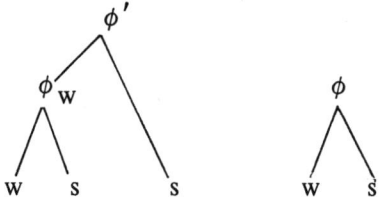

b. Le cittá vecchie sono belle.

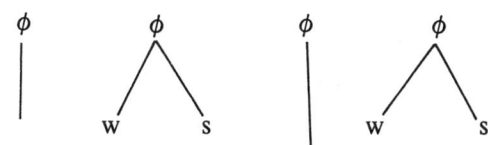

(7) a. Credo che mangerá bene da Francesco.
  'I think he'll eat well at Francesco's.'

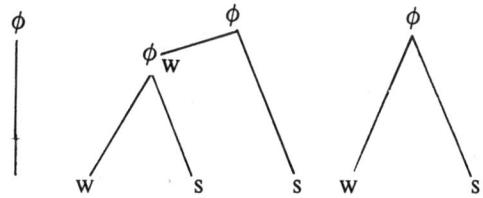

b. Credo che mangerá bene da Francesco.

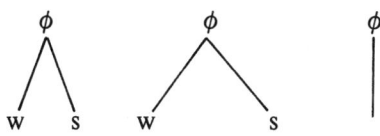

(8) a. Non so se troveró Marco.
  'I don't know if I'll find Marco.'

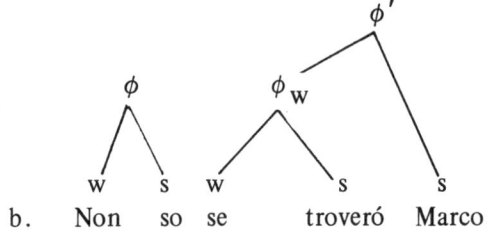

b. Non so se troverò Marco.

Since the phonological phrase (φ/φ') is the environment for the application of RS (given the appropriate phonological conditions at the word level and below), when RS occurs between X and a following non branching complement, this is an indication that restructuring has occurred. Note that this restructuring ensures that the rightmost word in a phonological phrase is always marked s. If, on the other hand, RS does not occur in this environment, this is an indication that the non-branching complement forms a separate φ. Finally, it should be noted that since φ restructuring makes reference to the non-branching nature of the complement of a given head, and thereby implicitly to its length, this directly reflects the observation that length plays a crucial role in determining the application of RS as well as other external sandhi rules[5].

2.2. *The intonational phrase: intonation contours.*

Once phonological phrases have been constructed, we can proceed to construct the intonational phrase (I), which consists of one or more φ/φ' and is "the domain over which an intonational contour is spread" (Selkirk, 1978:26). It has often been noticed that syllables at the end of sentences and other types of clauses are lengthened and often followed by a pause (cf. Cooper, 1976, among others), and in this way serve to indicate the end of intonational contours. Since performance factors such as rate of speech, style and length of the sentence may affect the number of intonational contours contained in an utterance, any rule for constructing I must allow for this variability. This does not mean, however, that the variability is without limits. Rather, there are certain syntactic factors that play a role in determining the domain of I. Certain syntactic structures, such as parentheticals and non-restrictive relative clauses, obligatorily form I's (cf. Selkirk, 1978). Other syntactic constituents, that is NP and S̄, determine the grouping of φ/φ' into I's, though other non syntactic factors may override these original divisions. We propose the following rules for constructing I:

(9) a. *I construction.*
   (i) Any displaced syntactic constituents, parentheticals and non-restrictive relative clauses obligatorily form at least one I.

(ii) Starting with the first ϕ/ϕ' of a sentence, join as many ϕ/ϕ' as possible into an I until either a) the end of the maximal projection of an N is reached, or b) another $\overline{S}$ begins. Once such an I is formed, proceed in the same way until the end of the main sentence is reached. Join any remaining ϕ's at the end of a sentence into an I.

b. *I constituency.*
I is right branching.

Since I's are right branching, the relative prominence of sister nodes is w s. If we assume that lengthening is typically a feature of strong rather than weak ϕ's, this accounts for the general observation mentioned above that lengthening tends to mark the ends of intonation contours. That is, in a right branching structure, the strongest element, i.e. the one dominated uniquely by s's, will always be the rightmost one. Since final lengthening appears to be independent of the direction of branching of the syntactic trees, this means that I is right branching not only in Italian but universally. The construction of I is illustrated below.

(10)

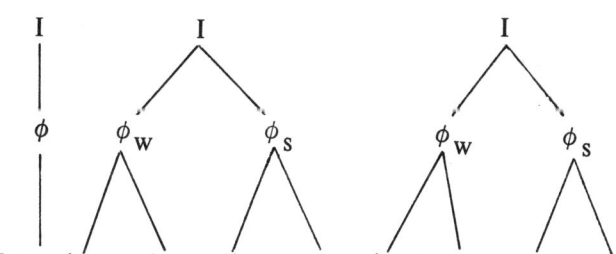

Marco ha venduto la bicicletta al fratellino di Marta
'Marco has sold the bicycle to the little brother of Marta.'

(11)

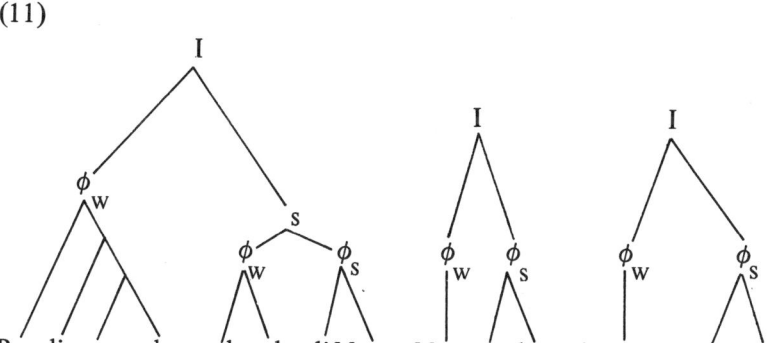

Pur di non andare col padre di Marco, Marta e Alice salterebbero le vacanze.
'Rather than going with Marco's father, Marta and Alice would miss their vacation.'

The I's thus constructed determine the domains over which an intonation contour is spread. Since I is a somewhat variable category, the groupings of ϕ/ϕ' into I's obtained by the rule in (9) represent only one of the possible divisions. In addition, there are restructuring rules that allow us to modify the original I's in case they are particularly long or particularly short (with the exception of those structures mentioned in (9ai) that obligatorily form I's).

(12)   *I restructuring*.
       a. Eliminate very short I's by joining them with adjacent I's.
       b. Eliminate very long I's by breaking them down into shorter I's.

We have deliberately left the formulation of the restructuring rules vague since we are not yet sure of exactly what factors determine restructuring, and since it seems that these factors include other than strictly linguistic considerations (e.g. physiological limitations, perceptual strategies, stylistic considerations). This is not to say, however, that restructuring is completely random. We have observed, for example, that whenever possible, a restructured I ends with the end of an NP (dominated in this case by other NP's).

When I's are restructured, the previous I structure is eliminated and new I's are built up according to the general branching and prominence convention. The number of I's would be reduced by (12a) and increased by (12b) in the examples given in (13) and (14), respectively.

(13)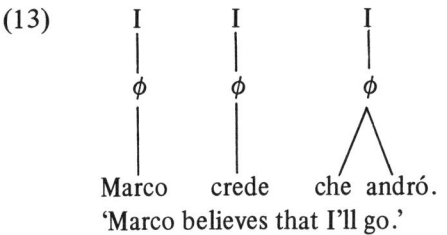
Marco crede che andró.
'Marco believes that I'll go.'

(14)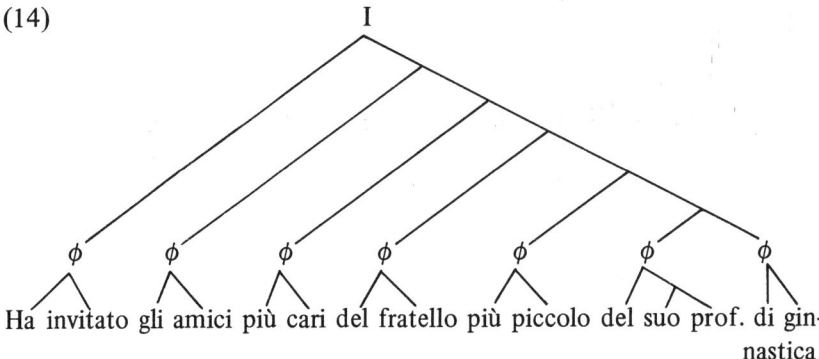
Ha invitato gli amici più cari del fratello più piccolo del suo prof. di ginnastica.
'He has invited the dearest friends of the youngest brother of his gym teacher.'

The three I's in (13) may be reduced to two I's by combining the two rightmost I's, or to one I that includes the entire sentence. The single I in (14) may be divided either into two I's such that the first includes the first three φ's and the second the remaining four φ's, or into three I's, such that the first includes the first three φ's, the second the next two φ's and the third the last two φ's.

We have seen above that, apart from constituents that have been moved, the syntactic categories that are crucial in the construction of I are NP and $\bar{S}$. That is, NP and $\bar{S}$ are barriers for I's.[6] Exactly why this should be the case is not clear to us, though it is interesting that precisely these two nodes are the bounding nodes for subjacency (cf. Rizzi, 1980), and are also barriers for government (see, among others, Bennis and Groos, 1980). They are thus barriers for syntactic, phonological and logical form rules.

Once the I's are built, we can proceed to construct the utterance (U), the highest prosodic category which corresponds to the highest category of syntactic structure (cf. Selkirk, 1978).

(15)   a. *U construction*.
       Join all I's in a root sentence (most generally the highest category of syntactic structure) into a U.
       b. *U constituency*.
       U is right branching.

The fact that U is right branching predicts that if, for example, three short I's such as those in (13) are restructured, the first and second I's can be dominated (directly or indirectly) by the same node labelled I only if the third I is also dominated by the same node. The second and third I's, on the other hand, can be joined to form a new I without necessarily including the first I. Either of these possibilities yields an unmarked pronunciation, that is, one with no particular emphasis. The structures in (16a) and (16b) are thus possible while the structure in (16c) is not.[7] The I's in parentheses are those node labels eliminated when restructuring occurs.

(16)   a.

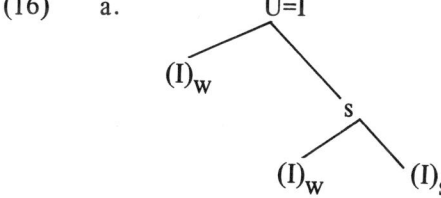

b.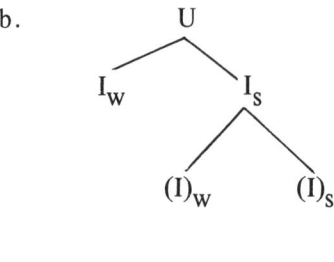

c.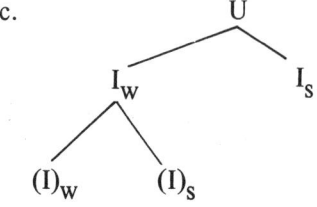

The fact that U is right branching means that the rightmost I will always be strong. Since length is one of the features associated with s, the fact that the rightmost I is strong may account for the generally observed lengthening at the end of an utterance. That is, the domain of lengthening will be under I_s, though exactly which elements are lengthened and to what extent, must be determined at a lower prosodic level.

Finally, assuming a model of grammar in which shallow structure, that is surface structures enriched with elements that are not phonetically realized such as PRO and traces (cf. Chomsky, 1975; 1980) is the input to the phonological component, it is reasonable to ask the following two questions: a) What role, if any, do these elements play in the phonology? b) Assuming that at least some of these elements do play a role, does their influence extend to the entire phonological component or is it restricted to a specific part of it? While it is clear that at least some prosodic rules do not take into consideration the presence of elements without a phonetic form (see, for example, (18b) below in which the Gorgia Toscana applies across a trace), it might be that other prosodic rules are sensitive to such elements (see Jaeggli (1980) who argues that traces marked for case, unlike traces not marked for case, block contraction in English). This is, of course, a very interesting and important problem, but we will not go into it further in this paper.

2.3. Further evidence for φ and I.

In this section, we will demonstrate that the prosodic categories established on the basis of RS and intonational contours allow us to account for additional phonological phenomena of Italian: the rule of stress retraction in Northern Italian and the Gorgia Toscana in Tuscan Italian.

2.3.1. Stress retraction (SR).
SR is a sandhi rule that applies in a sequence of word$_1$ word$_2$, if word$_1$ ends in a primary stressed vowel and word$_2$ has primary stress on its first syllable. In such cases, the primary stress is moved leftward away from the final syllable of word$_1$ to avoid this clash of primary stresses (e.g. *metá tórta* → *méta tórta* 'half cake').

Nespor and Vogel (1979) have shown that stress retraction is in a type of geographical complementary distribution with RS. That is, the former is found in northern varieties of Standard Italian while the latter is found in central and southern varieties. It follows from this that the prosodic category ϕ/ϕ' which defines the syntactic environments for RS also allows us to specify the syntactic environments for stress retraction, despite the difference in the phonological context for the two rules. That is, SR applies, as does RS, only when the two words in question are in the same phonological phrase. The sentence below provides examples of the environments for stress retraction or raddoppiamento sintattico, depending on the variety of Italian in question.

(17)
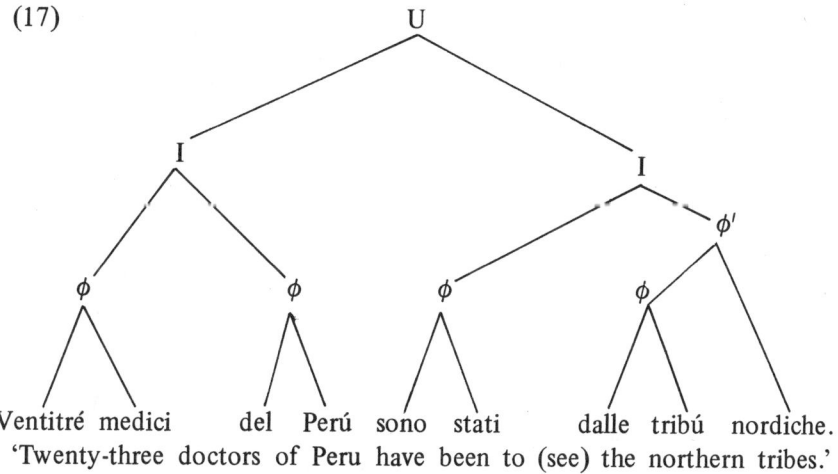
Ventitré medici del Perú sono stati dalle tribú nordiche.
'Twenty-three doctors of Peru have been to (see) the northern tribes.'

In this sentence there are three pairs of words in which the phonological context for SR (RS) is present: *ventitré medici, Perú sono, tribú nordiche*. In the first case, SR applies obligatorily since the words in question form a ϕ. SR also applies in the third case if restructuring has applied to form ϕ' as indicated in the prosodic tree. SR is blocked, however, in the second case since the two words belong to different ϕ's.

2.3.2. Gorgia Toscana (GT).

The next sandhi rule we will consider is the Gorgia Toscana. GT is traditionally described as a phonological phenomenon of Tuscan Italian that results in various degrees of so-called aspiration of the voiceless stops *p, t, k* in intervocalic position (cf. Giannelli and Savoia, 1979; Lepschy and Lepschy, 1977). The most common form of GT changes *p, t* and *k* into [φ], [θ] and [h], respectively (e.g. *la porta* → *la* [φ]*orta* 'the door', *la tavola* → *la* [θ]*avola* 'the table', *la casa* → *la*[*h*]*asa* 'the house').

Since the "aspiration" of *k* is the most widespread form of GT, we have limited our investigation to this particular phenomenon. On the basis of our recordings of over 900 sentences read by five speakers of Tuscan Italian from Florence and immediately surrounding areas, we have found that the domain of application of GT is I. It should be noted, however, that the Gorgia Toscana, unlike RS and SR, is not exclusively an external sandhi rule, but it applies in I both within and across words, as long as the proper segmental phonological environment exists. Thus, while in the cases of RS and SR, word junctures must be taken into account in addition to the prosodic domain of application, in the case of GT, no further specification is required. The environments for the Gorgia Toscana are illustrated below in (18a), (18b) and (18c).

(18) a.

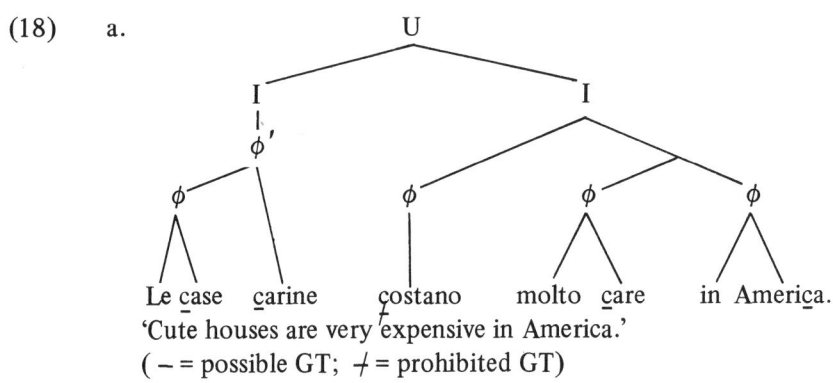

'Cute houses are very expensive in America.'
(– = possible GT; ≠ = prohibited GT)

b.

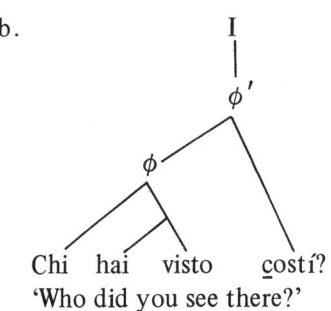

'Who did you see there?'

c.
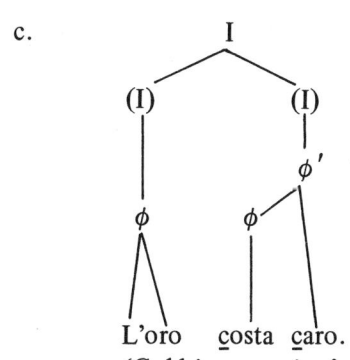
'Gold is expensive.'

In the sentence in (18a), GT occurs within the word (cf. *America*), within φ (cf. *case, care*) and within φ' (cf. *carine*), all of which are also obviously within I. GT is prohibited across I's (cf. *costano*), though in the unlikely case that the speaker utters the sentence so quickly that it is a single I, restructuring would then call for GT even in *costano*. In (18b) and (18c), GT occurs again in φ'. Furthermore, in (18c), since the two I's are so short, restructuring is very likely and GT can therefore also occur in *costa*.

3. THE UNIVERSAL CHARACTER OF φ.

In section 2.1., rules for constructing φ have been given. It should be noted that, while these rules make reference to the syntactic notion of lexical head, they do not refer to language particular syntactic structures of Italian. Instead, they make reference to the notion of recursive versus non recursive side of a phrase with respect to the head of the phrase. It would be very strange if only Italian prosodic categories needed to refer to such general notions as recursive and non-recursive side of a phrase. In this section we will show that these notions, in fact, allow us to determine the phonological phrase in all X-bar type languages.

3.1. The recursivity parameters.

In Graffi (1980), the following two parameters of core grammar are given:

(19) First Parameter of Core Grammar (p. 379).
Every language chooses a recursive side [(Chomsky, 1965)] with respect to the head of syntactic phrase categories.

(20) Second Parameter of Core Grammar (p. 382).
Some languages only exploit the recursive side with respect to the head; the remaining languages also exploit the non recursive side.[8]

That is, every language chooses a side with respect to the head for its complements (parameter I) and either the same side or the opposite side for its specifiers (parameter II).[9] These choices establish what is unmarked in a language, though it is nevertheless possible that some marked orders exist.

If we now look back at our rule for constructing ϕ, we see that it depends crucially on which value (right or left) has been assigned to the first parameter of core grammar given above. That is, once the recursive side has been determined, we automatically know that ϕ will be built on the opposite side of the head. It should be noted that if the second parameter is fixed in favor of the use of the non-recursive side as well as the recursive side, there will be many contexts for ϕ construction, whereas if the second parameter is fixed in such a way that only the recursive side is used, the contexts for ϕ construction are limited to marked cases if they exist. The fact that the basic syntactic structure of a language is taken into account in constructing ϕ implies that ϕ, rather than being an independent variable of the phonological component, is a dependent variable. This suggests that there are two distinct types of variables in the phonological component: independent variables such as those that specify opaque segments in harmony processes, and variables dependent on the syntax such as those that determine the domain of application of certain rules.[10] This is, of course, an empirical question. What we are saying is that there exists a category of external sandhi rules whose domain of application must be stated in relation to the basic order of the elements in a syntactic phrase. These rules will operate (a) to the left of the head in languages whose recursive side is to the right of the head, (b) to the right of the head in languages whose recursive side is to the left of the head. Furthermore, if there are sandhi rules that apply on the recursive side, this implies that they must also apply on the non-recursive side, but not vice versa. In such cases, the phonological phrase on the recursive side will have been created by a language specific rule. In the next section, we will illustrate the role the phonological phrase, as constructed on the basis of our rules, plays in relation to sandhi rules in languages other than Italian.

3.2. *The phonological phrase in other languages.*

In this section, we will examine sandhi rules in English and French whose domain of application is the phonological phrase. The first rule we will consider is stress retraction in English and the second is liaison in the colloquial style of French. We will also briefly compare Selkirk's (1978) proposal to account for English stress retraction and French liaison since it is, in fact, quite similar to ours. Finally, we will discuss a prediction our ϕ construction rule makes for Japanese.

Rule (3) given above for constructing ϕ yields phonological phrases similar to those yielded by the rule Selkirk (1978) gives for constructing ϕ in English. Our rule is to be preferred, however, since it is more general in that it can construct ϕ's in any X-bar type language and since it provides a principled way for determining the direction of branching of the prosodic trees in ϕ.

As Selkirk points out, ϕ is the domain of application of the rhythm rule that retracts stress to eliminate clashes of primary stresses, as in *thirtéen mén* → *thírteen mén* (cf. Liberman and Prince, 1977, for details of this phenomenon).[11] In as much as our ϕ is the same as Selkirk's, the two proposals account for the same facts. It seems, however, that an additional category, ϕ', is necessary in English, as in Italian, in order to account for all cases of stress retraction. Consider the following examples.

(21) a. John gládly persevéres.
      b. John pérseveres gládly.

(22) a. Given the chance, rabbits quíckly reprodúce.
      b. Given the chance, rabbits réproduce quíckly.

While in (21a) and (22a) the verbs *persevere* and *reproduce* have final stress, this is not the case in (21b) and (22b), where they are directly followed by a word with initial primary stress. Thus, it is not the case that retraction occurs only to the left of the head of a phrase. Instead, the domain of application of the rhythm rule in English appears to be identical to the domain of stress retraction in Italian. That is, a restructuring rule such as the one given above in (5) is also required to construct ϕ' in English.

Note that, as in Italian, ϕ' is constructed only when the complement in question is non branching. Thus, retraction occurs as we have seen in (21b) and (22b), but not in the sentence in (23), where the complements are branching.

(23) a. John persevéres gládly and diligently.
      b. Given the chance, rabbits reprodúce véry quickly.

Although Selkirk (1978) does not discuss French in detail, she does mention that the phonological phrase is also the domain of application of liaison. As we mentioned above, the ϕ's constructed in right branching languages are the same in Selkirk's proposal and the one presented here. It follows, therefore, that both accounts adequately handle liaison. That is, liaison applies in colloquial French within a ϕ, as illustrated in (24), but not across ϕ's, as illustrated in (25), where the relevant consonants are underlined.

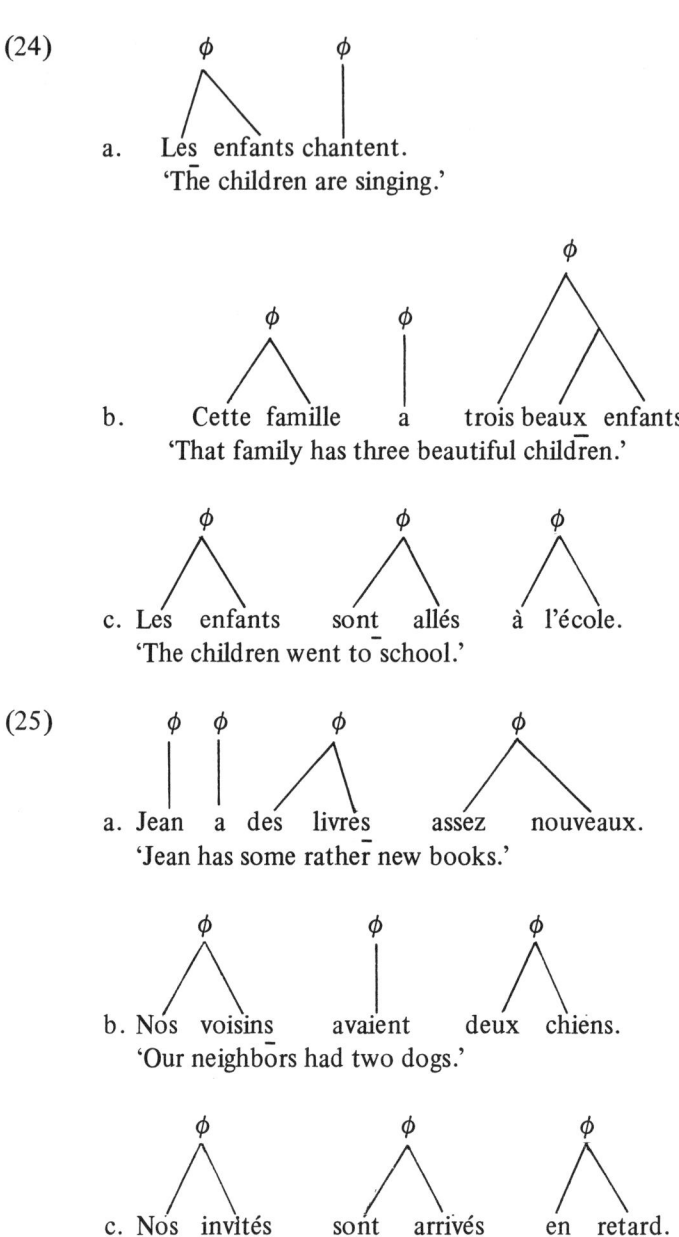

It should be noted, however, that liaison differs from the other rules that operate in the domain of the phonological phrase discussed so far in that it does not apply in the additional ϕ' environment. Thus, while liaison occurs in the sentence above in (24), the ϕ domain, it does not occur in those in (26), the ϕ' domain.

(26)

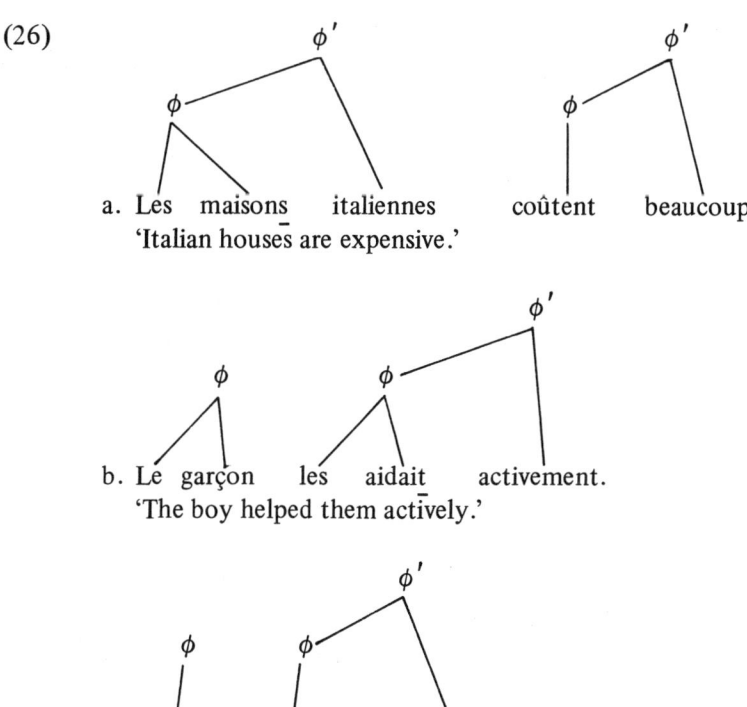

a. Les maisons italiennes coûtent beaucoup.
'Italian houses are expensive.'

b. Le garçon les aidait activement.
'The boy helped them actively.'

c. Marc viendrait aujourd'hui, ...
'Marc would come today, ...'

This does not necessarily mean that ϕ' does not exist in French. It might in fact turn out that there are other sandhi rules that apply within the domain of ϕ'.

The empirical evidence for the phonological phrase we have given thus far is based on data from right branching languages. We have shown that in these languages external sandhi rules treat everything to the left of the head of a phrase plus the head itself as one constituent (ϕ). The prediction made by our statement of ϕ constituency as formulated in (3b) is that in left branching languages sandhi rules make use of phonological constituents that are the mirror image of ϕ's in right branching languages. We do not, however, have enough empirical evidence about sandhi rules in left branching languages to make an explicit claim. It is interesting to note, though, that a study by McCawley (1977) of accent in Japanese, a left branching language, seems to confirm the left branching nature of phonological phrases in that language. McCawley claims that if a constituent of more than one word is read "as a single phrase", then it is the accent of the first constituent that predominates, exactly the opposite of what happens in right branching languages. McCawley points out further that a rule that would account for this phenomenon in Japanese is the mirror image of the nuclear stress rule of English (cf. Chomsky and Halle, 1968). Since we have assumed, following Wheeler (1981), that the prominence relation is s w in left branching trees and w s in right branching trees, and since the predominant accent of a constituent cannot fall on a w element, the prosodic category that is the domain of application of the stress rule mentioned by McCawley should be left branching. What remains to be investigated is if that category is ϕ as constructed in (3a), or a category that is the result of a restructuring rule, or still a different category. More data than those provided by McCawley are, however, needed in order to establish the exact environment of the rule.

4. I AND U IN OTHER LANGUAGES

4.1. Intonational Phrase.

The rule given in (9ai) for constructing I in Italian is, in fact, quite general in that it makes use of such notions as displaced syntactic constituents, parentheticals and non-restrictive relative clauses. The part in (9aii), however, makes use of the syntactic categories NP and $\bar{\text{S}}$ and is thus formulated in such a way that it is a possible rule only for right branching languages. We have suggested above that the fact that NP and $\bar{\text{S}}$ are relevant for the construction of I might somehow be related to the fact that they are binding nodes for subjacency and barriers for government. We could thus hypothesize that our rule would be adequate for constructing I's in all languages in which NP and $\bar{\text{S}}$ function in this way. We expect, however, that it would not be difficult to modify the rule to account for other types of languages as well, though in the absence of relevant data, we will not do so here. In the remainder of this section, we will discuss rules in two right branching languages, English and Spanish, that operate in the I domain, as constructed by the rule in (9).

We will first consider the flapping of *t* and *d* in American English. It has been noted that flapping not only occurs within words, but also across word boundaries (see, for example, Kahn, 1976). It is obvious that flapping does not occur across all words, but rather it appears to be limited to those within the domain of I. Thus, flapping occurs in the examples in (27), and is blocked in those in (29); the relevant consonants are underlined.

(27)

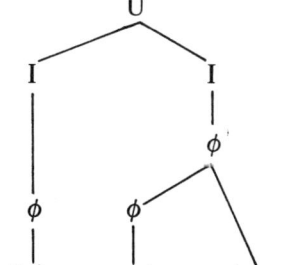

a. John met Anne.

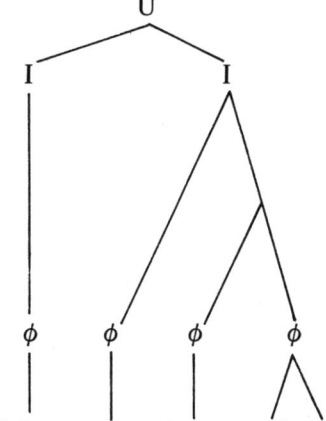

b. John met Anne and Sue.

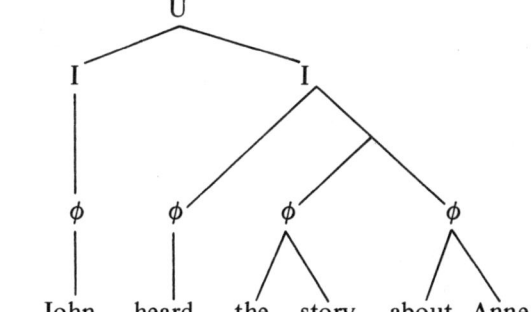

c. John heard the story about Anne.

(28)

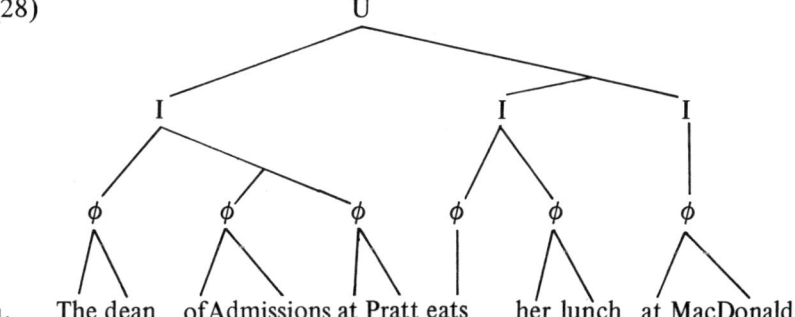

a. The dean of Admissions at Pratt eats her lunch at MacDonalds.

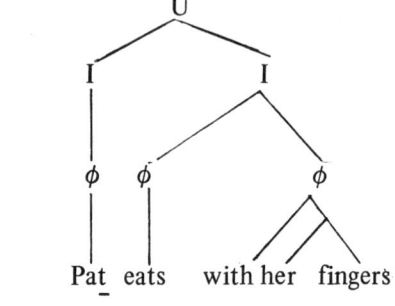

b. Pat eats with her fingers

c. Roger, alias the rat, eats only cheese.

While in the examples in (27) flapping is obligatory, since the t's are necessarily within an I, the examples in (28) are slightly more complicated. That is, flapping does not occur because the *t*'s are at the end rather than within an I. As mentioned above, however, restructuring may take place to eliminate sequences of particularly short I's. In (28b), for example, where the first I contains only one word, the sentence is likely to be pronounced as a single intonational phrase. In this case, in fact, flapping occurs. In (28a), since the I's are relatively long, restructuring, and therefore flapping, are highly unlikely, if possible at all. Finally, in (28c), where *alias the rat*, a parenthetical, is obligatorily in I, flapping can never occur.

The second sandhi rule operating within I that we will consider is nasal assimilation in Spanish. It has frequently been observed that nasals assimilate in point of articulation to the following consonant across word boundaries as well as within words (cf. Navarro Tomás, 1957; Harris, 1968; Hooper, 1976, among others)[12]. Exactly across which words nasals assimilate, however, has never been adequately specified. Examination of the following examples shows that the appropriate domain of nasal assimilation is the intonational phrase constructed exactly as in Italian.

(29) a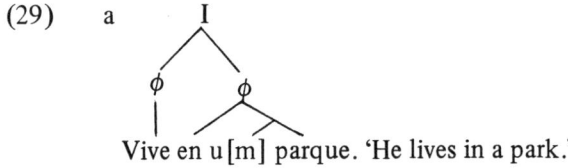

Vive en u[m] parque. 'He lives in a park.'

b.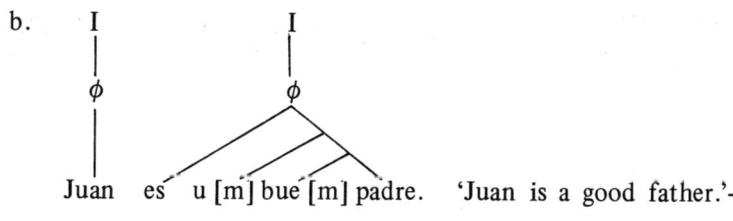

c.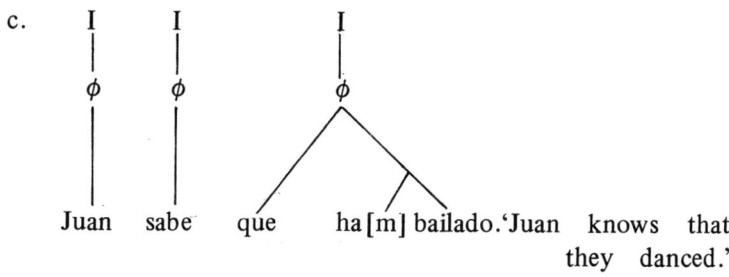

d.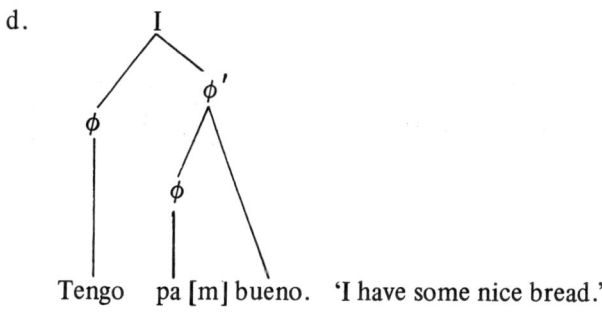

e.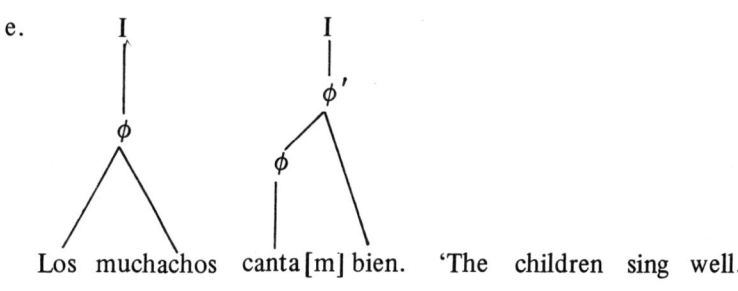

f.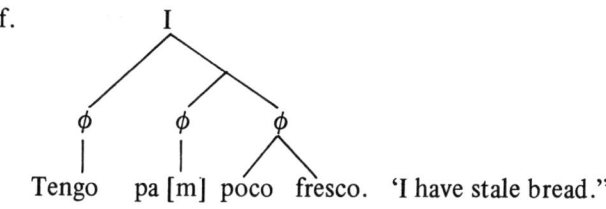

g.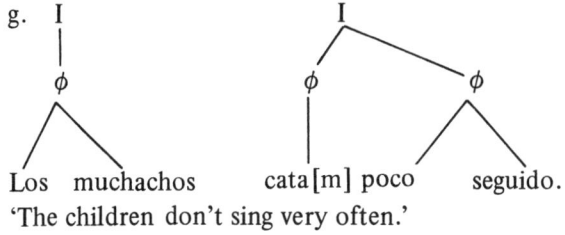
'The children don't sing very often.'

(30) a. 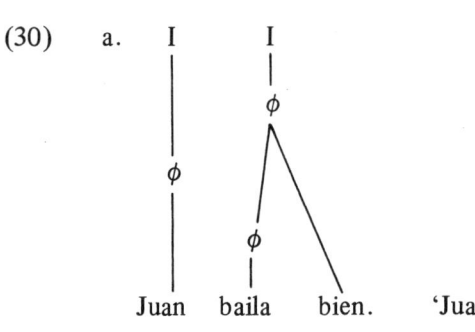 'Juan dances well.'

b.
Dicen que vienen. 'They say they will come.'

c.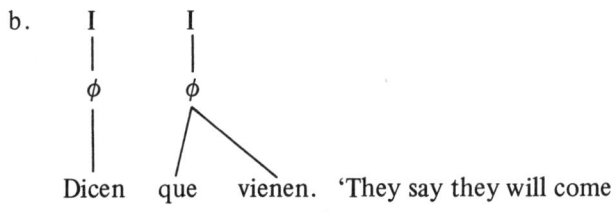
'The brother of the wife of Juan travels very often with Maria.'

d.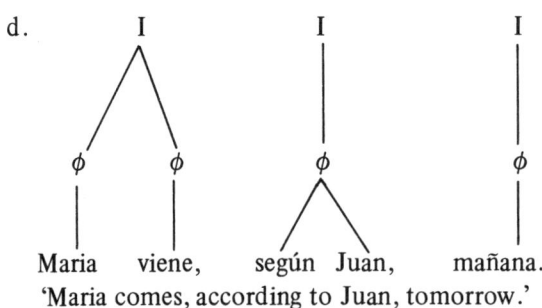
'Maria comes, according to Juan, tomorrow.'

In the sentences in (29), nasal assimilation applies obligatorily, since all the nasal plus consonant sequences in question are within I. Note, however, that the organization of the relevant words in phonological phrases does not affect the application of nasal assimilation. That is, in (29) *a, b* and *c*, assimilation occurs within ϕ, in (29) *d* and *e* within ϕ' and in (29) *f* and *g* across ϕ's. in the sentences in (30), on the other hand, the nasal and the consonant are in different I's and assimilation, therefore, does not take place. Sentences (30) *a* and *b*, however, are likely to be restructured to avoid very short I's within a sentence, and in this case, assimilation takes place. Such a restructuring is very unlikely in (30c) given the length of the I's, and it is prohibited in (30d) where the parenthetical, *según Juan*, obligatorily forms an I on its own.

4.2. UTTERANCE.

We have not yet found any rules in Italian whose domain is U. There are, however, two phenomena in standard English as spoken in England that occur in U: the linking-r and the related, intrusive-r.

While final *r*'s are usually deleted in the English in question, if the following word begins with a vowel, the *r* is retained as a "linking-r". As the sentences in (31) show, the final *r* is retained before any word beginning with a vowel as long as the words are in the same U. That is, the *r* is pronounced within ϕ (31a), across ϕ's within I (31b) across I's (31c) and even at the end of a parenthetical (31d).

(31) a. He has the prope*r* attitude.
 b. The rule*r* of that country is a tyrant.
 c. The drive*r* arrived late today.
 d. The crime, according to Arthu*r*, is the work of a band of thieves.

When a word ends with a vowel, specifically [ə], [ɔ] or [a], and the next word begins with a vowel, an *r* is introduced, yielding a sequence similar to that produced by the linking-r. The intrusive *r* is also found between any two words in the same U, as well as within words, as we see below.

(32) a. The cat has been claw - r - ing at the furniture all afternoon.
 b. I bet you don't dare eat a raw - r - aubergine.
 c. They go to America - r - in the spring of every leap year.
 d. His far-fetched idea - r - appeals to everyone.
 e. The great continent, Asia, - r - evokes mysterious images.

In (32a), the intrusive *r* is found word internally, in (32b) within a ϕ, in (32c) across ϕ's within I, in (32d) across I's and in (32e) at the end of a parenthetical.

5. PROSODIC STRUCTURE AND SPEECH PERCEPTION.

In this paper we have shown that the grammar, that is, the theory of competence, must include a hierarchically organized prosodic component as part of the phonology. We hypothesize now that the prosodic units justified in the theory of competence are also units of performance, that is, both production and perception. In the remainder of this paper, we will investigate the implications of this hypothesis further, limiting ourselves, however, to perception and further, to Italian data. Specifically, we will argue that it is the units of the prosodic structure of a sentence that determine the first level of processing in perception. This means that a listener will not be able to distinguish between the possible meanings of ambiguous sentences if they have the same prosodic structure, whether or not their syntactic structure is the same. In order to disambiguate such sentences, the listener must resort to other types of information such as contextual cues.

This proposal makes predictions that contrast with those of Lehiste (1973:112), among others, according to which sentences that can be disambiguated are ones "for which a difference in meaning is correlated with a difference in surface [syntactic] constituent structure", and sentences that cannot be disambiguated are those that "have only one bracketing, although the constituents may bear different labels". While Lehiste's study deals with English, we do not think this is what accounts for the difference between Lehiste's and our proposals. That is, although the actual syntactic and prosodic structures may differ from language to language, we assume that a principle so fundamental as the role of the different components of the grammar in perception cannot be language specific. The crucial difference lies thus in the fact that Lehiste refers only to syntactic structure while we claim that it is necessary to refer to the prosodic structure, which, although it is based on syntactic structure, is not isomorphic to it.

We will now examine some sentences in Italian which demonstrate that disambiguation in perception depends on prosodic constituents rather than syntactic ones. The relevant sentences are those in which the same sequence of words, can be analyzed syntactically in different ways but which nevertheless yield identical prosodic structure. Consider the sentences in (33) and (34) in which a difference in meaning is correlated with a difference in syntactic structure.

(33) Ha toccato il quadro con la matita.
 a. 'He touched the picture with (containing) the pencil.'
 b. 'He touched the picture with (using) the pencil.'

(34) Ho mangiato i pasticcini con la cioccolata.
 a. 'I ate donuts with (containing) chocolate.'
 b. 'I ate donuts (together) with chocolate.'

The *a* interpretations in (33) and (34) correspond to the syntactic structures in which the PP is a complement of the NP, while the *b* interpretations correspond to syntactic structures in which the PP is a complement of the VP. Despite these syntactic differences, the prosodic structures corresponding to the different interpretations are identical at the φ level. There is, nevertheless, a difference at the I level. The prosodic structures of the *a* and *b* examples are given in (35) and (36) respectively.

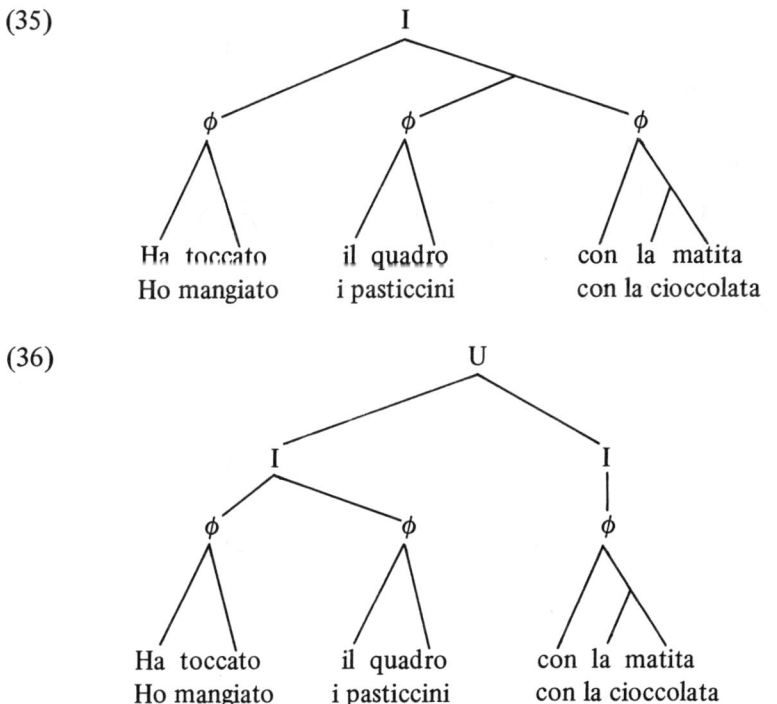

(35)

(36)

It should be noted, furthermore, that the two I's in (36) may be restructured to form a single I since they are both quite short (cf. (12a)). If this restructuring occurs, as it typically would in such a case, the two sentences can no longer be disambiguated since their prosodic structures become identical, despite their different syntactic structures. If, on the other hand, restructuring does not take place and the sentences in (36) contain two intonational contours, these sentences can only have the interpretations given in (33b) and (34b).

There are other sentences, however, in which different syntactic structures obligatorily give rise to different prosodic structures and may thus be disambiguated on the basis of phonological information, as illustrated by the sentences in (37) and their configurations given in (33b) and (34b).

(37) La vecchia legge la regola.
      a. 'The old law regulates it.'
      b. 'The old lady is reading the rule.'

(38) a.

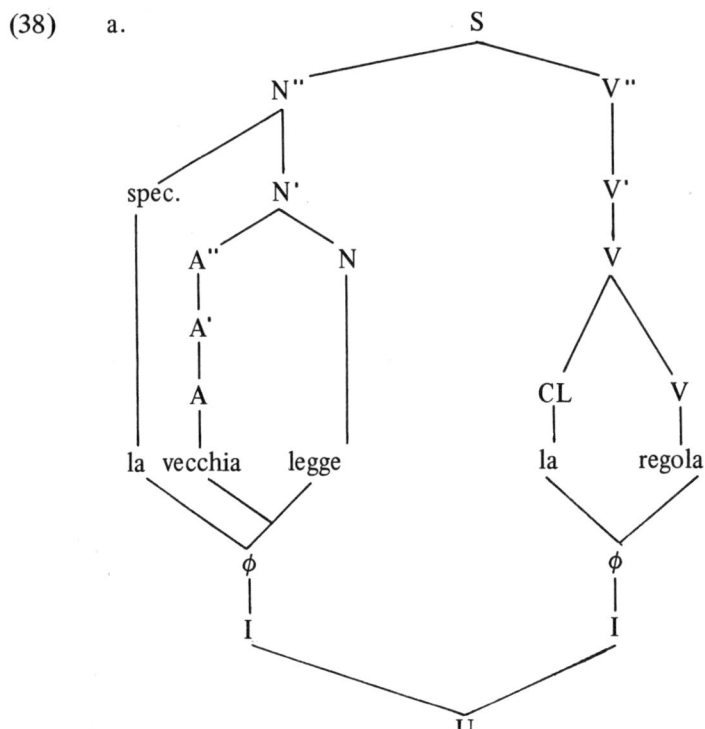

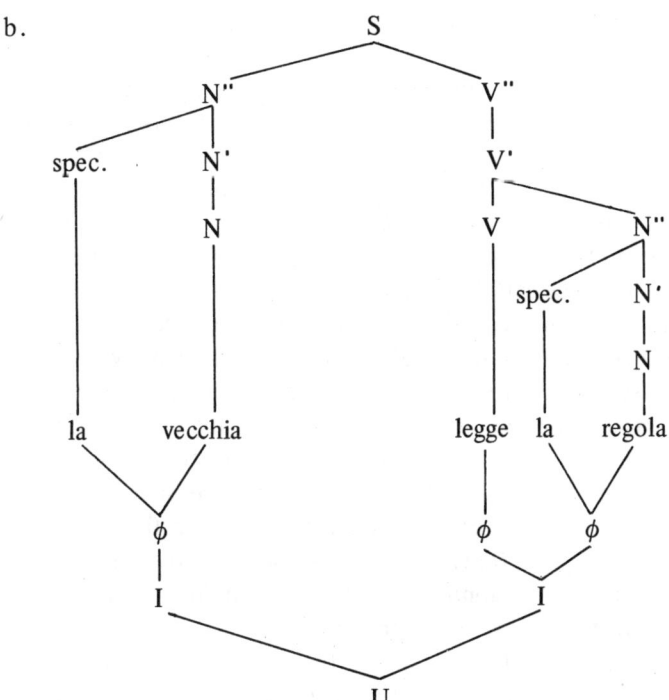

In (38a), there are only 2 φ's, while in (38b) there are 3. This comes as a result of the different functions of the words *vecchia* and *legge* in the two sentences. In (38a), *legge*, the noun 'law' is the head of the phrase and incorporates what is to its left, including, in this case, *vecchia*, the adjective 'old', into a φ. In (38b), on the other hand, the verb *legge* '(she) reads', as head of the VP, forms a φ by itself. *Vecchia*, here the noun 'old lady', is the head of the NP and thus forms a φ along with its preceding determiner.

Our analysis thus shows that syntactic structure plays a role in the perception of sentences, however this role is only indirect. According to a theory of perception in which each level of linguistic representation in the native speaker's competence corresponds to a level of representation computed by the processor, there must obviously be a level of processing corresponding to the syntactic structure. Our proposal does not imply that the syntactic level is no longer relevant, but rather that the syntactic units do not themselves form the initial units of processing. Instead, the syntactic units allow us to construct the prosodic units which then serve as the perceptual units at the initial level of processing. It is for this reason that syntactic distinctions that are not reflected in the prosodic structure are not perceived at this initial level.

6. CONCLUSIONS

In this paper, we have provided an analysis of the domains of application of rules of external sandhi in Italian. These domains cannot be adequately defined in terms of syntactic categories. The first of these, the phonological phrase, extends over the left side of a phrase and not the right side. This asymmetry had already been observed by Napoli and Nespor (1979), Rotenberg (1978) and Clements (1978), who argue that in Italian, French, Hebrew and Ewe certain phonological rules must make references to either left or right branches of a syntactic tree. The second prosodic category, the intonational phrase, in addition to not necessarily being isomorphic to any syntactic category, also exhibits a certain amount of variability based on such non syntactic factors as length and rate of speech.

Starting from the observations that syntactic phrases in X-bar type languages are themselves asymmetric in that one side is recursive and the other is not, we have built prosodic categories on the basis of two external sandhi rules in Italian. We have shown that these prosodic categories are the domain of application of other sandhi rules in Italian, French, Spanish, British and American English.

The prosodic categories above the word level, as constructed in this paper, have interesting theoretical consequences in that they can be built only after a syntactic parameter of core grammar has been determined. Therefore, although prosodic structures differ in left and right branching languages, this coice is not made in the phonology independently of the syntax.

Finally, we have shown, on the basis of Italian data, that prosodic categories are used in perception at the first level of processing, in that speakers cannot disambiguate sentences with identical prosodic structures independently of whether their syntactic structures are identical or different.

ACKNOWLEDGEMENTS

We would like to thank Jan Edelman, Yuki Kuroda, Anneke Neijt, Donna Jo Napoli, Mauro Scoretti and Milos Stejskal for their helpful suggestions and criticisms. We would also like to thank all of the people who helped us with their intuitions about their native language and in particular Bernard Bichakjian, Emanuela Cresti, Enzo Lo Cascio, Anita de Meijer Concas, Massimo Moneglia and Yuri Okabe. Finally, we are grateful to the many speakers of Italian who spent a lot of time talking into a tape recorder.

FOOTNOTES.

1. Napoli and Nespor (1979) was originally written and circulated as a manuscript in (1976).
2. See footnote 1.

3.   The data consist of tape recordings and oscilloscopic measurements of sentences containing contexts for SR spoken by six speakers of standard Italian in Rome, six in Palermo, and five in Florence. The data were gathered as part of a larger project supported in part by the Faculty of Letters of the University of Amsterdam.
4.   By non-recursive side, we mean the side opposite the recursive side.
5.   P. Verluyten (personal communication) has suggested that length also plays a role in the application of liaison in French.
6.   They are not absolute barriers since, as we have seen, a restructuring of I can, under certain circumstances, take place with the effect that I can extend over NP and $\bar{S}$ (cf. (13)).
7.   If in sentence (13) special emphasis is placed on the word *crede*, (16c) is the correct structure, as seen by the fact that this word bears the label *s* only in (16c). The predictions that prosodic trees make in cases of emphasis are very interesting but we will not go into them any further in this paper, since they raise a whole series of independent questions.
8.   Our translation.
9.   This applies of course, only to X-bar type languages, as opposed to W-star type languages. See Hale (1981) for the distinction between X' and W* languages.
10.   Some phonological rules might also need to refer directly to the syntax, such as rules that must specify syntactic categories, but we will not consider this type of rules in this paper.
11.   Our use of an acute accent does not say anything about the absolute value of the stress of the syllable bearing it, but simply that it bears more stress with respect to other syllables in the word.
12.   While there are some minor differences in the assimilation patterns within words and across word boundaries, such as the behavior of nasal + glide sequences, we are not concerned with them here.

References

Allen, M.R. (1978), *Morphological Investigations*. Doctoral Dissertation. University of Connecticut.
Al-Mozainy, H. (1981), *Vowel Alternations in a Bedouin Hijazi Arabic Dialect: Abstractness and Stress*. Doctoral Dissertation. University of Texas, Austin.
Anderson, S.R. (1976), Nasal consonants and the internal structure of segments. *Language 52,* 326–344.
Anderson, S.R. (1978), Syllables, Segments and the Northwest Caucasian Languages. In: *Bell & Hooper (eds.),* 47–59.
Anderson, S.R. (1979), On the Subsequent Development of the 'Standard Theory'. In: *Dinnsen (ed.),* 2–31.
Anderson, S.R. (1980), Problems and perspectives in the description of vowel harmony. In: *R. Vago (ed),* 1–49.
Arekambe, D. (1972), Aspects of the phonology of Gokana. Long Essay. University of Ibadan, Nigeria.
Aronoff, M. (1976), *Word Formation in Generative Grammar*. Linguistic Inquiry Monograph, 1. Cambridge, Mass., M.I.T. Press.
Asinyirimba, J.O. (1972), The phonology of Gokana. Long Essay. University of Ibadan, Nigeria.
Barratt, L. (1981), Prenasalized Stops in Guaraní. Where the Autosegment Fails. *Linguistic Analysis 7,* 187–202.
Battistella, E. (1979), Igbo Vowel Harmony. *Cunyform papers in Linguistics 5–6,* 108–124.
Becker, L. and D. Massamba (1980), Ci-Ruri Tonology (A Preliminary View). *Studies in the Linguistic Sciences.* Urbana, Illinois.
Bell, A. and J.B. Hooper (eds.) (1978), *Syllables and Segments*. Amsterdam.
Bendor-Samuel, J.T. (1960), Some problems of segmentation in the phonological analysis of Terena. *Word 16,* 348–355.
Benjamin, G. (1976), An Outline of Temiar Grammar. In: *P. Jenner et al. (eds.),* Part I.
Bennis, A. and A. Groos (1980), The government-binding theory: an overview. *GLOW Newsletter.* Foris Publications, Dordrecht.
Bing, J.M. (1979), *Aspects of English Intonation*. Doctoral dissertation Amherst: University of Massachusetts.
Bing, J.M. (1980), Linguistic rhythm and grammatical structure in Afghan Persian. *Linguistic Inquiry 11:3,* 437–63.
Booij, G. (1981), Rule Ordering, Rule Application, and the Organization of Grammars. In: W. Dressler (ed.)., *Phonologica 1980* (Proceedings of the 4th International Phonology Meeting).
Brame, M. (1974), The Cycle in Phonology: Stress in Palestinian, Maltese, and Spanish. *Linguistic Inquiry 5,* 39–60.
Broselow, E. (1979), Cairene Syllable Structure. *Linguistic Analysis 5,* 345–82.
Brosnahan, L.F. (1960), A word list of the Gokana dialect of Ogoni. *Journal of West African Languages 1,* 43–52.
Brosnahan, L.F. (1964), Outlines of the phonology of the Gokana dialect of Ogoni. *Journal of West African Languages 4,* 43–48.
Camilli, A. (1941), I rafforzamenti iniziali. *Lingua Nostra 3,* 170–174.
Carlson, G. and T. Roeper (1980), Morphology and subcategorization: Case and the unmarked complex verb. In: *Hoekstra, Van der Hulst and Moortgat (eds.),* 123–165.

Carrier, J. (1979), *The Interaction of Phonological and Morphological Rules in Tagalog: A Study in the Relationship between Rule Components in Grammar.* Doctoral dissertation. Cambridge, Mass., M.I.T.

Carter, H. (1962), *Notes on the Tonal System of Northern Rhodesian Plateau Tonga.* London: Her Majesty's Stationery Office.

Carter, H. (1971), Morphotonology of Zambian Tonga: Some Developments of Meeussen's System – I. *African Language Studies 12.*

Carter, H. (1972), Morphotonology of Zambian Tonga: Some Developments of Meeussen's System – II. *African Language Studies 13.*

Carstairs, A. (1981), *Constraints on Allomorphy in Inflexion.* Ph.D. dissertation. University of London.

Chen, M.Y. (1979), Metrical structure: Evidence from Chinese poetry. *Linguistic Inquiry 10:3*, 371–420.

Chinchor, N. (1979), On the treatment of Mongolian Vowel Harmony. *Cunyform Papers in Linguistics 5–6*, 171–187.

Chomsky, N. (1955), *The Logical Structure of Linguistic Theory.* [publ. in 1975 New York: Plenum Press].

Chomsky, N. (1965), *Aspects of the Theory of Syntax.* Cambridge, Mass. MIT Press.

Chomsky, N. (1970), Remarks on Nominalization. In: R.A. Jacobs and P.S. Rosenbaum (eds.), *Readings in English Transformational Grammar.* Waltham, Mass: Ginn & Co., 184–221.

Chomsky, N. (1975), *Reflections on Language.* New York, Pantheon.

Chomsky, N. (1980), *Rules and Representations.* New York, Columbia University Press.

Chomsky, N. and M. Halle (1968), *The Sound Pattern of English.* New York: Harper and Row.

Clark, E. and H. Clark (1979), When Nouns Surface as Verbs. *Language 55*, 767–811.

Clark, M. (1979), *A Dynamic Treatment of Tone with Special Attention to the Tonal System of Igbo.* PhD dissertation, University of Massachusetts at Amherst. [Distributed by the Indiana University Linguistics Club.]

Clements, G.N. (1976), Vowel harmony in nonlinear generative phonology: An autosegmental model. [Later published by *Indiana University Linguistics Club*, 1980.]

Clements, G.N. (1976a), The Autosegmental treatment of Vowel Harmony. In: W.U. Dressler and O.E. Pfeiffer (eds.). *Phonologica 1976*, Innsbruck.

Clements, G.N. (1977), Tone and Syntax in Ewe. In: Clements, G.N. (ed.), *Harvard Studies in Phonology* Vol. 1, 75–186.

Clements, G.N. (1977a), Neutral Vowels in Hungarian Vowel Harmony. An Autosegmental Interpretation. *North Eastern Linguistic Society 7*, 49–64.

Clements, G.N. (1978), Tone and Syntax in Ewe. In: D.J. Napoli (ed.), *Elements of Tone, Stress and Intonation.* Georgetown University Press, 21–99.

Clements, G.N. (1979), Review article of Elimelech, A tonal Grammar of Etskatǫ. *Journal of African Languages and Linguistics 1*, 95–108.

Clements, G.N. (1981), Akan vowel harmony: a non-linear analysis. In: G.N.Clements (ed.), *Harvard Studies in Phonology* Vol. II, 108–177.

Clements, G.N. (1981a), The hierarchical representation of tone. G.N. Clements (ed.), *Harvard Studies in Phonology* Vol. II, 50–108.

Clements, G.N. (1982), Principles of Tone Assignment in Kikuyu. In: *Clements and Goldsmith (eds.).*

Clements, G.N. and K. Ford (1979), Kikuyu Tone Shift and its Synchronic Consequences. *Linguistic Inquiry 10*, 179–210.

Clements, G.N. and J. Goldsmith (eds.) (1982), *Autosegmental Studies in Bantu Tonology*. Foris Press.

Clements, G.N. and J. Keyser (1981), A Three-Tiered Theory of the Syllable. *Center for Cognitive Science Occasional Papers* #19.

Cohen, M. (1974), Topics in Tonga Tone. Unpublished paper. Department of Linguistics, Cambridge, MA., MIT.

Conklin, H. (1956), Tagalog Speech Disguise. *Language 32*, 136–139.

Conklin, H. (1959), Linguistic Play in its Cultural Context. *Language 35*, 631–636.

Cooper, W.E. (1976), *Syntactic Control of Timing in Speech Production*. Ph.D. dissertation, MIT.

De Chene B. and S. Anderson (1979), Compensatory Lengthening. *Language 55*, 505–536.

Diffloth, G. (1976), Minor-syllable Vocalism in Senoic Languages In: *P. Jenner et al. (eds.)*, Part I.

Dinnsen, D. (ed.), (1979), *Current Approaches to Phonological Theory*. Bloomington.

Dixon, R.M.W. (1977a), Some Phonological Rules of Yidin^y. *Linguistic Inquiry 8*, 1–34.

Dixon, R.M.W. (1977b), *A Grammar of Yidin^y*. Cambridge University Press, Cambridge, England.

Donegan, P. and D. Stampe (1979), The Study of Natural Phonology. In: *Dinnsen (ed.)*, 126–174.

Ekundare, J.F. (1972), Gokana phonological system. Long Essay. University of Ibadan, Nigeria.

Elimelech, B. (1976), A Tonal Grammar of Etsakǫ. *UCLA Working Papers in Phonetics 35*.

Emeneau, M. (1967), Echo-words in Toda. In: *Collected Papers*. Annamalai University, Annamalainagar.

Emonds, J. (1980), Word Order in Generative Grammar. *Journal of Linguistic Research. 1*, 33–54.

Esau, H. (1973), *Nominalization and Complementation in Modern German*. Amsterdam/London: North Holland.

Ewen, C. (1980), *Aspects of Phonological Structure with Particular Reference to English and Dutch*. Ph.D. University of Edinburgh.

Fiorelli, P. (1958), Del raddoppiamento da parola a parola. *Lingua Nostra 19*, 122–127.

Freidin, R. (1978), Cyclicity and the Theory of Grammar. *Linguistic Inquiry 9*, 519–549.

Fudge, E. (1969), Syllables. *Journal of Linguistics 5*, 253–87.

Fujimura, O. (ed.) (1973), *Three Dimensions in Linguistic Theory*. Tokyo, TEC.

Fujimura, O. (1979), An Analysis of English Syllables as Cores and Affixes. *Zeitschrift für Phonetik, Sprachwissenschaft und Kommunikationsforschung*.

Fujimura, O. and J. Lovins (1978), Syllables as Concatenative Units. In: *A. Bell and J.B. Hooper (eds.)*, 107–121.

Garcia-Bellido, P. (1980), Trilled vs. Flapped /r/: Some remarks on the syllable structure of Spanish, *North Eastern Linguistic Society* 10, 109–25.

Gianelli, L. and L.M. Savoia (1979), L'indebolimento consonantico in Toscana. *Rivista Italiana di Dialettologia*, 23–58.

Goldsmith, J. (1974), English as a Tone Language. Ms., MIT [Later published in *Communication and Cognition* 1977, and *Phonology in the 1980's*, ed. by D. Goyvaerts.]

Goldsmith, J. (1976), Autosegmental Phonology. *Indiana University Linguistics Club.* [Published by Garland Press, 1979.]
Goldsmith, J. (1976a), An overview of autosegmental phonology. *Linguistic Analysis* 2, 23–68.
Goldsmith, J.A. (1976b), Tone melodies and the autosegment. In: R.K. Herbert (ed.), *Proceedings of the Sixth Conference on African Linguistics.* (Ohio State University Working Papers in Linguistics, no. 20), 135–147.
Goldsmith, J. (1979), The Aims of Autosegmental Phonology. In: *Dinnsen (eds.).* 202–23.
Goldsmith, J. (1981), Towards an Autosegmental Theory of Accent: The Case of Tonga. *Indiana University Linguistics Club,* 1981.
Goldsmith, J. (1981a), English as a Tone Language. In: D. Goyvaerts (ed.), *Phonology in the 1980's.* Gent 1981.
Goldsmith, J. (1982), Accent in Tonga. In: *Clements and Goldsmith (eds.).*
Goldsmith, J. In preparation. The Ki-Langi Verb.
Graffi, G. (1980), Universali di Greenberg e grammatica generativa. *Lingua e Stile XV.3,* 371–390.
Green, M. and G. Igwe. (1963), *A Descriptive Grammar of Igbo.* Oxford University Press.
Hale, K. (1981), On the position of Walbiri in a typology of the base. *Indiana University Linguistics Club.*
Halle, M. (1959), *The Sound Pattern of Russian.* The Hague: Mouton.
Halle, M. (1978), Formal vs. Functional Considerations in Phonology. *Indiana University Linguistics Club.*
Halle, M. (1980), Colloquium at University of Southern California.
Halle, M. and J.R. Vergnaud (1978), Metrical Structures in Phonology. Unpublished ms. MIT.
Halle, M. and J.R. Vergnaud (1980), Three Dimensional Phonology. *Journal of Linguistic Research 1,* 83–105.
Halle, M. and J.R. Vergnaud (1981), Harmony Processes. In: W. Klein and W. Levelt (eds.), *Crossing the Boundaries in Linguistics.* Dordrecht: Reidel, 1–23.
Haraguchi, S. (1977), *The Tone Pattern of Japanese: An autosegmental theory of tonology.* Tokyo: Kaitakusha.
Haraguchi, S. (1977a), Seisei on'inron no dookoo. *Eigogaku* (English Linguistics) 16, 2–36.
Haraguchi, S. (1978), Remarks on the metrical treatment of <-ory>. *Eigogaku* (English Linguistics) 19, 2–13.
Haraguchi, S., Hirose, Y., Mikami, S., Seki, S., Takezawa, K. and Tabata, T. (1980), Inritsu riron no chooboo (An overview of metrical theory). *Eigogaku* (English Linguistics) 23, 2–39.
Harris, J. (1969), *Spanish Phonology.* Cambridge, Mass., MIT Press.
Harris, J. (1980), Nonconcatenative Morphology and Spanish Plurals. *Journal of Linguistic Research 1,* 15–31.
Harris, J. (M.S.), Spanish Syllable Structure. To appear in a volume in M.I.T. Press.
Hayes, B. (1980), Aklan stress: Disjunctive ordering or metrical feet? *North East Linguistic Society 10,* 179–89.
Hayes, B. (1981), A Metrical Theory of Stress Rules. Unpublished 1980 Doctoral dissertation, MIT, Cambridge, Mass., Revised version distributed by the Indiana University Linguistics Club, Bloomington, Indiana.

Hockett, C.F. (1955), A Manual of Phonology. *International Journal of American Linguistics 21*, No. 4 , Part I. Baltimore: Waverly Press.
Hoekstra, T., H. van der Hulst and M. Moortgat (1980), *Lexical Grammar*. Dordrecht.
Hooper, J. (1976), *An Introduction to Natural Generative Phonology*. New York: Academic Press.
Howard, I. (1975), Can the 'Elsewhere Condition' Get Anywhere?. *Language 51*, 109–127.
Huang, C.-T.J. (1980), The metrical structure of terraced-level tones. *North East Linguistic Society 10*, 257–70.
Hyman, L.M. (1972), Nasals and nasalization in Kwa. *Studies in African Linguistics 3*, 167–205.
Hyman, L. (1977), On the Nature of Linguistic Stress. In: L. Hyman (ed.), *Studies in Stress and Accent*. Scopil 4.
Hyman, L.M. (1978), Historical tonology. In: V. Fromkin (ed.), *Tone: A Linguistic Survey*. Academic Press.
Hyman, L. (1981), The Accentual Treatment of Tone in Eastern Bantu. Paper read at the 1981 Conference on African Linguistics, Stanford, California.
Hyman, M. (In preparation) The representation of length in Gokana.
Hyman, L.M. and R.G. Schuh. (1974), Universals of tone rules: Evidence from West Africa. *Linguistic Inquiry 5*, 81–115.
Hyman, L.M. and B. Comrie. (1981), Logophoric reference in Gokana. *Journal of African Languages and Linguistics 3*, 1.
Ingria, R. (1980), Compensatory lengthening as a metrical phenomenon. *Linguistic Inquiry 11*, 465–495.
Jaeggli, O.A. (1980), Remarks on To Contraction. *Linguistic Inquiry, 11*, 239–245.
Jenner, P., L. Thompson and S. Starosta (eds.) (1976), *Austroasiatic Studies*. Parts I and II, University Press of Hawaii, Honolulu.
Jensen, J.T. (1980), The metrical structure of Swedish accent. *North East Linguistic Society 10*, 371–82.
Kahn, D. (1976), *Syllable-Based Generalizations in English Phonology*. M.I.T. dissertation, reproduced by Indiana University Linguistics Club.
Kaye, J.D. (1971), Nasal harmony in Desano. *Linguistic Inquiry 2*, 37–56.
Kaye, J. (1974), Morpheme Structure Conditions Live! *Montreal Working Papers in Linguistics 3*, 55–62.
Kean, M.-L. (1974), The Strict Cycle in Phonology. *Linguistic Inquiry 5*, 179–203.
Kenstowicz, M. and Ch. Kisseberth (1977), *Topics in Phonological Theory*. New York: Academic Press.
Kiparsky, P. (1968), Linguistic Universals and Linguistic Change. In: E. Bach and R. Harms (eds.), *Universals in Linguistic Theory*. New York: Holt, 171–202.
Kiparsky, P. (1968 = 1973), How Abstract is Phonology? *Indiana University Linguistics Club*. Also in Fujimura (1973).
Kiparsky, P. (1973), Abstractress, opacity, and global rules. In: *Fujimura (1973)*, 57–86.
Kiparsky, P. (1973a), Elsewhere in Phonology. In: Kiparsky, P. and S. Anderson (eds.), *Festschrift for Morris Halle*. New York: Holt, Rinehart and Winston.
Kiparsky, P. (1977), The rhythmic structure of English verse. *Linguistic Inquiry 8*, 189–247.
Kiparsky, P. (1979), Metrical Structure Assignment is Cyclic. *Linguistic Inquiry 10*, 421–442.
Kiparsky, P. (1981), Remarks on the Metrical Structure of the Syllable. In: W. Dressler (ed.), *Phonologica 1980*. (Proceedings of the Fourth International Phonology Meeting).
Kiparsky, P. and C. Kiparsky (1971), Fact. In: D.D. Steinberg and Leon A. Jakobovits (eds.), *Semantics*. Cambridge: University Press.

Kirshenblatt-Gimblett, B. (ed.) (1976), *Speech Play*. University of Pennsylvania Press, Philadelphia.
Kisseberth, Ch. (1970), On the Functional Unity of Phonological Rules. *Linguistic Inquiry 3*, 3–33.
Koutsoudas, A., G. Sanders and C. Noll (1974), On the Application of Phonological Rules. *Language 50*, 1–28.
Ladd, D. Jr. (1980), *The Structure of Intonational Meaning*. Bloomington: Indiana University Press.
Laughren, M. (1982), An Autosegmental Account of Tone in Zulu. In: *Clements and Goldsmith (eds.)*.
Leben, W. (1971), Suprasegmental and segmental representation of tone. *Studies in Afr. Ling. Suppl. 2*, 183–200.
Leben, W. (1973), Suprasegmental Phonology. *Indiana University Linguistics Club*.
Leben, W. (1978), The representation of tone. In: V. Fromkin (ed.), *Tone: A Linguistic Survey*. Academic Press.
Leben, W. (1980), A metrical analysis of length. *Linguistic Inquiry 11*, 497–509.
Lee, B. (1982), *On the Role of Well-formedness Conditions in Phonology*.
Lehiste, I. (1973), Phonetic disambiguation of syntactic ambiguity. *Glossa 7*, 107–122.
Lepschy, A.L. and G. Lepschy (1977), *The Italian Language Today*. London: Hutchinson.
Liberman, M. (1975), *The intonational system of English*. Ph.D. Dissertation. MIT. Distributed by *Indiana University Linguistics Club*.
Liberman, M. and A. Prince (1977), On stress and linguistic rhythm. *Linguistic Inquiry 8*, 249–336.
Lieber, R. (1980), *On the Organization of the Lexicon*. Ph.D. dissertation, M.I.T.
Linell, P. (1979), *Psychological Reality in Phonology*. Cambridge: Cambridge University Press.
Lowenstam, J. (1979), *Topics in Syllabic Phonology*, MIT diss.
Luce, J. (1981), *A Phonetic Investigation of Accent in Tonga and English*. Ms., Indiana University.
Lunt, H.G. (1973), Remarks on nasality: the case of Guarani. In: Stephen R. Anderson and Paul Kiparsky (eds.), *A Festschrift for Morris Halle*, 131–139. New York: Holt, Rinehart and Winston.
Mahapatra, K. (1976), Echo-formation in Gtaʔ In: P. Jenner et al. (eds.), Part II.
Marantz, A. (1981), Re-reduplication. To appear in *Linguistic Inquiry*.
Marchand, H. (1969), *The Categories and Types of Present-day English Word-formation*[2]. München: C.H. Beck.
Mascaró, J. (1976), *Catalan Phonology and the Phonological Cycle*. Ph.D. dissertation, M.I.T. Reproduced by the Indiana University Linguistics Club.
Massamba, D. (1982), Tone in Ci-Ruri. In: *Clements and Goldsmith (eds.)*.
Massamba, D. In preparation. PhD dissertation, Indiana University.
McCarthy, J. (1977), CT. *North East Linguistic Society 7*, 209–17.
McCarthy, J. (1979), *Formal Problems in Semitic Phonology and Morphology*. Doctoral dissertation, Cambridge, Mass., MIT.
McCarthy, J. (1979a), On Stress and Syllabification. *Linguistic Inquiry 10*, 443–465.
McCarthy, J. (1981), A Prosodic Theory of Nonconcatenative Morphology. *Linguistic Inquiry 12*, 373–418.
McCarthy, J. (1981a), Prosodic structure and expletive infixation. Unpublished.

McCarthy, J. (to appear), Prosodic Organization in Morphology.
McCawley, J. (1973), Some Tonga Tone Rules. In: Stephen R. Anderson and Paul Kiparsky (eds.), *A Festschrift for Morris Halle*. New York: Holt, Rinehart and Winston.
McCawley, J. (1977), Accent in Japanese. In: L. Hyman (ed.) *Studies in Stress and Accent*. Southern California Occasional Papers in Linguistics 4, 261–302.
McCawley, J. (1978), What is a Tone Language. In: V. Fromkin (ed.), *Tone: A Linguistic Survey*. New York: Academic Press.
Meeussen, A.E. (1963), Morphotonology of the Tonga Verb. *Journal of African Linguistics* Vol. 2, Part I.
Mohanan, K.P. (1981), *Lexical Phonology*, Ph.D. dissertation, M.I.T.
Moortgat, M., H. van der Hulst and T. Hoekstra (eds.) (1981), *The Scope of Lexical Rules*. Dordrecht: Foris [Linguistic Models 1.]
Nanni, D.L. (1977), Stressing words in <-ative>. *Linguistic Inquiry 8: 4*, 752–63.
Napoli, D.J. and M. Nespor (1979), The syntax of word-initial consonant gemination in Italian. *Language 55*, 812–841.
Nash, D. (1979), Yidin^y Stress: A Metrical Account. *Cuny form papers in Linguistics 7–8*, 112–130.
Navarro Tomás, T. (1957), *Manual de pronunciación española*. New York: Hafner.
Nespor, M. and I. Vogel (1979), Clash avoidance in Italian. *Linguistic Inquiry 10*, 467–482.
Odden, D. (1980), Associative tone in Shona. *Journal of Linguistic Research 1*, 37–53.
Odden, D. (1982), Stem Tone Assignment in Shona. In: *Clements and Goldsmith (eds.)*.
Okotie, F. (1972), Phonemic analysis of Gokana. Long Essay, University of Ibadan, Nigeria.
Osburne, A. (1979), Segmental, Suprasegmental, Autosegmental: Contour tones. *Linguistic Analysis 5*, 161–83.
Paul, H. (1896), Über die Aufgaben der Wortbildungslehre. *Sitzungsberichte der königl. bayer. Akademie der Wissenschaften, philosophisch-philologische und historische Classe*, 692–713. München.
Pesetsky, D. (MS), *Russian morphology and lexical theory*. M.I.T.
Phinney, M. (1980), Evidence for a rhythm rule in Quebec French. *North East Linguistic Society 10*, 369–82.
Pike, K. and E. Pike (1947), Immediate constituents of Mazatec Syllables. *International Journal of American Linguistics 13*, 78–91.
Pratelli, R. (1971), Le renforcement syntactique des consonnes en Italien. *La linguistique 6*, 39–50.
Price, R. and S. Price (1976), Secret Play Languages in Saramakka: Linguistic Disguise in a Caribbean Creole. In: *B. Kirshenblatt-Glimblett (ed.)*.
Prince, A. (1976), *Applying Stress*. MS.
Prince, A.S. (1980), A metrical theory for Estonian quantity. *Linguistic Inquiry 11*, 511–562.
Pulleyblank, D. (1981), *Tone and the Cycle in Tiv*. Ms., MIT.
Rardin, R. (1975), *Studies in Derivational Morphology*. Ph.D. dissertation, M.I.T.
Riemsdijk, H.C. van (1978), *A case study in syntactic markedness*. Foris Publications.
Riemsdijk, H.C. van and N.S.H. Smith (1973), Zur Instabilität komplexer phonologischer Segmente. In: A.P. ten Cate and P. Jordens (eds.), *Linguistische Perspektiven*. [Referate des VII Linguistischen Kolloquiums Nijmegen, 26–30 September 1972, *Linguistische Arbeiten 5*]. Niemeyer 1973.

Ringen, C. (1980), Hungarian Vowel Harmony. In: *R. Vago (ed.)*, 135–154.
Rischel, J. (1964), Stress, Juncture, and Syllabification in Phonemic Description. *Proceedings of the IXth International Congress of Linguistics*, 85–93.
Rischel, J. (1972), Compound Stress in Danish without a Cycle. *ARIPUC 6*, University of Copenhagen.
Rizzi, L. (1980), Violations of the WH Island Constraint in Italian and the Subjacency Condition. *Journal of Italian Linguistics 5*, 157–196.
Rotenberg, J. (1978), *The syntax of phonology*. Ph.D. dissertation. MIT.
Rubach, J. (1981), *Cyclic Phonology and Palatalization in Polish and English*. Warsaw, Wydawnictwa Uniwersytetu Warszawskiego.
Schane, S.A. (1979a), The rhythmic nature of English word accentuation. *Language 54*, 559–602.
Schane, S.A. (1979b), Rhythm, accent, and stress in English words. *Linguistic Inquiry 10*, 483–502.
Selkirk, E. (1972), *The Prase Phonology of English and French*. Ph.D. dissertation. MIT.
Selkirk, E. (1974), French liaison and the $\overline{X}$ notation. *Linguistic Inquiry 5*, 573–590.
Selkirk, E. (1977), French schwa. Unpublished.
Selkirk, E. (1978), On prosodic structure and its relation to syntactic structure. Paper presented at the Conference of the Mental Representation of Phonology. Distributed by *Indiana University Linguistics Club* in 1980.
Selkirk, E. (1980), The role of prosodic categories in English word stress. *Linguistic Inquiry 11*, 563–605.
Selkirk, E. (1980a), Prosodic domains in phonology: Sanskrit revisited. In: M. Aronoff and M.L. Kean (eds.), *Juncture*. Saratoga, C.A. Anma libri.
Selkirk, E. (1981), English Compounding and the Theory of Word Structure, In: *Moortgat, Van der Hulst and Hoekstra (eds.)*, 229–279.
Sherzer, J. (1976), Play Languages: Implications for (Socio)Linguistics. In: *B. Kirshenblatt-Gimblett (ed.)*.
Siegel, D. (1974), *Topics in English Morphology*. Ph.D. Dissertation, M.I.T.
Siegel, D. (1977), The Adjacency Condition and the Theory of Morphology. *North East Linguistic Society 8*.
Singh, R. (1981), The English Negative Prefix *in-*. *Montreal Working Papers in Linguistics 17*, 139–143.
Stampe, D. (1972), *A Dissertation on Natural Phonology*. Garland Press.
Stanley, R. (1967), Redundancy Rules in Phonology. *Language 43*, 393–436.
Stein, M.J. (1980), Something else. *North East Linguistic Society 10*, 401–12.
Stemberger, J.P. (1980), Length as a suprasegmental: Evidence from speech errors. Unpublished.
Strauss, S. (1979), Against Boundary Distinctions in English Morphology. *Linguistic Analysis 5*, 387–419.
Strauss, S. (1979a), Stress Assignment as Morphological Adjustment in English. Paper presented at the Linguistic Society of America Winter Meeting, Los Angeles.
Thrainsson, H. (1978), On the Phonology of Icelandic Preaspiration. *Nordic Journal of Linguistics 1*, 3–54.
Toman, J. (1980), *Wortsyntax*. Ph.D. dissertation, University of Köln.
Vago, R. (1980), A Critique of Suprasegmental Theories of Vowel Harmony. In: *Vago (ed.)*, 155–183.
Vago, R. (ed.), (1980a), *Issues in Vowel Harmony*. Amsterdam.

Van der Hulst, H.G. (1981), De structuur van fonologische representaties. *GLOT 4*, 1–33.

Vergnaud, J.-R. (1977), Formal properties of phonological rules. In: *Butts, R.E. and Hintikka, J. (eds.). Basic problems in methodology and linguistics.* Dordrecht-Holland: D. Reidel, 299-318.

Vergnaud, J.-R. (1979), A Formal Theory of Vowel Harmony. In: *Vago (ed.)*, 49–63.

Vogel, I. (1977), *The Syllable in Phonological Theory; with special reference to Italian.* Stanford University, diss.

Vogel, I. (1978), Raddoppiamento as a Resyllabification Rule. *Journal of Italian Linguistics, 3.1,* 15–28.

Welmers, W. (1959), Tonemics, Morphotonemics and Tonal Morphemes. *General Linguistics 4,* 19.

Wheeler, D. (1979), A Metrical analysis of Stress and related processes in Southern Paiute and Tübatulabal. *University of Mass. Occasional Papers 5,* 145–174.

Wheeler, D.W. (1981), *Aspects of a categorial theory of phonology.* Ph.D. Dissertation. Amherst.

Whitney, W.D. (1889), *Sanskrit Grammar.*[2] Cambridge, Mass., Harvard University Press.

Williams, E. (1971), Underlying Tone in Margi and Igbo. *Linguistic Inquiry 7 (1976).*

Williams, E. (1981), On the Notions "Lexically Related" and "Head of a Word". *Linguistic Inquiry 12,* 245–274.

Williamson, K. (1973), More on nasals and nasalization in Kwa. *Studies in African Linguistics 4,* 115–138.

Williamson, K. (1979), Preliminary reconstruction of Ogoni group. Ms., University of Port Harcourt.

Wolff, H. (1959), Niger-Delta Languages I: Classification. *Anthropological Linguistics 1.*

Wolff, H. (1964), Synopsis of the Ogoni languages. *Journal of African Languages 3,* 38–51.

Woo, N. (1969), Prosody and Phonology. *Indiana University Linguistics Club.*

Yip, M. (to appear), *Chinese Secret Languages* – A form of Reduplication.

Zide, N. (1976), A note on Gta? Echo forms. In: *Jenner et al. (eds.),* Part II.

Zwicky, A. (1970), The Free-Ride Principle and Two Rules of Complete Assimilation in English. *Papers from the Sixth Regional Meeting, Chicago Linguistic Society.* Chicago, Illinois.

Index of Names

Allen, M.R. 131, 140, 174
Al-Mozainy, H. 196, 197, 222
Anderson, S.R. 2, 3, 5, 17, 18–22, 29, 30, 44, 45, 112, 129, 177, 178
Arekambe, D. 129
Aronoff, M. 131, 134, 136, 143
Asinyirimba, J.O. 129, 130

Barratt, L. 22
Battistella, E. 22
Bendor-Samuel, J.T. 22, 112
Benjamin, G. 208, 221, 222
Bennis, A. 235
Booij, G. 132
Brame, M. 145
Brosnahan, L.F. 113, 121, 127, 129

Camilli, A. 227
Carlson, G. 174
Carrier, J. 222
Carter, H. 59, 62, 69, 76
Carstairs, A. 140
Chinchor, N. 22
Chomsky, N. 2, 7, 63, 140, 146, 147, 150, 153, 157, 159, 169, 225, 236, 239, 244
Clark, E. 134, 140, 174
Clark, H. 134, 140, 174
Clark, M. 49
Clements, G.N. 5, 11–17, 19–21, 29, 40, 42, 49, 56, 57, 63, 66, 67, 83, 111, 126, 127, 144, 177, 179, 185, 194, 225, 254
Cohen, M. 69
Comrie, B. 118, 129
Conklin, H. 199–201, 222
Cooper, W.E. 232

De Chene, B. 29

Diffloth, G. 222
Dixon, R. 98, 100, 101, 106, 110
Donegan, P. 200

Edelman, J. 254
Ekundare, J.F. 122, 129
Elimelech, B. 11
Emeneau, M. 202
Emonds, J. 230
Esau, H. 134
Ewen, C. 5, 18, 23

Fabb, N. 174
Feinstein, M. 191
Fiorelli, P. 227
Ford, K. 11–16, 56, 66, 67, 126, 179, 185, 194
Freidin, R. 157
Fudge, E. 30, 38
Gianelli, L. 238
Gil, D. 188, 189, 190
Goldsmith, J. 5, 10, 13–16, 24, 26, 49, 50, 53, 57, 60, 61, 63–71, 74, 75, 78, 81, 125, 177, 180, 181, 191, 195, 197
Graffi, G. 239
Green, M. 111
Groos, A. 235

Hachipola, J. 59
Hale, K. 255
Halle, M. 1, 2, 7, 13–17, 21–23, 24, 26, 28, 30, 33, 37, 43, 45, 61, 63, 83, 129, 140, 146, 147, 150, 157, 159, 169, 177–180, 185, 189, 191, 195, 225, 226, 230, 244, 255
Haraguchi, S. 14–17, 56, 67, 93, 126

Index of Names

Harris, J. 132, 144, 191, 246
Hayes, B. 30, 33, 34, 35, 36, 44, 83, 103, 105, 110, 131, 150, 155, 158, 161, 166, 178, 179, 181, 183, 185–187, 188, 190
Hockett, F. 111
Hoekstra, T. 1, 2
Hooper, J. 246
Howard, I. 173
Huang, C. 40
Hulst, H.G. van der, 2, 4, 22, 23, 44, 45, 83
Hyman, L.M. 23, 63, 113, 118, 122 128, 129, 130, 186, 190

Igwe, G. 111
Ingria, R. 29, 180

Jaeggli, O.A. 129, 236

Kahn, D. 38, 42, 188, 244
Kaye, J.D. 112
Kenstowicz, M. 167, 174
Keyser, J. 19, 29, 42
Kiparksy, P. 2, 32, 39, 50, 65, 83 92, 97, 98, 131, 136, 138, 143, 148, 158, 172, 173
Kiparsky, C. 138
Kisseberth, Ch. 167, 174
Kooij, J.G. 1
Koutsoudas, A. 136
Kuroda, Y. 254

Ladd, D. 63
Laughren, M. 63
Leben, W. 10, 12, 13, 28, 45, 129, 180, 181, 188
Lehiste, I. 250
Lepschy, A.L. 238
Lepschy, G. 238
Liberman, M. 30, 32, 37, 83, 105, 131, 143, 150, 178, 225, 226, 241
Lieber, R. 133, 174
Linell, P. 174
Lowenstam, J. 43
Luce, J. 61
Lunt, H.G. 112

Madugu, G. 129
Mahapatra, K. 202, 203, 205, 207, 208

Marantz, A. 28, 191, 221
Marchand, H. 173, 174
Mascaró, J. 131, 153, 158, 166
Masamba, D. 63
McCarthy, J. 24–26, 28, 83, 178, 179, 181, 183–185, 189, 191, 192, 196, 198, 199, 221, 222, 223
McCawley, J. 49, 69, 243, 244
Meeussen, A.E. 53, 69, 73, 77
Mohanan, K.P. 132, 139, 140
Moortgat, M. 1, 2

Napoli, D.J. 225, 228, 254, 255
Nash, D. 110
Navarro Tomás, T. 246
Neijt, A. 254
Nespor, M. 31, 225, 228, 237, 254, 255
Noll, C. 136

Odden, D. 11, 13, 50
Oehrle, R. 174
Okotie, F. 129
Osburne, A. 12

Paul, H. 134
Pesetsky, D. 131, 140
Pike, E. 38
Pike, K. 38
Poser, B. 71
Postal, P. 172
Pratelli, R. 227
Price, R. 201
Price, S. 201
Prince, A. 30, 32, 33, 37, 39, 83, 105, 131, 143, 150, 178, 189, 191, 225, 226, 241
Pulleyblank, D. 60, 132

Rardin, R. 174
Riemsdijk, H.C. van 5, 229
Rischel, J. 143
Rizzi, L. 235
Roeper, T. 174
Rotenberg, J. 41, 254
Rubach, J. 131, 150, 154

Sanders, G. 136
Savoia, L.M. 238

Index of Names

Schane, S.A. 44, 84, 86, 87, 88, 89, 90, 93, 94, 95, 107, 108, 109
Schuh, R.G. 190
Scoretti, M. 254
Selkirk, E. 30–34, 36–38, 41, 83, 93–95, 97, 107–109, 132, 161, 189, 226, 232, 235, 240, 241
Sherzer, J. 200, 201
Siegel, D. 131, 132, 139, 143
Singh, R. 139
Smith, N.S.H. 4, 5, 22, 23, 44, 45
Stampe, D. 200
Stanley, R. 124, 168, 170
Stejskal, M. 254
Stemberger, J.P. 180
Strauss, S. 132, 139

Teele, N.J. 83
Thraínsson, H. 24
Toman, J. 134

Vago, R. 19, 21, 22

Vergnaud, J.R. 13, 14, 15, 16, 17, 21, 22, 23, 26, 28, 30, 33, 43, 45, 83, 178, 191, 195, 226, 230
Verluyten, P. 255
Vogel, I. 31, 42, 227, 237

Watanabe, M. 95
Wheeler, D. 1, 36, 39, 43, 226, 229, 244
Whitney, W.B. 132
Williams, E. 12, 13, 14, 67, 132, 133
Williamson, K. 113, 122, 129
Withgott, M. 184
Wolff, H. 129
Woo, N. 6

Yip, M. 12, 191, 222
Younes, M. 223

Zide, N. 203, 206, 222
Zoranen, G. 129
Zwicky, A. 172
Zubizaretta, M.L. 44

Subject Index

Ablaut 141, 132
Absolute slicing hypothesis 5, 6 see also *segment*
Abstractness 2, 146, 148, 158, 170 see also *Alternation Condition*
Accent (language) 47, 57, 66 see also *star*
Accent association rule 49 see also *initial association rule*
Accent component 52
Accent hop 53, 55–57, 59
Accent rules 48, 49, 53, 60, 76
Accent shift 52, 81
Accent subordination 47 see also stress levels
Acquisition 15, 37, 172
Affix 10, 20, 134, 187
  neutral– (#) 32
  non-neutral– (+) 32
  see also *derivation, infix, prefix, suffix*
Affix tier, 194
Affricate 5
Alternation condition 131, 148–150, 171 see also *abstractness, RAC, revised alternation condition*
Ambisyllabicity, 38, 39, 42, 43, 188 see also floating C
Ambiguity 250, 252
Archisegments 10, 12, 124, 167, 168
Aspiration 24
Association
  – convention (universal) 17, 20, 21, 38, 44, 194, 201, 202, 210, 211, 212 see also *Wellformedness Condition, Williams' rule*
  – line 3, 9, 13, 14, 18, 50, 66, 191
  – rule (language-specific) 23, 49, 181, 191, 195, 197, 209, 212, 213, 215, 216 see also *initial association rule, multiple association, dis(as)-sociation, reassociation*
Association rule (w.r.t. syllables) 38
Asterisk see *star*
Atomic feature 5–7
Autosegment 8
  free, unassociated– 22, 49, 50, 69, 73 see also *floating tone*
Autosegmental phonology 3, 8, 48, 65, 125
Autosegmental rules 48
Auxiliary reduction rules 87 see also *vowel quality, reduction*

Bahuvrihi compound 139 see also *compound*
Barrier (for government) 235, 244, 255
Base melody 207
Basic tone melody 47, 52, 59, 60, 75
  – association/assignment 48, 49, 53–57, 62
Bidirectionality see *directionality*
Binarity 31, 40, 83, 84, 181, 182
Blank see *archisegments*
Blocking (in morphology) 134–136
Blocking segments 21, 22 see also *opaque segments*
Boundaries 3, 4, 38, 41, 97, 113, 114, 118–120, 126, 132, 133, 139, 150, 151, 214, 225, 246, 255 see also *affix*
Boundary strength 139
Boundedness 13 see also *foot, bounded–*
Bounding node 235
Branching 36, 37, 105, 181–184, 229, 230, 233, 243
Branching segment 19 see also *complex segment*
Bracketing 139, 145
  – erasure 140, 141 see also opacity (in morphology)

Subject Index

Categorial phonology 39
Clitics 76, 78, 110, 145
Co-articutation (of autos. tiers) 9, 13, 65
Coda 38, 39
Compensatory lengthening 28, 29, 180
Complementary distribution 122, 179
Complex segment 4, 5, 18, 19, 27, 39, 195 see also *affricate, (pre)nasality, short diphthong, subsegmental phenomena*
Compounds 32, 87–89, 130, 133, 138, 139, 141, 172, 174
Concrete phonology 2, 147
Co-occurence restriction 38 see also *phonotactic restrictions, morpheme structure conditions*
Copying 4, 26, 109, 187, 201, 210, 211 see also *reduplication*
Contour tone see *tone*
CV-level/skeleton 9, 24, 25, 28, 29, 42, 191, 194, 196 see also *tier, basic-*
Cyclicity 32, 58, 59, 62, 63
Cyclic phonology 131, 147
Cyclic rule, 132, 140, 143–145, 152–171

[Delayed release] 5, 6
Degemination 146
Dependency phonology 18, 23
Deletion (rule) 11, 16, 26, 29, 50, 55–58, 60, 61, 66, 69, 75, 78, 79, 80, 101, 104, 109, 110, 178, 180, 185
Derivation 131
Derivational Simplicity Criterion 172
Derived words 32
Destressing 87, 108, 144, 155–156
Detail rule 85
Directionality 19, 20, 44, 50, 177, 178, 179, 185–187
Dis(as)sociation 13
Disjunction in SD's 7, 97
Disjunctive application/ordering 50, 163, 165, 169, 170, 173 see also *Elsewhere Condition*
Dissimilation rule 11, 13
Distinctness 137, 160, 170
Domains of rule application 3, 19, 37, 41, 44, 111, 112, 131, 167, 228, 234, 238, 240, 241, 244, 254
Domain Problem 167

Domain span rule 41
Dominance 31, 188
Dominant node 183 see also *recessive node*
Double L deletion 57, 60
Downdrift 6, 7, 37
Downstep 60, 74, 77, 78, 186
Duplication problem 167, 168

EC see *Elsewhere Condition*
Echo-word (formation) 202, 203, 206–208
Elsewhere condition (EC) 50, 51, 136, 137, 159, 160, 163–165, 169, 172
Empiricial domain 3, 4, 17, 30, 42
Endocentricity 133, 135
English stress rule (ESR) 32, 155, 161–166, 175
Exocentricity 139
Extrametricality 34, 86, 161, 162, 188, 189

Feature changing rule 161, 167 see also *structure changing rule*
Final vowel deletion 55, 58
Flapping 184, 185, 244, 246
Floating tone 11, 15, 73, 74, 76, 185
Floating C 41
Fixed stress 32
Foot 4, 17, 32, 33, 84, 185, 226
  binary– 181, 182
  bounded– 34, 35, 181
  degenerate– 34, 36
  disyllabic– 102
  monosyllabic– 34, 36
  Q insensitive– 35, 36
  Q sensitive– 34, 40
  ternary– 34
  tonal– 40
  unbounded– 34, 35, 36, 181
Foot assignment 161–163
Foot formation (tonal) 32, 40
Foot structure 97
Foot tree 33
Foot span rule 41
Free autosegment see *autosegment*
Free ride 148, 172
Fundamental frequency 48

Games (language–, word–) 11, 194, 196, 197, 199, 200

Subject Index

Generalized left branch condition 230
Gestures 23, 24
Glide formation 79, 80
Gorgia Toscana (GT) 227, 236–238
Government 244
Grid 63, 226

Harmony 4, 19, 29, 42, 43, 240
  consonant– 4
  vowel– 4, 18, 19, 20, 177, 178, 187
  labelling– 105
  directional vs non-directional (dominant)– 43, 177
Hierarchical structure 226
  in morphology 32
  morpho-syntactic– 3, 4, 31
  phonological– 4, 17, 24, 30
  see also *metrical–, prosodic–*
Hierarchical theory (HT) 84
High flop 52, 55
Head
  in morphology 133
  lexical– 228, 239
  -of foot 33
Heavy Constraint (HC) 85, 90

Indentity rule 137, 160
Independence (of autos. tiers) 10
  see also *stability*
Inert (unaccented) 51
Infix 183, 192, 193, 198, 200–202, 215, 222
Inflection 131, 137–139, 146
Initial association rule 15, 126
  see also *accent association rule*
Initial Constraint (IC) 85, 89
Insertion (rule) 13, 50
Integrity (of segments) 5
Intervocalic voicing 153
Intonation 227, 234
Intonational phrase (I) 31, 232, 236, 244
I-constituency 233
I-construction 232
I-restructuring 234, 251, 252, 255
Intrusive-r 245

Labelling (S/W) 31, 32, 103, 105, 106, 110, 163
  –w.r.t. syllables 39

–harmony 105
Length 8, 18, 28, 29, 61–63, 105, 199, 222, 236, 254, 255
  consonant– 25, 28, 42
  Vowel– 7–11, 29, 35, 40, 97, 99, 102, 106, 110, 149, 172, 206
Lengthening 13, 100, 103, 104, 172, 227, 232, 233
Levels
  in morphology 131, 136, 139, 145, 192, 196, 199, 209
  in phonology 36, 37
  see also *foot, intonational phrase, phonological word, syllable*
Level problem 167,
Level tone see *tone*
Lexical entry 9, 20, 49, 134, 137, 159, 160, 169
Lexical phonology 2, 131
Lexical representation 66
Lexical stress 32
Lexical syntax 2
Lexical tone system/language 15, 16
Lexicalization 171
Lexicon 2, 131, 132, 161, 166
Liaison 241, 242
Linear theory (LT) 84
Linking-r 245
Locality 62, 102, 105, 222
Loudness 47, 61

Many-to-one association 195, 204, 205, 206, 210, 216, 221
  see also *matching condition, multiple association*
Mapping
  w.r.t. autos.tiers 10, 12, 13, 66, 67–69, 71, 73–76, 82, 126, 194, 199
  w.r.t. phonological and grammatical hierarchy 31, 32, 226, 227
Markedness 13, 15, 17, 22, 23, 67, 158, 159, 169, 172, 195, 213, 230, 235, 240
Matching convention/rule 195, 199, 204
Meeussen's rule 53, 55, 57, 58, 60, 61, 75–78, 81
Melody
  tonal– 10, 15, 16, 26
  non-tonal– 20, 25, 26
Metrical phonology 30, 83
Metrical rule 19

Metrical structure 31
  see also *hierarchical structure*
Metrical structure erasure 164
Monomoraic diphthong 206
  see also *short diphthong*
Monomorphemic word 31
Morpheme
  as autosemental tier 26
  defective– 10
  segmentless– 10, 20, 22
  tonal– 10
  toneless– 10
Morpheme structure rule (MSR) 146, 158, 167, 168
Morphememic template 192, 193, 194, 208, 210
Morphemic tier 192, 203, 205
Morphology 2, 48, 131, 191
Morphologization 150
Morphophonological rule 174
Multiple association 61, 62, 69, 74, 204, 206, 290
  see also *matching condition, many-to-one association*
Multi-tiered vs one–tiered 12, 13

Nasal assimilation 121, 245, 246
Nasal-bearing unit (NBU) 111, 112
  see also *P-bearing unit*
Nasality 22, 23, 111, 187
  intrinsic– 129
  paradigmatic–111
  syntagmatic– 111
  pre– 5, 18, 22, 111
  post– 111
Naturalness Condition 172
Natural Phonology 2
  see also *concrete phonology*
Neutral segments 21
Neutralization rule 148, 150, 152, 153, 158, 171
  absolute– 152
  contextual– 152
Nominative Island Condition (NIC) 158
Non-concatenative morphology 4, 24, 191, 220
Non-restrictive clause 240, 244
Non-segmental theories 4
Non-structure changing application 163
Nuclear stress rule 143, 244
Nucleus 38–40, 206

Obligatory Contour Principle (OCP) 8, 40,
Onset 38–40
Opacity Condition
  in morphology 205, 212, 214, 218, 221
  in phonology 140
  in syntax 158
Opaque segments 21, 23, 43, 44, 127, 178, 179, 240

Parameters 37, 195, 226, 227, 240
Parentheticals 232, 244, 245, 250
P-bearing unit 17, 21
  see also *nasal bearing unit, tone bearing unit*
Perception 250, 253
Percolation 43, 134, 188
Performance 250
Phonemic core 65, 68, 72
Phonemic level 146
Phonetic interpretation 14, 31, 36, 204, 211
Phonological constituent structure 41
  see also *hierarchical structure*
Phonological domain see *domain*
Phonological grammar 39
  see also *categorial grammar*
Phonological phrase (φ) 227, 228, 230, 232, 236, 237, 240, 242, 254
φ-constituency 229
φ-construction 228
φ-restructuring 230, 232
Phonological word 4, 30, 32
Phonotactic restriction/rule 38, 174
  see also *co-occurence restriction, morpheme structure condition*
Phrasal stress 90
  see also *nuclear stress rule*
Phrase phonology 144
Pitch accent system/language 15, 16, 47, 48
Post-accent 52
Post-stress destressing 157
Pre-accent 52
Pre-stress destressing 155, 156
Prefix 20, 198, 208
Prevocalic lengthening 160
PRO 236
Production 250
Productivity 136, 140

Subject Index

Projection 17, 19, 40, 179, 180, 188, 189 see also *P-bearing unit*
Prosodic structure 31
see also *hierarchical structure*
Prosodic templare (tier) 191, 192, 208, 209
Prosodic word 226 see also *phonological word*

Raddopiamento Sintattico (RS) 225, 227–229, 232, 237, 238
Rate of speech 232, 254
Readjustment rules 31
Reassociation 13, 26, 57, 62, 193
Recessive accent placement 71
Recessive node 182, 183, 187
Recoverability 205
Recursivity parameters 239
Reduction 85, 97, 98
Redundancy rule 72, 167, 169
Reduplication 11, 27, 28, 109, 124, 130, 193, 198, 210, 213, 219, 221
Resyllabification (rule) 52
see also *syllabification*
Revised Alternation Condition (RAC) 152. 153, 158
Rhyme 17, 38, 40, 179, 180
Rhythmic constraints 84, 87
Rhythm rule, 85, 91, 92, 93, 110, 143, 156, 241 see also *Stress Retraction*
Root 145, 146
Root tier 192, 194, 196, 198, 199, 209
Rule application 2, 41, 78, 80, 154
see also *domains, (non)-structure changing application, vacuous application*
Rule formulation 2, 50
Rule ordering 2, 154, 168, 215
Rule schema 11

Sandhi rule 225, 227, 232, 238, 240, 243, 254
Segment(ation) 3, 5, 8, 18
see also *absolute slicing hypothesis*
Segmental analysis 23, 30, 108, 120, 123, 124
Segmental features 13, 22, 72, 128, 129
Segmental level 9
Segmental rule 19
Segmental theory (strict-) 3, 5, 7,
Sentence phonology 144

Sentence stress 143
Short diphthong 195
see also *monomoraic diphthong*
Short vowel see *length*
Sonority 38, 39
Sound change 171
SPE see *standard theory*
S-placement 84
Stability 12, 29, 180
Standard Theory 4, 5, 10, 33, 37, 85, 87, 147, 225, 229
Star(*) 15, 16, 52, 180
Stray Syllable Adjunction 34, 103
[Stress] 33, 107
Stress 140, 143, 144, 145
—of verbs 140, 143
see also *phrasal stress, sentence stress, lexical stress*
Stress assignment 32, 33, 99, 100, 107, 108
Stress clash 92, 94
see also *Rhythm rule*
Stress levels 33, 63, 85
see also *accent subordination*
Stress Retraction (SR) 227, 236, 237, 238, 240, 241
Stress shift 89, 91, 93, 102, 105, 108, 109
Stress-timed language 36
Strict Cyclicity Condition (SCC) 146, 154, 158–160, 162–164, 171, 173
Strong Retraction Rule (SRR) 161–166, 175
Structure-changing application 163, 165
Subcategorization 133, 134
Subjacency 235, 244
Subsegmental phenomena 4, 5, 18, 111
see also *complex segment, short diphthong*
Suffix 20, 117
primary— 132
secondary— 132
Suprasegmental phenomena 2, 3, 5, 18, 112, 125
Syllabification 110, 145, 158, 161
see also *resyllabification*
Syllable (structure) 3, 4, 12, 17, 18, 28, 30, 37, 38, 65, 128, 144, 145, 160, 191, 226, 232
—count 97, 100, 106
—duration 47

276 Subject Index

open/closed– 35, 37, 40
–weight 35, 39, 42, 161, 181
Syllable span rule 41

Tensed S Condition 158
Three dimensional phonology 23, 65
Tier 3, 8, 9, 12, 13, 18, 23, 24, 26, 62, 65, 72, 191, 192
   basic– 24, 25
   see also *CV-level*
Tonal feet 40
Tonal displacement 51
Tonal melody 49, 68
Tone (language) 6, 47, 48, 57, 177, 179, 187
   contour– 6, 7, 9, 11, 13, 18, 29, 68 70
   level– 6, 113
Tone-bearing unit 5, 9, 16, 17, 19, 72, 179, 186, 194
   see also *P-bearing unit projection*
Trace 236
Transformational rule (in phon.) 80
Trisyllabic shortening 147, 148, 150–152, 154–157, 159, 167, 172

Unassociated element, see *autosegment*
Unboundedness 11, 19

Underlying representation 148, 149
Utterance (U) 235, 244, 245
U-constituency 235
U-construction 235

Vacuous application 58, 167
Velar softening 153, 154
Vocalic melody (tier) 192, 194, 196, 202, 203, 207
Voicing assimilation 180
Vowel merger 56, 57
Vowel quality 35

W* 255
Weak cluster 7, 37
Weakening Convention (WC) 84, 87, 108, 109
Well-formedness Condition (WFC) 14, 15, 49, 50, 56, 61, 62, 66–71, 75, 76, 81, 82, 180, 181, 95, 207
   see also *association conventions*
Williams' rule 67
Word phonology 144, 154
Word tree (formation) 33, 36

X-bar 227, 239, 241, 254, 255

Zero-derivation 135, 139, 140–143, 174

LIBRARY

as you